T0314216

*Globalization and
America's Trade Agreements*

Globalization and America's Trade Agreements

William Krist

Woodrow Wilson Center Press
Washington, D.C.

Johns Hopkins University Press
Baltimore

EDITORIAL OFFICES

Woodrow Wilson Center Press
One Woodrow Wilson Plaza
1300 Pennsylvania Avenue, N.W.
Washington, DC 20004-3027
Telephone: 202-691-4029
www.wilsoncenter.org

ORDER FROM

Johns Hopkins University Press
Hopkins Fulfillment Services
P.O. Box 50370
Baltimore, MD 21211-4370
Telephone: 1-800-537-5487
www.press.jhu.edu/books/

Library of Congress Cataloging-in-Publication Data

Krist, William.
    Globalization and America's trade agreements / William Krist.
       pages cm
    ISBN 978-1-4214-1168-2
    1. Free trade—United States. 2. United States—Commerce. 3. United States—
Commercial treaties. 4. United States—Commercial policy. 5. United States—
Foreign economic relations. I. Title.
    HF1756.K84 2013
    382′.973—dc23
                                                                              2013019577

To my wife, Barbara,
for putting up with too many lost evenings and weekends

Contents

Tables

Preface

In the wake of the devastation of World War II, U.S. policymakers set out to build a new international architecture to govern world trade. A new international institution was created, the General Agreement on Tariffs and Trade (GATT), and under its auspices eight rounds of multilateral negotiations were held between 1947 and 1995. Along with the GATT negotiations, the United States has entered into bilateral and regional trade agreements with twenty nations, and its trade competitors have also entered into many bilateral agreements. These agreements have resulted in the elimination of many nontariff barriers to trade and have reduced developed-country tariffs on nonagricultural goods from an average of 40 percent to less than 4 percent today. This has led to huge growth in world trade and given an enormous boost to overall global economic growth.

U.S. trade agreements have promoted its foreign policy interests in addition to its commercial objectives. The reduction of trade barriers after World War II enabled Europe and Japan to recover economically, and without this, much of Western Europe would probably have fallen under the Soviet Union's orbit. More recently, U.S. policymakers have negotiated bilateral and regional trade agreements to promote a number of its foreign policy interests, such as its post-9/11 agreements with Middle Eastern countries to reduce the potential for terrorism, and its agreements with its neighbors in the Americas to reduce the flow of narcotics and illegal immigrants into the United States.

In 1995, as a result of the last successful round of multilateral negotiations—which enormously expanded the rules governing international trade to include agriculture, services, and intellectual property, as well as a robust dispute settlement mechanism—the GATT was renamed the World Trade Organization (WTO). This followed the 1994 U.S. agreement to create the North American Free Trade Agreement (NAFTA), which removed almost all barriers to trade between the United States, Mexico, and Canada.

Although the free trade community viewed the creation of NAFTA and the WTO as enormous successes, these agreements stimulated a huge backlash against globalization. Organized labor saw the WTO and NAFTA as a threat to the American worker, a concern notably captured by Ross Perot in his 1992 campaign for the presidency when he said that the movement of jobs from the United States to Mexico would create "a giant sucking sound." Environmentalists viewed the new agreements as a threat to the ability of governments to protect endangered species and deal with concerns such as global warming. And the developing countries came to believe that they had been sold a bill of goods with the WTO, which many saw as balanced in favor of the developed countries and against the developing countries' interests.

In spite of antiglobalization protests, a new round of multilateral trade negotiations, the Doha Development Round, was launched in November 2001. In the wake of the September 11, 2001, terrorist attacks, this round was advocated as important for promoting economic development in the poorer countries—and this, it was argued, would reduce the potential for impoverished nations to be used as recruiting grounds for terrorist groups. Along with pursuing these new multilateral negotiations, the United States has negotiated bilateral and regional trade agreements with twenty nations. A few of these, primarily the agreements with Australia and South Korea, have significant commercial implications, but most were negotiated primarily for foreign policy reasons and as a spur to the multilateral trade round.

The trade community argues that additional trade liberalization will boost economic growth and that this will better enable countries to protect the environment and improve workers' standards of living. But critics of U.S. trade agreements remain largely unconvinced. By and large, U.S. labor unions continue to oppose the nation's trade agreements, and the developing countries remain skeptical about the possible benefits of a successful Doha Round. Moreover, the free trade paradigm is increasingly being questioned in the light of the success that a number of countries, including China and South Korea, have had through a neomercantilist trade model that aggressively promotes exports and limits imports.

The world trade system today is extremely unbalanced, given that the United States has experienced a large trade deficit for the past ten years, while China and other nations have enjoyed corresponding trade surpluses. Many economists view this situation as unsustainable.

Today, the Doha Round trade negotiations have basically collapsed, and the three most recent U.S. trade agreements—with Colombia, Panama, and South Korea—were only approved by Congress after a four-year delay. Additionally, the American public views the U.S. trade agreements program with a great deal of skepticism.

In a presentation at the Woodrow Wilson Center on March 5, 2003, Murray Weidenbaum, who had been chairman of the Council of Economic Advisers under President Ronald Reagan, challenged the trade community to seriously consider the concerns of the trade critics. In his address, he said: "Moving to the high middle ground on globalization is difficult and will take time. Developing a feeling of trust, or at least common understanding, is a badly needed precondition. But in order to achieve real progress, we must 'break the ice' by taking the concerns of the critics seriously and responding with constructive action rather than just more talk."

The objective of this book is to help break the ice. The first three chapters set out the context of U.S. policy on trade agreements—first, with a broad review of developments since the policy was enacted in 1934; second, with an overview of the nation's trade agreements that are in force; and third, with a brief summary of the economic theory underlying the U.S. trade agreements program. Chapter 4 examines the commercial impact of U.S. trade agreements, and chapter 5 looks at the foreign policy rationale of these agreements. The next three chapters consider the major concerns of the critics—first, the interests of the developing countries; second, the impact of U.S. trade agreements on environmental protection; and third, the agreements' impact on U.S. labor. The final chapter makes recommendations vis-à-vis the major steps needed to gain broader appeal.

In addition to setting out ideas for how trade liberalization can be reconceived in a way that benefits the U.S. economy broadly, as well as the economies of its trade partners, it is hoped that this book can be useful to the academic community and to those in the general public that would like to have a better understanding of U.S. trade agreements.

These agreements today are far more complex than was the case twenty-five years ago, and they have a far greater impact on the U.S. economy and domestic policies. This book seeks to provide the historical context for these changes and the theoretical framework for understanding how trade affects labor, the environment, and economic development.

Acknowledgments

I am very grateful for all the support given me by the Woodrow Wilson International Center for Scholars. President and CEO Jane Harman, Executive Vice President Michael Van Dusen, and former president Lee Hamilton have created an environment at the Center conducive to rigorous and nonpartisan scholarship, and they have provided enormous support to the Center's scholars, without which I never could have completed this project.

My special thanks go to Kent Hughes, director of the Program on America and the Global Economy at the Wilson Center, who reviewed numerous drafts and was generous with his time in brainstorming some of the critical issues in trade policy. And special thanks also go to Geoff Dabelko, who brought me to the Center and contributed to my thinking on the nexus of trade and the environment. Joe Brinley, director of the Wilson Center Press, provided invaluable help in preparing my manuscript for publication and encouragement to finish this project.

I also owe special thanks to several people who reviewed drafts of this book and gave me invaluable comments, including two former deputy U.S. trade representatives, Ambassador Alan Wolff and Ambassador Michael Smith, as well as Charles Blum and Joe Papovich, former senior officials at the Office of the U.S. Trade Representative, and Bruce Petersen, an economist and good friend.

The Wilson Center also provided a number of outstanding research assistants whose help was invaluable: Jonathan Bennett, Lindsay Bernsen, Darwin Brack, Rachel Callahan, Debbie Chung, Trenton Feasel, Icaro Gama, Anthony Gauspohl, Susan Guarda, Hala Hanna, Takanori Hayashi, Can Kevenk, Dani Litovsky, Alexander Moscoso, Carl Oberg, and Shaila Rajamani. Although each one only worked with me for a short time, their energy and enthusiasm were inspirational.

The library staff at the Wilson Center—Dagne Gizaw, Michelle Kamalich, and Janet Spikes—were invariably helpful in finding research material. And my colleagues at the Center—Zdenek David, Dennis Kux, Bill Milam, and John Sewell—never failed to make the times spent on research and writing enjoyable.

Many of the excellent programs presented at the Wilson Center helped shape my views, as did my years working on trade policy in the Office of the U.S. Trade Representative, on Capitol Hill, at the U.S. Department of Commerce, and in the private sector. Many individuals gave me invaluable help in my career and in understanding trade policy. I will always owe deep gratitude to Ambassador William Brock, Senator William Roth, Congressman Sam Gibbons, Forrest Abbuhl, Bill Kelly, Dick Heimlich, Fred Montgomery, Harold Bratt, Dick Matheisen, and many others too numerous to mention.

I would also like to thank a number of people who shared ideas with me, including Peter Allgeier, Jim Bacchus, Don Eiss, Geza Feketekuty, Skip Jones, and Dick Self, among others.

Needless to say, however, I myself bear full responsibility for the contents of this book and for any mistakes it may contain.

*Globalization and
America's Trade Agreements*

Chapter 1

U.S. Trade Policy in Crisis

The United States has led the world in an unprecedented reduction of barriers to international commerce during the past sixty-five years. The major tool in liberalizing world trade has been to negotiate multilateral reciprocal trade agreements in which America and its trade partners agree to mutually reduce trade barriers. Today this approach is under serious attack. The outcome of the debate on U.S. trade agreements policy will have enormous consequences for both the nation's economy and its foreign policy.

Following World War II, America's leaders believed that it was critical to establish international trade rules that would lead to a steady reduction of barriers to trade. Policymakers believed this was necessary to enable the world economy to recover from the devastation of the Great Depression and the war, and that it would help prevent international disputes that could lead to future conflicts.

Accordingly, the United States and its allies negotiated the General Agreement on Tariffs and Trade (GATT) in 1947 and, under the GATT's auspices, the United States led the world in eight rounds of multilateral negotiations to reduce trade barriers. Only several dozen countries participated in the earliest rounds, but by the end of the last successful round in 1995, the Uruguay Round, 125 countries participated.

In 1950, the developed countries' tariff rates averaged 40 percent; but fifty years later, after the implementation of most of the Uruguay Round concessions, they had fallen to an average of 4 percent. Additionally, nontariff barriers such as quotas and arbitrary standards were also removed. Spurred by this enormous liberalization of trade barriers, world

1

trade exploded; imports and exports, which accounted for only some 10.9 percent of the U.S. gross national product in 1947, rose to 30.6 percent in 2008 before the global financial and economic crisis. Most economists believe this growth in trade contributed enormously to U.S. economic growth in the post–World War II years.

The reduction of trade barriers, of course, was not the only cause of this increase in trade, but it was probably one of the most important factors. Other developments, such as better and cheaper transportation and communications, also played a significant role.

By 1995, U.S. efforts to liberalize trade had achieved enormous success. The just-completed Uruguay Round not only substantially reduced trade barriers but also transformed the postwar GATT into a more extensive system of international trade rules that covered services and intellectual property, as well as goods, and that included binding dispute settlement procedures. In recognition of this strengthened role, the GATT was renamed the World Trade Organization (WTO).

In addition to the Uruguay Round, U.S. trade negotiators had completed negotiations for the North American Free Trade Agreement (NAFTA). This agreement, which expanded a 1989 agreement with Canada to include Mexico, went into effect January 1, 1994, and required the elimination of substantially all barriers to trade between the three countries, thereby creating a duty-free market of some 450 million people that accounted for 24 percent of total world gross domestic product.

The WTO and NAFTA generated increased concern about "globalization" and the role of America's trade agreements among a broad swath of the American public.[1] Although there are many aspects of "globalization," the focus in this book is on economic globalization, which refers to the interdependence of national economies whereby companies and workers compete across borders, and goods, services, and capital can flow relatively freely around the world.

1. There are many definitions and aspects of "globalization," including its economic, political, and social dimensions. My focus here is on the economic dimension; the KOF Institute defines economic globalization as characterized by "long distance flows of goods, capital and services as well as information and perceptions that accompany market exchanges." KOF also publishes an index of globalization by country and region and year going back to 1970. "KOF Index of Globalization," http:// globalization.kof.ethz.ch/.

Some early dispute settlement cases in both the WTO and NAFTA led the environmental community to view U.S. trade agreements as an enemy of better protection of the environment. Labor in the United States increasingly viewed trade liberalization as a mechanism to transfer good jobs from the United States to the rest of the world. The development community was similarly concerned, but for the opposite reason—that is, that the trade agreements would open developing countries up to competition from the developed nations that would destroy their infant industries. Additionally, the developing countries believed that the Uruguay Round was unfair to them by requiring them to adopt expensive new rules, such as for the protection of intellectual property, while not providing expanded market access for the products they produce.

These concerns bubbled over into mass protests against globalization and the WTO in late November 1999. The WTO had hoped to launch a new round of multilateral negotiations to further liberalize trade, including trade in agriculture products and services, at its Ministerial Meeting in Seattle. However, labor unionists, environmentalists, prodemocracy groups, human rights advocates, and others (even including some middle-aged hippies wanting to relive the Vietnam War protests) took to the streets in what became known as the Battle in Seattle. After four days of sometimes violent protests, on December 3, 1999, the WTO Ministerial Meeting collapsed in failure amid tear gas and antiglobalization protests. (Although the protests were an indication of public concerns regarding trade policy, most observers believe that the Ministerial Meeting collapsed because there was an insufficient consensus among the main participants to launch a new multilateral round.)

Two years later, in November 2001, following the horrific terrorist attacks of September 11, 2001, the WTO negotiators were finally able to launch the new round. In the context of the terrorist attacks, this new round, dubbed the Doha Development Round, had an ostensible emphasis on promoting economic development in the poorest countries.[2]

2. The official name for this round of multilateral negotiations is the "Doha Development Agenda." However, all other trade rounds have been called "rounds." Because that terminology is more informative than "agenda," the Doha negotiations are referred to as the "Doha Development Round" in this book. Trade negotiating rounds have generally been named after the city where the negotiations were launched or took place, and that was the case with the Doha Round, which was

In the early 2000s, in addition to seeking multilateral negotiations to further remove global barriers to trade, the United States sought to negotiate regional and bilateral agreements.[3] The rationale for negotiating bilateral and regional agreements was to press forward on market liberalization and to provide incentive for countries to complete the Doha Round. The biggest regional U.S. agreement was to be a "Free Trade Area of the Americas" that would include all the nations in South, Central, and North America, except for Cuba. Although significant progress was made, these negotiations collapsed in 2005, primarily over disagreements between the United States and Brazil.

U.S. negotiators did have some successes, however, implementing free trade agreements (FTAs) with the six nations of the Caribbean Basin, as well as with Chile, Peru, Singapore, Australia, Bahrain, Morocco, Oman, Colombia, Panama, and South Korea. Congress, which must approve trade agreements for them to become law, had grave concerns about the labor provisions in the Colombia agreement and with the threat of unfair competition from reducing trade barriers with South Korea, and it refused to approve the agreements until the Obama administration had renegotiated the relevant provisions.

Today the United States and the rest of the world are only slowly emerging from the 2008–9 global financial and economic crisis, the worst such event since the Great Depression of the 1930s. Most economists believe that further reducing world barriers to trade could strengthen economic growth. Unfortunately, the multilateral negotiations in the Doha Round have so far failed, and some countries have imposed new barriers to trade, which could jeopardize future economic growth.

Many policymakers and businesspeople view the lack of progress in trade liberalization as a temporary problem, and believe that these obstacles would be overcome if the trade community did a better job of making its case for the benefits of trade. Some free traders view globalization as inevitable; in this view, the United States may have some setbacks, but over time globalization will inevitably continue. However, this is not necessarily the case. A better course of action is to seriously

launched in Doha, Qatar. The Kennedy and Dillon rounds were exceptions to this practice and were named after a key individual responsible for the round.

3. In 2001, the United States did have two bilateral free trade agreements already in place with Israel and Jordan, in addition to NAFTA.

consider the critics' concerns and to develop a trade policy that better promotes broad U.S. interests.

The "Golden Era of Globalization" and Its Aftermath

Today's globalization has a precedent in the period from 1896 to 1913, when world trade roughly doubled. A century ago, capital moved freely across borders, and European investors eagerly bought bonds that financed economic development in the United States, South America, and Australia. Unlike the current period of globalization, people in 1900 could move across many borders freely, without passports. The market for goods, then as now, was basically global.

Late-nineteenth-century globalization was driven largely by improvements in transportation and communications. Early in the century, countries built canals and railroads, and refrigeration techniques were greatly improved. Later, the costs of shipping declined as steamships replaced sailing ships and the telegraph dramatically lowered the costs of communication. Trade around the world became much more possible and affordable.

Trade policy also played a role. David Ricardo's theory of comparative advantage, which suggested that all nations were better off engaging in international trade, had become highly influential.[4] A number of countries signed treaties to cut trade barriers, and some countries were unilaterally reducing barriers to trade. In 1888, for example, Italy signed treaties with Spain and Switzerland, and Mexico signed agreements with Britain, Japan, and Ecuador.[5] The United States reached three major trade agreements in the 1800s and early 1900s—with Canada (1855–66), Hawaii (1876–1900), and Cuba (1903–34).[6]

This golden age ended on June 28, 1914, when an assassin's bullet killed Archduke Franz Ferdinand and Europe descended into World

4. David Ricardo's theory of comparative advantage was set out in 1817 and published four years later in *On the Principles of Political Economy and Taxation* (London: John Murray, 1821).

5. Robert Pahre, *Politics and Trade Cooperation in the Nineteenth Century* (Cambridge: Cambridge University Press, 2008), 160–61.

6. Douglas A. Irwin, *From Smoot-Hawley to Reciprocal Trade Agreements: Changing the Course of U.S. Trade Policy in the 1930s*, NBER Working Paper 5895 (Cambridge, Mass.: National Bureau of Economic Research, 1997), 10.

War I. When the war finally ended in 1918, the world trade system was in tatters. Unfortunately, the United States turned its back on international cooperation, and the victorious European powers demanded harsh reparations from Germany.

After the war, the United States was in deep recession, with unemployment of about 20 percent. In the early 1920s, however, the U.S. economy took off, spurred by new technologies such as the automobile and radio, Federal Reserve policies of low interest rates and an expanded money supply, and deep cuts in business taxes. Responding to business pressures, Congress raised import tariffs several times during the 1920s.

By 1924, good economic times began to spread to Europe and the Roaring Twenties were in full force. However, as a result of loose monetary policy, several bubbles formed, first a housing bubble, which popped in the mid-1920s, and then greatly inflated prices on the New York Stock Exchange. The stock market bubble, of course, ended with the stock market crash beginning October 29, 1929, which ultimately led to a fall of 89 percent in the Dow stock index by July 1932.

In the face of the stock market collapse, policymakers made several serious mistakes. Although economists continue to debate the causes of the Great Depression, two major policy failures stand out. First, the Federal Reserve, which had pursued too loose a policy in the 1920s, now let the money supply shrink by a third by 1933. Second, policymakers failed to act as some major banks failed.

However, trade policy also played an enormous role. On June 16, 1930, President Herbert Hoover signed the Smoot-Hawley Act, which substantially raised U.S. tariffs on imports. This legislation had started out as a bill that would have only raised tariffs on some agricultural products. Unfortunately, other congressmen and senators inserted their own proposals for duty increases, and by the time the bill passed Congress, tariffs were to be raised on some 890 products.

Other countries immediately retaliated or even took preemptive action as the bill was being debated in Congress. For example, in May 1930 Canada imposed new tariffs on products that accounted for about 30 percent of its imports from the United States. Britain abandoned its traditional free trade stance and signed preferential trade agreements with its multiple colonies that discriminated against nonmembers such as the United States. And Germany signed bilateral trade agreements with the Eastern European nations, while Japan sought to establish a Greater East Asia Co-Prosperity Sphere.

The result was that world trade plummeted 66 percent between 1929 and 1934.[7] High tariffs were a factor in the drop in trade, as was the drop in income because of the worldwide Depression of the early 1930s.

Although most economists do not believe that the Smoot-Hawley tariff was the major cause of the Great Depression, almost all believe that it was an enormous policy mistake; in fact, 1,028 economists wrote President Hoover as the bill was being passed by Congress urging him not to sign the legislation.[8] With the world deep in the Depression, however, it was a mistake that could not be simply reversed once tariffs were raised, given that politically the United States could not then unilaterally reduce tariffs with unemployment running at more than 20 percent. It required an ingenious policy initiative—the Reciprocal Trade Agreements Act—to begin the process of expanding world trade.

The Reciprocal Trade Agreements Act of 1934

By 1934, unemployment in the United States had reached 21.7 percent. President Franklin D. Roosevelt, elected in 1932, recognized that the Smoot-Hawley tariffs had been an enormous mistake; however, he could not unilaterally reduce them without congressional approval. And Congress would not have granted approval with almost a quarter of all Americans unemployed.

In theory, the president could have negotiated trade treaties with other countries to reduce foreign trade barriers. However, under Article 1, Section 8, of the U.S. Constitution, it is Congress—not the president—that has the power to impose and collect import duties and to regulate commerce with foreign nations. Accordingly, any such agreement would need to have been submitted to the Senate as a treaty, which would require a two-thirds vote of approval. Additionally, because changing tariffs is a revenue measure, the agreement would need to be approved by the House of Representatives. In the economic and political environment of 1934, it would have been impossible to obtain congressional approval for a treaty that reduced U.S. tariffs.

7. U.S. Department of State, http://future.state.gov/when/timeline/1921_timeline/Smoot_tariffhtml.
8. See, e.g., Jude Wanniski, "Why Wall Street Crashed," January 8, 2005, http://www.polyconomics.com/ssu/ssu-050108.htm.

Roosevelt's secretary of state, Cordell Hull, came up with an in-genious solution. Working with Congress, he developed legislation—the Reciprocal Trade Agreements Act (RTAA)—to give the presi-dent authority to negotiate trade agreements that would reduce U.S. tariffs in exchange for reciprocal concessions from other countries. In a major break from the past, agreements negotiated under this au-thority would not require congressional approval; that is, Congress delegated its constitutional authority to impose tariffs to the execu-tive branch for the period the RTAA was in effect. Congress was will-ing to do this because most members recognized their mistake in the logrolling exercise that resulted in the Smoot-Hawley tariff bill and because the approach of mutually negotiating tariff reductions with the U.S. trade partners picked up support from industries anxious to expand export sales.

The stated purpose of the RTAA, which the president signed on June 12, 1934, was "expanding foreign markets for the products of the United States (as a means of assisting in the present emergency in re-storing the American standard of living, in overcoming domestic un-employment and the present economic depression, in increasing the purchasing power of the American Public."[9] To achieve this purpose, the act gave the president authority for three years to enter into bi-lateral trade agreements with foreign governments that could increase or decrease any existing rate of duty by up to 50 percent. The RTAA specified that "the proclaimed duties and other import restrictions shall apply to . . . all foreign countries."

The Department of State under Secretary Hull had the lead in negoti-ating these agreements, supported by an interagency committee that in-cluded the Commerce, Agriculture, and Treasury departments. The first agreement was with Cuba in 1934, followed by Belgium, Haiti, and Swe-den in 1935, and by Brazil, Canada, Colombia, Finland, France, Guate-mala, Honduras, the Netherlands, Nicaragua, and Switzerland in 1936. The RTAA was reauthorized in 1937, 1940, and 1943; by 1945, when the RTAA was extended again, the United States had negotiated agree-ments with twenty-eight countries. Because of the approach of reducing U.S. tariffs only on products where the partner was principal supplier, the duty reductions were not large. In fact, the U.S. Tariff Commission

9. Chapter 474, 48 Stat. 943, 19 U.S.C., Sect. 350 (a).

calculated that the average U.S. tariff only declined from 46.7 percent to 40.7 percent for the first thirteen country agreements.[10]

After World War II, President Harry Truman used the RTAA as authority to negotiate the first multilateral trade round after World War II, the Geneva Round, which was concluded between the United States and twenty-two other countries in 1947 and reduced tariffs on a wide variety of products.[11] The results of the Geneva Round were then codified into the newly negotiated General Agreement on Tariffs and Trade,[12] which President Truman implemented by executive order under the authority of the RTAA.[13]

The fundamental pillar of the GATT, enshrined in Article I, is the most-favored-nation (MFN) clause, which requires all signatories to grant the same trade treatment to all members that is granted to any member. To the original architects of the postwar GATT system, bilateral agreements were anathema. They believed that the web of special agreements spun by Germany, the United Kingdom, and Japan after World War I had contributed to the political tensions that spurred World War II. Additionally, they believed that bilateral or regional agreements generally caused more harm to nonmembers than benefit to the members. Accordingly, the GATT sought to ensure that the trade rules and benefits applied equally to all members.

From 1934 to 1962, the RTAA was extended eleven times; during that period, the stated U.S. objective for trade agreements remained the same: to strengthen the United States commercially by expanding its exports through mutual tariff reductions. Following the Geneva Round, four more rounds were held between 1949 and 1961, although these only reduced trade barriers to a minor extent.

10. Irwin, *From Smoot-Hawley to Reciprocal Trade Agreements*, 28.

11. For a description of the GATT multilateral trade rounds, see World Trade Organization, "The GATT Years: From Havana to Marrakesh," http://www.wto .org/english/thewto_e/whatis_e/tif_e/fact4_e.htm.

12. The United States had envisioned an International Trade Organization, which would have broad authority for trade policy, economic development, investment, and other elements of commercial policy. Although the International Trade Organization was approved by the United Nations in 1949, President Truman withdrew it from congressional approval in 1950 when it was clear it lacked the votes to pass.

13. U.S. trade partners implemented the GATT as a treaty, which has a higher legal standing than an executive order. E.g., under U.S. law, a treaty overrides state law, whereas state law trumps an executive order.

Each of the bilateral agreements negotiated before World War II and the first five multilateral rounds negotiated under the GATT only achieved modest results. Because tariff reductions would be made on an MFN basis, there was concern that some countries might try to benefit from other countries' concessions without reducing their own high duties. To minimize the potential for such "free riders," the RTAA specified that the United States could only reduce tariffs on products where the "primary" supplier of the product to the United States also agreed to reduce its own tariffs.

This approach proved to be very restrictive, and it limited the extent of trade liberalization. Negotiations were conducted on a "request-offer" basis, whereby a country would request specific concessions from its negotiating partners, which then would offer specific commitments, and this cumbersome process would continue until a package of limited concessions was put together.

Although these trade rounds reduced the tariffs imposed by members on imports from other members, GATT members were free to impose any trade barriers they wanted to on nonmembers. In fact, the United States imposed Smoot-Hawley level tariffs on imports from the Soviet Union and other Communist Bloc countries from 1951 until 1974, when the president selectively waived these duties on some Communist Bloc countries while retaining them on others, and Smoot-Hawley tariffs still apply to North Korea and Cuba.

The rationale for trade agreements was generally stated in terms of promoting U.S. commercial interests, but it was recognized that trade was also important to its foreign policy interests. As President Roosevelt said in his 1945 message to Congress requesting that the trade agreements act be renewed, "We cannot succeed in building a peaceful world unless we build an economically healthy world."[14] (Ironically, the first step listed by President Roosevelt to "build an economically healthy world" was "to improve currency relationships." This was never done, and today the world's out-of-kilter currency exchange system is still the greatest danger to the world trade system.)

In 1962, Congress passed new legislation to authorize the president to negotiate trade agreements for three years. This new legislation, the Trade

14. Roosevelt's message to Congress asking that the Trade Agreements Act be renewed is available at http://www.presidency.ucsb.edu/ws/index.php?pid=16597&st=bretton&st1=#axzz1reBUWyfF.

Expansion Act, continued the basic concept underlying the RTAA of reducing U.S. tariffs in exchange for reciprocal concessions from U.S. trade partners. However, it made a major change to the previous approach by providing that any agreements would have to be approved by Congress rather than be automatically implemented under presidential authority.

Under the mandate of the Trade Expansion Act, President Kennedy negotiated a major multilateral trade round—the Kennedy Round—which reduced U.S. tariffs on industrial products by almost one-third. The breakthrough came because negotiators agreed on a formula for reducing tariffs that the developed countries would apply across the board with only limited exceptions, rather than the request-offer approach used in previous rounds.

Although the Kennedy Round focused on reducing tariffs, it included a code addressing antidumping practices. Congress passed most of what the administration had negotiated, but it included language prohibiting U.S. adherence to the agreement on antidumping. This, understandably, infuriated U.S. trade partners, which felt that they had agreed to a whole package that included this change to U.S. law.

Presidential authority to negotiate trade agreements expired after 1967. However, by the early 1970s, it was recognized that the nontariff barriers maintained by many countries were substantially damaging the potential of U.S. exports. President Nixon accordingly sought and obtained new authority to negotiate via the Trade Act of 1974.

Because of the experience with the Kennedy Round, in which Congress refused to pass one element of the negotiated package, U.S. partners had made it clear that they would not enter into negotiations unless the United States provided better assurances that the whole package would be approved. Accordingly, the Trade Act of 1974 embodied another innovation, the so-called fast track provision, which specified that Congress would vote up or down on any agreement without amendment and within ninety legislative days. With this assurance, the United States successfully negotiated the Tokyo Round trade agreement, which was approved in 1979.

Like the Kennedy Round, the Tokyo Round significantly reduced tariffs, with the nine major industrial nations cutting their duties by one-third, and thus bringing their duties down to an average of 4.7 percent. Even more important, for the first time the Tokyo Round addressed nontariff barriers to trade. Throughout the early years of the GATT, high tariffs were the primary tool used by governments to restrict trade. By the end of the Kennedy Round, however, tariffs had been substantially reduced, and nontariff measures became more visible and more prevalent.

Although the Tokyo Round was very successful in further opening up trade for industrial products, virtually no progress was made with regard to agricultural trade. The United States and a number of other countries continued to maintain high tariffs on agricultural products, and many countries, including the United States, limited imports of many agricultural products by quota restrictions. Additionally, the European Union, the United States, and others provided significant subsidies to their domestic producers, thereby greatly distorting world trade patterns.

In September 1986, the GATT launched the Uruguay Round at its Ministerial Meeting in Punta del Este. By the time this round concluded in 1994, in addition to continued reductions of tariffs, agreements had been reached on services, the protection of intellectual property, and investment. The developed countries agreed to give up several protectionist systems, including the Multi-Fibre Arrangement on textiles and the future use of "voluntary restraint agreements." It also set out a framework for rules on agriculture, although it did not significantly liberalize existing practices. Unlike the Tokyo Round, the Uruguay agreement was set out as a "single undertaking," which meant that countries had to take either the whole package or none of it, with the exception of the government procurement, civil aircraft, bovine meat, and dairy agreements, which remained plurilateral agreements.

Negotiators also agreed on a new binding dispute settlement system with timelines for deciding a dispute. Countries that were injured by other country practices that violated the agreement now had a robust mechanism to obtain compensation or to authorize retaliatory measures. In recognition of this new status for world trade rules, the GATT was renamed the WTO.

The current multilateral trade round, the Doha Development Round, was launched in 2001. These negotiations were supposed to improve the developing countries' ability to participate in the world trade system, and to substantially liberalize trade in agriculture and services as well as further reduce barriers to trade in nonagricultural products.

The Spread of Bilateralism

As noted above, the fundamental pillar of the GATT was that all concessions were to be granted to all GATT member countries. GATT members were free to apply any duties they wished to nonmembers, but members were to receive MFN treatment. The original GATT included an exception to this rule for countries that formed a customs union or free trade area subject to review by the GATT membership.[15]

Early on, however, the MFN principle faced challenges. Both the United Kingdom and France were permitted to retain the preference agreements they had granted to their colonies. Then, in 1957, Germany, France, Italy, Belgium, Luxembourg, and the Netherlands formed the European Economic Community (EEC), which was to eliminate barriers to trade between the six, establish a common external tariff, and implement a common agricultural policy.[16] The United States fully supported the EEC, which was viewed as a mechanism to ensure that there would be no future wars between France and Germany and that it would be a buffer against the expansion of the Soviet Union.

While supporting the formation of the EEC, other European countries were concerned that their economic interests would suffer, as their exports to these six nations would face discrimination compared with sales by EEC members. Accordingly, in 1960 the United Kingdom, Austria, Denmark, Norway, Portugal, Sweden, and Switzerland launched the

15. A customs union is formed by two or more countries that eliminate trade barriers between themselves and adopt a common external tariff, whereas the members of a free trade area eliminate barriers between themselves but each retains its own external tariffs.

16. The EEC began as a customs union between Belgium, France, Germany, Italy, Luxembourg, and the Netherlands. The EEC then expanded in 1973 to include Denmark, Ireland, and the United Kingdom; and it expanded again in the 1980s to include Greece, Spain, and Portugal. In 1993, the EEC further evolved from a customs union to become an economic union, renamed the European Union, with the intent to have common commercial regulations and the free movement of labor and capital. Austria, Finland, and Sweden joined in 1995. And in 2004 Cyprus, the Czech Republic, Estonia, Hungary, Latvia, Lithuania, Malta, Poland, Slovakia, and Slovenia joined. In 2007, Romania and Bulgaria joined, bringing the European Union's membership to twenty-seven states. Croatia is expected to become the twenty-eighth member of the EU in July 2013.

European Free Trade Area, which would eliminate tariffs on trade among themselves while allowing each to maintain its own external tariff.

The United States, however, shied away from preferential trade agreements until 1985, when the United States entered into a bilateral FTA with Israel, which was negotiated primarily for foreign policy reasons. Israel was seen as a staunch U.S. ally in the Middle East, and the agreement was intended to cement that relationship. Additionally, there was a minor commercial interest: Israel had negotiated an FTA with the European Communities that would place U.S. exporters at a commercial disadvantage vis-à-vis their European competitors. It was felt that a United States–Israel FTA would counter that commercial disadvantage.

In 1989, the United States entered into its second postwar FTA, this time with Canada, as can be seen in table 1.1. This agreement, which was primarily motivated by commercial considerations, built on the Automotive Products Trade Agreement signed in 1965, which led to duty-free trade in autos and parts.

Two years later, in June 1990, U.S. president George H. W. Bush announced the Enterprise for the Americas Initiative, which envisioned an eventual FTA that would extend from "Anchorage to Tierra del Fuego." The objectives of this negotiation were based on both foreign policy and commercial considerations. From a commercial perspective, the Free Trade Area of the Americas (FTAA) would open up major markets, particularly Brazil and Argentina. From a foreign policy perspective, it was envisioned that an FTAA would foster stability and democracy in U.S. neighbors to the south.

In 1994, the United States, Canada, and Mexico launched NAFTA, under which all trade barriers were eliminated, including agricultural barriers, and investment was opened up; the agreement also included side pacts on environment and labor. However, the agreement did not require the United States to curb its huge agricultural subsidies.

In 2001, Jordan became the next country with which the United States negotiated a bilateral FTA. The U.S. motive for negotiating this agreement was entirely political. The agreement, built on a system that the United States had earlier implemented, allowed goods manufactured in Jordan in "qualified industrial zones" to enter the U.S. duty free, provided that the product incorporated a specified level of raw materials and parts from Israel. The intent of both the qualified indus-

Table 1.1. U.S. Bilateral and Regional Free Trade
Agreements

Agreement	Date Implemented
Israel	September 1, 1985
Canada	January 1, 1989
Mexico (as part of NAFTA)	January 1, 1994
Jordan	December 7, 2001
Chile	January 1, 2004
Singapore	January 1, 2004
Australia	January 1, 2005
Morocco	January 1, 2006
CAFTA-DR	
El Salvador	March 1, 2006
Honduras	April 1, 2006
Nicaragua	April 1, 2006
Guatemala	July 1, 2006
Dominican Republic	March 1, 2007
Costa Rica	January 1, 2009
Bahrain	August 1, 2006
Oman	January 1, 2009
Peru	February 1, 2009
South Korea	March 15, 2012
Colombia	May 15, 2012
Panama	October 31, 2012

Note: NAFTA = North American Free Trade Agreement;
CAFTA-DR = Central American Free Trade Agreement–
Dominican Republic.
Source: World Trade Organization, "Regional Trade Agree-
ments Information System," http://rtais.wto.org/UI/Public-
SearchByMemberResult.aspx?MemberCode=840&lang=1&
redirect=1.

trial zones and the FTA was to promote peace between Israel and its neighbors.

Shortly after the September 11, 2001, terrorist attacks, the United States launched an initiative to promote peace in the Middle East by announcing the intention to negotiate a Middle East Free Trade Agreement, which would extend from the Persian Gulf to the Atlantic Ocean. A flurry of negotiations and agreements resulted, including agreements with Morocco (2006), Bahrain (2006), and Oman (2009). The hope was that an FTA including both the Arab nations and Israel would promote peace in the Middle East and, by stimulating long-term economic growth, would discourage terrorism.

As progress on the Doha Development Round and on the Free Trade Area of the Americas waned, the United States turned increasingly to bilateral negotiations. Robert Zoellick, the U.S. trade representative, articulated a strategy of "competitive liberalization," under which the United States would pursue bilateral and regional FTAs partially for their own sake and also to spur broader multilateral negotiations.

In September 2003, FTAs were signed with Chile and Singapore, and in August 2004 with Australia and five Central American Common Market nations (Costa Rica, El Salvador, Guatemala, Honduras, and Nicaragua). The Dominican Republic subsequently joined this latter agreement, which became known as the Central American Free Trade Agreement–Dominican Republic (CAFTA-DR). Subsequently, FTAs were implemented with Colombia, South Korea, and Panama.

Currently, the United States is engaged in negotiations with eleven other countries (Australia, Brunei, Canada, Chile, Japan, Malaysia, Mexico, New Zealand, Peru, Singapore, and Vietnam) for a regional trade agreement called the Trans-Pacific Partnership (TPP). The hope is that a successful negotiation could produce a template for future negotiations with other Asian-Pacific countries. The TPP would build on agreements that the United States already has with Australia, Canada, Chile, Mexico, Peru, and Singapore.

The United States is also in talks with the European Union to launch negotiations for an FTA to be called the Trans-Atlantic Trade and Investment Partnership. These negotiations are expected to begin in 2013. Given the enormous commercial importance of the United States and the EU, a successful negotiation would likely have enormous commercial impact.

The Making of Trade Agreements Policy

Congress has the power to regulate commerce with other nations under the U.S. Constitution, as noted above, whereas the president has the authority to conduct foreign policy. Accordingly, both Congress and the administration are heavily involved in the formulation of U.S. trade policy. The formulation of trade policy is very political, because changes in U.S. trade barriers and access to other markets have an economic impact on all states and congressional districts and on all industries—and hence have a large influence on voters.

As a result of the experience with the Smoot-Hawley tariff bill, Congress has often delegated authority to negotiate trade agreements to the president under what has been known as "fast track authority" and more recently as "trade promotion authority." This authority was last granted to the president in legislation establishing the WTO in 1994, and it was extended in the Trade Act of 2002; this authority expired on July 1, 2007, and the president currently does not have delegated trade negotiating authority.[17]

Even when the president does have trade promotion authority, however, Congress still exercises enormous power over the whole process of negotiating trade agreements. First, of course, Congress can refuse to approve the agreement; for example, Congress refused to pass the South Korean agreement until improvements had been made to better protect the ability of the U.S. auto industry to do business in South Korea, and Congress refused to pass the Colombia agreement until more actions had been taken to protect workers' rights. Second, in granting the president negotiating authority, Congress defines the objectives of the negotiations and the terms of the authority, including such aspects as the maximum depth of tariff cuts permissible and the number of years the president has this authority.

Third, Congress requires the administration to consult closely with the relevant committees as negotiations proceed, and it requires the Office of the U.S. Trade Representative (USTR) to provide detailed briefings on a regular basis to interested committees. If Congress has concerns, it can hold oversight hearings or even threaten to withhold appropriations through its budgetary responsibilities.

Congress, of course, is very sensitive to the concerns of the public. As noted, currently there are significant concerns among the broader public regarding globalization and U.S. trade agreements, and this has played a major role in congressional refusal to grant the president negotiating authority and in requiring changes to the Colombian and South Korean FTAs.

Even when the president does have trade promotion authority and has consulted closely with Congress as the negotiations proceed, however, it often can be extremely difficult to obtain congressional approval

---

17. A number of congressmen and senators have indicated an interest in legislation to give the president new negotiating authority, and such legislation may well pass Congress and be signed into law later in 2013.

of an agreement after negotiations have been completed. For example, Congress delayed passage of the agreements with South Korea, Colombia, and Panama for several years and forced the administration to go back and negotiate some changes to these agreements. The reality is that some important segments of the private sector have to lobby aggressively and effectively for approval of the agreement, and opposition by important segments needs to be minimized.

Within the administration, the president sets the broad parameters of the U.S. approach to trade policy, including the negotiation of trade agreements, within the constraints set out by his legislative mandate. Until 1963, the key agency responsible for administering trade policy under the president's guidance was the Department of State. Under congressional pressure, however, President Kennedy created a new Office of the Special Trade Representative (STR) in the White House. At that time, Congress believed that the Department of State was giving too little attention to U.S. commercial interests. The intent of the new office was to have a balance of U.S. commercial, foreign policy, and other interests.[18]

In the Trade Act of 1974, Congress expanded STR's responsibilities, gave the office a legislative charter, and made STR accountable to both the president and Congress. STR's responsibilities were again expanded in 1979, and STR was renamed the Office of the United States Trade Representative, a White House office headed up by the U.S. trade representative, a Cabinet-level officer.

USTR chairs an interagency committee process that develops positions for negotiations and makes recommendations to the president in the case of significant differences in positions between agencies on the negotiations. This interagency process, which includes nineteen federal agencies and offices, operates at two levels.[19] The Trade Policy Staff

18. Interestingly, the first STR (later to be called USTR) was Christian Herter, who had been secretary of state two years previously, and was one of the major U.S. political figures in the early 1960s.

19. The federal departments on the TPSC and TPRG are Agriculture, Commerce, Defense, Energy, Health and Human Services, Homeland Security, Interior, Justice, Labor, State, Transportation, and Treasury; and the agencies are the Council of Economic Advisers, the Council on Environmental Quality, the Environmental Protection Agency, the Agency for International Development, the National Economic Council, the National Security Council, the Office of Management and Budget, and, as a nonvoting member, the U.S. International Trade Commission.

Committee (TPSC) is at the senior civil service level and meets frequently to develop positions or options. When the TPSC is unable to reach a consensus, the issue is taken up by the Trade Policy Review Group (TPRG), which is at the undersecretary level. In the event that the TPRG is unable to reach a consensus or considers that the issue requires presidential approval, the National Economic Council will submit final options to the president for decision.

USTR has enormous power in this whole process. First, USTR chairs both the TPSC and the TPRG and determines what issues get taken up and how the options will be set out. Second, USTR has the lead in international negotiations, which gives it enormous leverage in the policy process. As a small agency of some two hundred people, USTR can develop its positions relatively quickly, well before larger agencies have had a chance to get guidance from the political level, which gives USTR substantial credibility in interagency debates.

Finally, and perhaps most important, USTR is mandated by U.S. law and historically has had extremely close relations with the congressional committees most responsible for trade policy: the House Ways and Means Committee and the Senate Finance Committee.[20]

The career staff at USTR is generally at a very senior level. USTR normally recruits career officials who have made significant contributions in one of the agencies—such as the State, Treasury, Commerce, or Agriculture departments—or have had senior positions on a congressional staff, generally the House Ways and Means Committee or the Senate Finance Committee.

Although most career officials in USTR have had some economics, only a few have graduate degrees in economics, while an increasing number have law degrees. Most of the U.S. trade representatives have backgrounds in law and politics, as can be seen in the appendix, and only one since 1977 has had prior experience in business or agriculture. Many of the career staff at USTR believe that free trade is inherently good and that the more a trade agreement lowers trade barriers, the better.

Trade-negotiating authority since 1974 has included a requirement that USTR establish advisory committees from the private sector. Currently, some seven hundred individuals serve on twenty-eight advisory

---

20. In 1981 newly elected President Reagan wanted to abolish USTR and was sharply reminded by Congress that USTR was legislatively mandated.

committees, representing various industries, agricultural sectors, and other expertise, such as environmental interests.[21] Each of these committees is required to report to Congress on its views of any trade agreements negotiated by the administration. Other than the specialized committees, such as environment and labor, the advisory committees are heavily dominated by large multinational firms.

USTR's role is to develop and implement a policy that promotes U.S. economic and commercial interests, within the limitations of domestic U.S. politics and with the need to gain an international consensus for trade liberalization. Because this is essentially a job of balancing objectives and constraints, few parties to the process obtain all they want. Historically, the view in USTR—only half-jokingly—is that if everyone is unhappy, then it must be the right policy.

Conclusion

The U.S. approach to trade agreements has achieved enormous success since the RTAA was passed in 1934. Trade liberalization, largely driven by U.S. policy on trade agreements, has benefited it and the world economically, and these U.S. agreements have advanced U.S. foreign policy interests.

However, today the outlook for continued multilateral trade liberalization is uncertain. The Doha Development Round negotiators have been unable to reach an agreement. The United States, the European Union, and Japan have been unwilling to make substantial changes in current agricultural programs, and the advanced developing countries—particularly India, China, and Brazil—have been unwilling to significantly reduce their industrial tariffs. Many other developing countries have been skeptical about new trade agreements, believing that they got a raw deal in the last trade round, the Uruguay Round.

Negotiations for bilateral and regional FTAs are also struggling. A major regional agreement sought by the United States, the Free Trade Agreement of the Americas, failed due to the unwillingness of the United States to open up its agricultural trade and that of its partners, particularly Brazil, to reduce tariffs on industrial goods and commit to disci-

21. See USTR's Web site for a listing of advisory committees and their recommendations: http://www.ustr.gov/about-us/intergovernmental-affairs/advisory-committees.

plines on services. The South Korea, Colombia, and Panama agreements faced strong opposition in Congress and had to be renegotiated before Congress finally gave approval.

Presidential authority to negotiate agreements under fast track procedures expired in July 2007. However, even when this authority was in place, some agreements barely passed Congress; for example, CAFTA passed the House by just two votes, and congressional leadership had to hold the vote open for close to an hour in order to round up the necessary votes.

Among the American public, support for trade agreements such as the WTO and NAFTA is at low levels. For example, according to a September 2010 NBC News / *Wall Street Journal* poll, 53 percent of respondents felt that U.S. trade agreements have hurt the country, and only 17 percent felt that they have helped.[22] And many believe that the country's huge structural trade deficit and its growing indebtedness to other nations threaten the stability of its economy and of the international commercial system.

In fact, the multilateral system of trade rules so painstakingly developed since World War II is increasingly being undermined by trade barriers and distortions not addressed by the rules. The GATT/WTO system is based on the expectation that there will be a roughly level playing field in the trade arena between countries. However, some countries, such as China, are pursuing neomercantilist policies that challenge this assumption and injure the U.S. economy.

Roger Altman, who was the U.S. deputy treasury secretary from 1993 to 1994, expresses the current crisis in trade policy in stark terms: "The long movement toward market liberalization has stopped, and a new period of state intervention, reregulation, and creeping protectionism has begun. Indeed, globalization itself is reversing. The longstanding wisdom that everyone wins in a single world market has been undermined."[23]

The trade policy community argues that trade liberalization is like riding a bicycle: Either we move forward or we fall off. Today, the United States is clearly in danger of falling off. Like the last period of globaliza-

22. The NBC News/*Wall Street Journal* poll is available at http://www.polling report.com/trade.htm.

23. Roger C. Altman, "Globalization in Retreat: Further Geopolitical Consequences of the Financial Crisis," *Foreign Affairs*, July–August 2009, 2–7. at 2.

tion, this era also has the potential to end badly. Governments have played a significant role in liberalizing trade since World War II, and they could just as easily play a role in shutting off trade.

Today, the United States needs a trade policy that recognizes that trade liberalization can have rough edges, and that liberalization needs to be consistent with other important national goals. It needs to be a policy that not only does no harm but also seeks to promote other important goals as appropriate. Such a policy needs to take the concerns of the critics seriously and respond with constructive action rather than just more talk.[24]

24. I hope Murray Weidenbaum will excuse this paraphrase of the quotation from his speech that was presented in the preface to this book.

Chapter 2

America's Trade Agreements

The General Agreement on Tariffs and Trade (GATT) steadily evolved from 1947 with just 23 members to become the World Trade Organization (WTO) with 159 members today. Under the GATT's auspices, eight rounds of multilateral trade negotiations were conducted. The first five rounds reduced tariffs on nonagricultural goods by only some 35 percent, and the sixth, the Kennedy Round, reduced them by about an additional 35 percent. The seventh, the Tokyo Round, cut an additional 35 percent and addressed many nontariff barriers. The last round—the Uruguay Round—again significantly cut developed-country nonagricultural tariffs, developed a structure for negotiations on agricultural goods and services, and produced agreements on trade-related intellectual property and on trade-related investment measures, as well as a robust dispute settlement system.

Similarly, U.S. bilateral and regional free trade agreements (FTAs) expanded from a simple 1985 agreement with Israel that only addressed tariffs on nonagricultural goods to a web of agreements with nineteen other countries that almost completely eliminate all trade barriers and have more extensive rules on intellectual property protection, services, and investment than the multilateral rules.

The North American Free Trade Agreement (NAFTA), which went into effect in 1994, and the newly created WTO, which resulted from the Uruguay Round negotiations, created a strong backlash against U.S. trade agreements. Efforts to conclude a new round of multilateral trade negotiations—the so-called Doha Development Round—which began in 2001 have essentially failed. Today, the major U.S. negotiations for new agreements are with eleven other Asian-Pacific countries, in what is called the Trans-Pacific Partnership negotiations, and with the European Union, in the Trans-Atlantic Trade and Investment Partnership negotiations.

America's trade agreements have changed dramatically over the last two decades. Before 1995, its key agreement was a relatively obscure arrangement headquartered in Geneva, known as the GATT. Though little known, the GATT had facilitated an enormous reduction in barriers to world trade through successive rounds of negotiations. By and large, however, the GATT was not a concern of the average American.

The United States also had an FTA with Israel in 1985 that had been implemented mostly for foreign policy reasons, and an agreement with its neighbor to the north, Canada, which went into effect in 1989. Few Americans were aware of the U.S. agreement with Israel, and its agreement with Canada enjoyed public support.

Then in 1994 the United States–Canada FTA was expanded to include Mexico in NAFTA. And in 1995 the GATT evolved into the WTO, which reaches significantly further into the American economy than the GATT did. Both the WTO and NAFTA aroused enormous public concern and debate regarding the implications of globalization.[1]

The world economy has also changed during the past two decades. Several developing countries—including China, Brazil, and India—developed successful export strategies to take advantage of the global market. China joined the WTO and has now overtaken Japan to become the second-largest economy in the world, and the U.S. trade deficit today with China is far larger than its deficit with Japan.

Business has also changed. Almost all large U.S. companies today are multinational, often earning more than half their profits overseas. Along with this, they have developed global supply chains to provide them with the parts and raw materials they need, and their distribution channels to sell in virtually all markets. Twenty years ago, it was possible to say what an "American" company was; today, that is far harder.

U.S. trade agreements both contributed to this globalization and were driven by it. As trade barriers were reduced in successive rounds of GATT trade negotiations, more and more companies entered world markets.

---

1. In 1983, Theodore Levitt published an article in the *Harvard Business Review* titled "The Globalization of Markets," which some credit with popularizing the concept of globalization in economics.

As they did, and evolved to become multinational organizations, in turn they pushed U.S. trade agreements to cover new areas, including investment rules, the protection of intellectual property, and trade in services.

Since 2000, the United States has entered into FTAs with seventeen additional countries. Its FTAs—as well as other countries' FTAs—build on the WTO rules, and FTA rules cannot conflict with WTO rules: they can go farther than the WTO rules, but they cannot undermine them.

The WTO is a broad agreement that applies to many countries, but it allows each member to maintain some restrictions on imports. In contrast, bilateral and regional FTAs remove almost all barriers to trade between the partners, providing traders with preferential access compared with exporters from other countries. The WTO is wide in its coverage of countries but leaves some trade barriers in place, whereas bilateral and regional FTAs apply only to the countries that are party to the agreement, but remove all or almost all barriers to trade between them.

Market Access and the GATT/WTO

The original 1947 GATT set out the basic principles that largely governed world trade over the next forty years and that would become the foundation for the WTO.[2] There were twenty-three original members, known as the "contracting parties." The GATT was to be a member-driven organization, but it had a very small secretariat in Geneva charged with administering the agreement for the members.

A fundamental pillar of the GATT/WTO is the most-favored-nation (MFN) concept. MFN (Article 1) requires each member to provide all other members with the most favorable trade treatment given to any member. If a member grants another member a tariff preference, it must grant the same preference to all other members. There are two important exceptions to this rule: the treatment of developing countries (e.g., the U.S. Generalized System of Preferences, which gives tariff preferences to many poor nations); and the formation of customs unions or free trade areas, such as NAFTA.

---

2. GATT 1947, and all the basic legal texts of the WTO, are available at http://www.wto.org/english/docs_e/legal_e/legal_e.htm.

A second fundamental GATT concept is national treatment (Article 3), which requires that members provide the same treatment to products once they have been imported into a member country as is provided to a "like" domestic product. This means, for example, that members cannot apply discriminatory taxes on imports after they have cleared the border.

Another important concept underlying the GATT is that barriers to imports and exports should be in the form of tariffs and not quotas that set a ceiling on the amount of possible imports (Article VIII). A fourth is that trade regulations are to be publicly available and administered in a uniform, impartial, and reasonable manner (Article X).

The first five rounds of multilateral trade negotiations under the GATT addressed tariffs, and bargaining was done on a product-by-product basis. Each country would submit a list of requests to its trade partners asking for tariff reductions on products of interest, and then it would submit a list of offers, that is, tariff concessions it was prepared to make. The goal was reciprocity, whereby countries made market access concessions roughly equivalent to the concessions made by other parties on products of interest. The negotiating process was cumbersome, and these first five rounds only resulted in a total reduction of tariffs on non-agricultural products of about 35 percent.

These tariff reductions, and the results of all subsequent rounds, were then *bound*, which meant that member countries notified their tariff schedules to the GATT and these were listed in annexes to the agreement. Under GATT/WTO rules, countries can apply tariffs lower than their bound rate, but they cannot apply higher duties unless they provide offsetting concessions to countries that are adversely affected by the new rates. In these situations, the country raising its duty past the bound rate and the affected countries enter into negotiations to resolve the issues, generally through offsetting concessions in other products. If an agreement cannot be reached, the adversely affected country may be authorized by the GATT to apply sanctions equal to the injury suffered.

The sixth round, the Kennedy Round, largely focused on tariffs, but instead of a product-by-product approach, the negotiators agreed to a formula that reduced tariffs by about one-third on industrial goods across the board. Countries could negotiate exceptions to the formula cuts, with negotiations again focused on achieving an overall balance of concessions between countries. Subsequent rounds—the Tokyo Round, the Uruguay Round, and now the Doha Round—all followed the approach of negotiating tariffs on the basis of a formula.

Along with the formula cuts, negotiators in the Tokyo Round agreed to eliminate barriers to trade for aircraft and parts; unlike the broader formula reduction on tariffs that applied to all members, however, this was a plurilateral agreement that applied only to the thirty countries that signed the agreement.[3] In the Uruguay Round, agreements applying to pharmaceuticals, medical equipment, steel, and paper products were also agreed to, whereby developed countries eliminated or enormously reduced all tariffs on these products.

In contrast to these sectors where greater than formula liberalization was achieved, footwear, textiles, and apparel were exempt from the Tokyo Round's formula cuts. These sectors employ relatively large numbers of unskilled workers and have difficulty competing with firms in low-wage countries. Further, these sectors have a great deal of political clout in a number of countries, and at that time they could have blocked approval of an agreement that they strongly opposed. Accordingly, not only were these sectors largely omitted from trade liberalization, but in 1974 some developed countries—including the United States, the EU member states, Canada, and Norway—imposed the Multi-Fibre Arrangement, which placed quantitative restrictions on the amount of textiles and apparel that could be imported.

Addressing Nontariff Measures

By the time of the Tokyo Round in 1973, tariffs on nonagricultural products had been substantially reduced. Accordingly, the negotiators increasingly turned attention to nontariff measures that restricted trade. Dealing with nontariff measures proved to be more complex than tariff negotiations, because many nontariff measures are generally qualitative and may have a legitimate purpose, although often they had a deliberately protectionist objective.[4] To separate protectionist aspects from legitimate functions, negotiators developed "codes of conduct," which specified what

3. WTO plurilateral agreements apply only to those countries that choose to sign on to the rights and responsibilities of the agreement, unlike the multilateral agreements, which apply to all WTO members. In addition to the aircraft agreement, the Tokyo Round also included plurilateral agreements on bovine meat and dairy products, although these are no longer in effect.

4. Originally nontariff measures were known as "nontariff barriers." The name change was in recognition that these measures often have a legitimate function.

could and could not be done in applying the various nontariff measures. (See table 2.1 for a listing of the areas covered in each round.)

For example, standards have a legitimate purpose of ensuring consistent quality for a country's consumers, but they can also easily be designed to prevent products produced in other countries from entering the market. Testing and certification procedures can also easily be used to block imports.[5] The standards code (known as "Technical Barriers to Trade") encouraged the use of international standards to the greatest extent possible. It also required that standards be adopted in a transparent way and be publicly available, that standards be the "least restrictive" necessary to achieve their objective, and that testing products for compliance not discriminate against imports. However, the code does not limit the ability of countries to adopt legitimate standards or to test domestic and imported products for compliance.

A second code of conduct developed in the Tokyo Round dealt with customs valuation. Up to that time, countries were free to determine how to value imports for the purpose of duty assessments. For example, the United States had a system called "American Selling Price" in effect for imports of chemicals; under this system, an imported product was arbitrarily valued at the same level as the price in the U.S. market for the same product, if that was higher than the import price. Clearly, arbitrarily raising the basis for assessing a duty could easily be used to minimize the impact of a lower tariff. Under the Tokyo Round code, a clear methodology for determining the value of an import was specified, which required the United States to give up the American Selling Price system of import valuation.[6]

---

5. E.g., a country might require all machines sold in the country to use a unique screw size, or it might require that all products have to be inspected by a government inspector, but then not provide any funding for the inspectors to travel overseas. As a result of either measure, foreign products would be effectively blocked from entering the market.

6. Interestingly, the U.S. chemical industry supported giving up the American Selling Price system, even though it meant giving up a method of import protection upon which the industry had relied for many years. The reason it supported this was that its products were blocked in other major markets by other valuation systems that also had to be changed to comply with the new code. In the Tokyo Round, as the American chemical industry supported these changes, it fundamentally changed its focus from national to global, and companies developed strategies to compete in the world market.

Table 2.1. Trade Rounds of the General Agreement on Tariffs and Trade / World Trade Organization

Name of Round	Years of Negotiation	Number of Participants	Main Issues
Geneva	1947	23	Tariffs
Annecy	1949	13	Tariffs
Torquay	1950	38	Tariffs
Geneva	1956	26	Tariffs
Dillon	1960–61	26	Tariffs
Kennedy	1964–67	62	Tariffs, antidumping
Tokyo	1973–79	102	Tariffs, government procurement, standards, customs valuation, import licensing, subsidies, safeguards
Uruguay	1986–94	123	Tariffs, textiles, agriculture, antidumping, intellectual property protection, investment, services, dispute settlement
Doha	2001–present	159	Tariffs, development, agriculture, services

Source: World Trade Organization, "Members and Observers," http://www.wto.org/english/thewto_e/whatis_e/tif_e/org6_e.htm.

Another code of conduct applies to import licensing. This code allows countries to maintain import licensing systems where they are legitimate, but prohibits the trade protectionist aspects of such systems.

Still another code negotiated in the Tokyo Round applies to government procurement. Basically all countries favor domestic suppliers in government procurement, and this code aims to open parts of this market segment to international competition. In the United States, procurement by government agencies accounts for roughly 20 percent of the economy, although a great deal of this is either defense related or salaries and transfer payments, which are not covered by this code. In many other countries, government procurement is a larger portion of the economy than is the case for the United States.

The Government Procurement Code differs from all other codes up to that time, which applied to conditions at the border, whereas the Government Procurement Code applies to goods after they have cleared customs at the border. However, the philosophy behind liberalizing government procurement is the same as for goods going to the private sector, and that is to promote global efficiency.

Forty-one countries, including the United States, had signed on to the Government Procurement Code as of February 2012. Each of these signatories has submitted a list of government agencies that will consider bids from firms in other code signatories on an equal footing with domestic bidders. The U.S. federal government notified a broad list of entities under the code, and thirty-seven states committed to open procurement to firms in other code signatories on listed entities. Other countries, such as the EU member states and Japan, made commitments comparable to that of the United States.

Under the code as negotiated in the Tokyo Round and as updated in the Uruguay Round, all signatories are required to accept bids from other signatories for all projects of listed entities over the threshold value. For the procurement of goods and services other than construction services by the United States, Canada, EU members, and a number of other signatories, this threshold is SDR 130,000 (SDRs are Special Drawing Rights)—equivalent to about $206,000—and for construction services, it is SDR 5 million, or just under $8 million.[7] Procurement by agencies not listed could be done under each country's own domestic laws.

Before the Government Procurement Code entered into force, as set out by the Buy America Act of 1933, the United States applied a preference margin of 6 percent for domestic suppliers and 12 percent for domestic small businesses; for defense procurement, the U.S. preference margin was 50 percent. Under the code, firms in other countries that are party to the agreement can now compete on bids above the threshold level on an equal footing with U.S. firms for those entities that the United States has listed. For entities not listed by the United States, firms in code signatories may still bid, but the historic 6/12/50 percent preference margins apply.

Signatories to the Government Procurement Code are free to discriminate against nonsignatories for all procurement. Nonsignatories to the

---

7. SDRs were created by the International Monetary Fund in 1969 and were designed to be an international reserve currency, along with the dollar. Originally the value of an SDR was based on gold, but today its value is derived from a basket of currencies, including the Japanese yen, the euro, the U.S. dollar, and the British pound. The value of an SDR varies as the value of these currencies change, but as of February 23, 2012, SDR 1 was equal to $1.55. Threshold levels for each of the signatories of the government procurement code are available on the WTO Web site at http://www.wto.org/english/tratop_e/gproc_e/thresh_e.htm.

code generally cannot bid on U.S. government contracts, regardless of whether the procurement is by a covered entity or not. This discrimination is deliberate and is intended to provide an incentive for countries to adhere to the code.

The standards, import licensing, customs valuation, and government procurement codes were all "plurilateral"; that is, members of the GATT could choose to sign on or not. The codes were designed to encourage countries to sign by limiting some benefits to signatories, such as opportunities to sell to governments under the procurement code or participating in the committee overseeing each code. However, nonsignatories enjoyed some of the benefits; for example, nonsignatories to the customs valuation code did not have to change their own system of valuation, yet they still enjoyed the certainty of the rules pertaining to valuation by those that did sign. Though most developed countries signed these codes, most developing countries in fact chose not to sign.

At the end of the Tokyo Round, the size and scope of the GATT had expanded enormously. When the GATT was launched in 1947, there were only twenty-three member countries, mostly the developed countries that had won the war, but also some developing countries, including India, Pakistan, South Africa, and Southern Rhodesia (now Zimbabwe). In the early 1950s, Germany, Austria, and Italy joined, and then in the early 1960s a wave of newly independent states, mostly poor developing countries, became members.

The Uruguay Round

The issues addressed in the Uruguay Round were extensive. Once again, tariffs on most nonagricultural products were reduced across the board on the basis of a formula; and this time, trade in textiles and apparel was opened up. The Multi-Fibre Arrangement on textiles and apparel was renamed the Agreement on Textiles and Clothing, which required that quotas on textiles and apparel be eliminated by 2005. (This happened on schedule, although the United States and a number of other countries still retain high tariffs on textiles and apparel products.)

For the first time, the Uruguay Round addressed trade in agricultural products in a comprehensive way, as only minimal agricultural liberalization had been achieved in previous rounds. The European Union had developed a highly protectionist Common Agricultural Policy, which included import restraints and domestic and export subsidies.[8] The United States and many other developed countries also have high tariffs on most agricultural imports, and the United States, as well as several other countries, dole out huge subsidies to domestic producers that allow them to underprice other country producers in world markets. Not only had almost no progress been made in the agricultural sector, but there was not even a framework for how to consider agricultural subsidies, which varied enormously from country to country.

However, in the Uruguay Round the negotiators agreed to reduce tariffs on agricultural products by 36 percent for the developed countries and by 24 percent for the more advanced developing countries. All members agreed to bind all their tariffs on agricultural products, although generally at high levels.

The negotiators also developed a framework for the various kinds of subsidies, categorizing them based on the extent to which they distorted trade and production. Direct export subsidies, such as payments based on the quantity of a product exported, were considered to be the most distortive. The developed countries agreed to reduce these by 36 percent by value, and the advanced developing countries agreed to cut their direct export subsidies by 24 percent.[9]

A second category was the subsidies that distorted trade, but where the country had placed limits on how much could be produced; these were placed in a so-called blue box. The United States notified only one blue box subsidy practice, and this was discontinued in 1996. The third category was the "amber box," which pertains to subsidies that have an impact on production but do not directly distort trade. Countries agreed

8. The Common Agricultural Policy (CAP) went into effect in 1962, replacing highly protectionist policies maintained by some of the original six European Community members (Germany, France, Italy, Belgium, Luxembourg, and the Netherlands). The objectives of the CAP were to provide reasonable income to farmers and thereby maintain a rural heritage and to provide food security. To achieve these objectives, imports were restricted and farmers received direct subsidies. To maintain a desired internal price, the EU bought excess product and then often dumped these products on world markets. In recent years, however, the EU has made major changes to the CAP system, which greatly reduces its trade distortions.

9. The European Union is far and away the largest user of direct export subsidies, and accounts for some 85 to 90 percent of all direct export subsidies. In contrast, the United States accounts for only 0.05 percent. Indirect export subsidies, such as export promotion and export credit guarantees, were also considered potentially distortive, but negotiators were unable to agree on how to address these practices.

to limit amber box subsidies to an index, the "Aggregate Measurement of Support"; the United States committed not to provide more than $19.2 billion in such programs, while the EU agreed to a level in euros equal to about $93 billion at that time, and Japan committed to a level in yen equivalent to about $43 billion.

Subsidies that did not distort production or trade were placed in a "green box," which had no limits on the amount of subsidy that could be provided. These included practices such as research, food stamps, and conservation.

Finally, there were two categories that the negotiators recognized were distorting but for domestic political reasons could not be addressed. The first was defined as support for a commodity that is less than 5 percent of the commodity's production value for developed countries and 10 percent for developing countries, and the second allowed non-product-specific support provided it is less than 5 percent of the total value of agricultural production for developed countries or 10 percent for developing nations.

Moving beyond Trade: Investment

In a very important move, the negotiators at the Uruguay Round broke radically new ground by addressing some extremely significant issues outside the traditional GATT focus on trade in goods—namely investment, services, and intellectual property protection.

The original GATT addressed investment in only a minor way, and only insofar as an investment distortion might have an impact on trade.[10] For example, the original GATT theoretically would have prohibited a local content rule that required all automobiles on the market to be manufactured in the country with 80 percent of the content from parts and components manufactured in the country. Such a rule, of course, would

---

10. As noted in chapter 1, in the 1940s negotiators of the post–World War II commercial architecture originally developed rules governing trade, investment, and competition policy to be incorporated in an International Trade Organization (ITO). However, when President Harry Truman realized that the Senate would not approve the ITO, he implemented only the General Agreement on Tariffs and Trade by executive order, leaving a major gap in rules on investment. The GATT rules that could impact investment were Article III concerning national treatment and Article XI on quantitative restrictions.

nullify the potential benefit of a tariff concession on automobile parts and components. However, the prohibitions in the original GATT were largely ignored, and by the 1980s, a number of investment practices had proliferated that had the effect of distorting trade and nullifying the benefit of trade concessions.

Investment rules have an enormous potential to distort trade. The WTO estimated that in 1995 about one-third of the $6.1 trillion total world trade in goods and services was intercompany trade, such as between a subsidiary of a company and its headquarters in a different country.

Accordingly, Uruguay Round negotiators developed the agreement on Trade-Related Investment Measures (TRIMs), which basically clarifies GATT Articles III and XI, particularly by including a short illustrative list of practices that are prohibited under these articles. For example, the TRIMs agreement makes it a clear violation of rules to require that an investor use products of domestic origin rather than imported products, or to require that an enterprise limit the use of imported products to the value of local products exported.

However, the TRIMs agreement is extremely limited. For example, it does not prohibit export performance requirements, limitations on the amount of equity that the foreign investor may hold, rules that a foreign investor must transfer technology to the country, or requirements that the foreign investor must conduct research and development locally. Additionally, the agreement does not address broader investment issues, such as the right to establish a foreign subsidiary or repatriate profits.

Unfortunately, these loopholes continue to distort trade and investment today.

Trade in Services

The original GATT also did not address services other than in a very minor way.[11] By the time negotiations in the Uruguay Round began in 1986,

---

11. The only reference to services was Article II.2(c), which specifies that contracting parties may impose fees on imported goods that are commensurate with the cost of the service provided. By implication, of course, this means that service fees on imported goods, such as charges to unload cargo, that are not commensurate with cost could be subject to dispute settlement.

however, GATT members had come to realize the importance of trade in services and had agreed to comprehensive negotiations.

Barriers to trade in services are radically different from barriers to trade in goods. All goods trade crosses borders in a highly visible way, and all governments—even those of the least developed countries—have customs officers at border posts to collect tariffs on imported products. Most measures to control trade in goods are imposed at the border, including tariffs, quotas, and import licensing.

In contrast, trade in services does not pass through customs posts. The ways that services can be traded are varied, and the potential barriers to this trade are very diverse. Generally, rules that affect trade in services are embedded in domestic regulations that affect the provision or consumption of services, such as regulations on banking, telecommunications, or electricity or water delivery, or rules aimed at protecting health or the environment. Services regulations may be imposed at the national level or a subnational level, or they may not be imposed by the government but by an industry association. Often these rules have been constructed from a domestic perspective without consideration of the potential impact on foreign suppliers.

And, of course, sometimes these rules have been constructed in a way to deliberately hold down the number of potential suppliers—often for valid reasons—such as requirements that doctors must be adequately trained. Even rules in such areas as visas can affect services trade by limiting the ability of customers to travel to other countries or the ability of providers to travel to consuming countries.

Regulations that can be barriers to services trade are not necessarily discriminatory. For example, a rule limiting currency exchange might have no effect on a local service provider but could discourage foreign providers from supplying the market. Conversely, regulations that are discriminatory may have a very legitimate domestic justification. For example, a central bank may impose more stringent capital requirements on a branch of a foreign bank than on a domestic branch for valid prudential reasons.

In the Uruguay Round, however, trade negotiators managed to devise a framework for defining trade in services that could set the stage for reducing barriers and distortions. The subsequent agreement—the General Agreement on Trade in Services (GATS)—follows some of the basic principles that govern trade in goods contained in the GATT. First, GATS extends MFN treatment to all the services and service suppliers of all other WTO members. The second principle is transparency: Members are required to publish all measures that have an impact on services trade of general application and to establish a national inquiry point to respond to requests from other member-country service providers. Additionally, members are required to set up appeals procedures that can be used by a firm that does not believe it is being treated fairly.

However, the real genius of the Uruguay Round negotiators was to categorize services trade by how it is supplied, and they defined four "modes" under which trade in services takes place. Mode 1 is where the service is exported from the provider in one country over the Internet, by mail, or via some other delivery mechanism directly to the consumer in another country. An example might be professional tax advice provided over the Internet to a consumer in another country.

Mode 2 pertains to consumption abroad, where the consumer of a service from one country travels to another country to purchase the service. An example would be a patient who travels to another country to have an operation performed by a specialist not available at home.

Mode 3 pertains to services provided through a commercial presence, whereby a firm establishes a facility in another country. For example, a Mode 3 commitment might be to allow foreign firms to make an investment in a specific services sector or to repatriate profits from those investments. Note that Mode 3 addresses the movement of a basic factor of production—that is, capital—and in this limited way, this aspect of GATS goes farther than the WTO investment provisions applicable to goods.

Mode 4 pertains to the presence of natural persons. For example, a doctor may travel overseas to oversee a highly technical operation, or migrant workers may travel from one country to another to assist on farms. Mode 4 represents movement across borders of another key factor of production: human capital.

The Uruguay Round negotiators then defined services in 12 broad sectors, which could be delivered through any of the four modes. The 12 broad sectors are business, communication, construction, distribution, educational, environmental, financial, health-related and social services, tourism, recreational-cultural-sporting, transportation, and other. Within these 12 broad sectors, there are some 160 specific service areas.[12] For

12. A list of the 12 sectors and 160 specific areas can be found at http://www.wto.org/english/tratop_e/serv_e/serv_e.htm.

example, business services include legal, taxation, architectural, engineering, accounting, and other specific service areas.

In addition to this basic framework, GATS also includes annexes on basic telecommunications and on financial services. These annexes call for more extensive commitments than is the case for other sectors.

Finally, each WTO member was required to submit a copy of its commitments to the GATT, which could apply to any of the four modes of delivery or any of the service sectors. These commitments could have all sorts of limitations, such as the number of suppliers to be permitted to supply the service. Additionally, commitments could be horizontal (i.e., apply to all sectors), or they could apply only to the specific service sector notified.

This structure gave each member "policy space" to pursue its own objectives, other than the obligations for MFN treatment and transparency. Accordingly, country schedules vary widely among WTO members, depending on the commitments each member chose to make. Developed countries tabled fairly extensive commitments, but generally these simply confirmed and "bound" existing practices, rather than representing real liberalization of access. Developing countries generally made far fewer commitments than developed countries. In fact, for many developing countries, commitments were limited to areas such as tourism, and more complex sectors were avoided. Even the least-developed members, however, undertook some binding commitments, such as committing to open their tourist markets to foreign hoteliers.

By and large, however, the 123 members of the newly established WTO did not liberalize trade in services, but instead only bound some of their current practices. Nonetheless, GATS was a breakthrough in establishing a framework for considering trade in services and including binding commitments by each member. For the first time, the trading community recognized the importance of liberalizing trade in services and set out a coherent framework for doing so.

Beyond Goods and Services to Intellectual Property

The third new issue introduced in the Uruguay Round was the protection of intellectual property, such as patents, copyrights, trade secrets, and trademarks. The original GATT did not address intellectual property, and instead rules governing intellectual property protection were developed in other international organizations, such as the World Intellectual Property Organization (WIPO). These rules covered such things as the definition of patents, trademarks, and copyrights; the mutual recognition of intellectual property developed in other signatories; the length of protection for patents, trademarks, and copyrights; and so forth.

The rules developed in WIPO and other organizations reflected the inherent tension between protection of intellectual property and diffusion of the benefits of the technology to the general public. The argument for protection is that it gives companies and individuals a period of exclusivity during which they can raise prices to profit from their innovation and recover the costs of their research. This provides incentives for research that will benefit all of society; proponents of intellectual property protection argue that without these protections, research in new products would be sharply diminished.

Conversely, such protection raises the costs of the products protected and may reduce availability. Nowhere is this tension greater than in the pharmaceutical sector, where research has developed cures for many diseases. However, the costs of these new drugs can often be extremely high during the period the producers have patent protection, making them unavailable to low-income individuals.

In terms of protecting intellectual property, WIPO had two critical limitations. First, only a limited number of countries were party to the agreement, and these were mainly developed countries. Piracy of intellectual property, however, was prevalent in a number of developing countries that were not party to the WIPO agreement, and often the counterfeit products produced in these countries found their way into the markets of developed countries. Second, WIPO did not have any dispute settlement mechanism or any sanctions for noncompliance; nor did WIPO require its members to provide criminal, civil, and administrative remedies against infringement of the rules.

Generally, the Uruguay Round negotiators did not attempt to recast the substance of the rules developed in WIPO; instead, with certain exceptions, they incorporated them in the agreement on Trade-Related Aspects of Intellectual Property Rights (TRIPS), which became an integral part of the final package. The developed countries were required to implement the TRIPS agreement within one year, and the developing countries were required to implement it within five years, whereas the least-developed countries had ten years to implement it.[13]

By including these rules in the Uruguay Round package, the negotiators immediately extended the requirement to protect intellectual property to all GATT/WTO members, not just the parties to WIPO. And just as important, they made compliance with these rules subject to the GATT/WTO dispute settlement procedures.

Dispute Settlement: A More Robust Mechanism

Perhaps the most important change to the GATT agreed to in the Uruguay Round, however, concerned dispute settlement. Under the original GATT, any member could bring a dispute to the membership if it felt the actions of another country "nullified or impaired" trade concessions it had received in exchange for its own concessions. GATT rules required that the countries consult first to see if they could resolve the dispute, but if not, the contracting parties could establish an independent panel of experts to consider the dispute. If the panel ruled against the accused member's action and the contracting parties accepted the panel's report, the offending member was supposed to bring its policy into compliance with the panel's ruling. Alternatively, the offending member could offer compensation to the party or parties injured by its action, generally by making new tariff concessions on products of export interest to the injured party. If the member refused to do this, the injured nation could be authorized to take retaliation, generally in the form of increasing duties on products imported from the offending member to restore the balance of trade concessions.

This system worked fairly well, at least initially, when the GATT membership was fairly small and the country representatives all knew each other and believed in the same underlying principles of the trading system. Over time, however, the system worked less and less well. A member facing an adverse panel report could delay consideration of the decision or of retaliation, because the GATT required a "consensus" to

---

13. In 2005 it was clear that the least-developed countries would not be able to implement the TRIPS agreement in the ten years specified in the Uruguay Round package. Accordingly, the WTO Council approved an extension to January 1, 2016, for least-developed countries to implement the TRIPS Agreement.

act, which was defined as agreement by all members. So a member whose practice was found in violation could delay the process indefinitely.

By the 1970s, however, some countries—and particularly the United States—were becoming frustrated with the GATT dispute settlement mechanism. The trade rules did not cover a broad range of nontariff barriers that countries were using to block trade, and the United States faced serious international competition from both Europe and Japan.

In the U.S. Trade Act of 1974, which provided the president authority to negotiate a new trade round, a frustrated Congress included a provision (Section 301) that authorized the president to take retaliatory action to force the removal of foreign trade actions that were discriminatory or unreasonable and that restricted U.S. commerce. The Office of the U.S. Trade Representative could initiate a case, or an industry could file a petition to launch an investigation, which would force action if the investigation confirmed the facts.

The United States used Section 301 authority aggressively, and because of the size of the U.S. market, other countries generally removed the offending practice. One of the largest Section 301 cases involved Japanese semiconductors in the mid-1980s. At that time Japan effectively blocked foreign access through a system of cartels whereby Japanese manufacturers of semiconductors and users, such as computer producers, only purchased from each other and refused to purchase non-Japanese semiconductors. In contrast, the U.S. semiconductor market was very open. The Japanese companies used this imbalance in access to price high in their domestic market and sell at prices below cost in foreign markets, particularly the United States—a practice known as dumping. Even though the semiconductor market had been started by the United States and long dominated by it, by the mid-1980s the U.S. semiconductor companies were on the ropes and facing the prospect of bankruptcy.

The U.S. industry initiated a Section 301 petition, and the Office of the U.S. Trade Representative launched negotiations with Japan. When the negotiations were not successful, the United States retaliated and obtained a commitment from Japan to open its market, using a benchmark that foreign suppliers would have at least a 20 percent market share, and the Commerce Department took action to prevent dumping.[14] The result

14. Commerce imposed a system called "Fair Market Value" (FMV), which was determined by traditional dumping methodology based on an industry with increasing costs. However, the costs of semiconductors fall dramatically when production is

of these actions, along with actions to promote research and development, was that the U.S. industry regained its competitive position. Without this action, it is very possible that companies such as Texas Instruments, Intel, and Micron would no longer be in existence.

Voluntary restraint agreements (VRAs) were another practice that had grown up by the 1990s. Under these practices, large countries used their market power to induce exporting nations to "voluntarily" limit their exports or face more severe restraints. Both U.S. Section 301 and VRAs were strongly opposed by smaller nations; and in the Uruguay Round, as the price for the new dispute settlement mechanism, countries agreed that VRAs would now be a violation of WTO rules, and the United States agreed to modify Section 301 to commit to use the WTO dispute mechanism and retaliate only when authorized by a dispute settlement panel.

Under the new dispute settlement system, time limits were placed on panel consideration and the length of time the contracting parties had to consider the panel report. No longer could one member block adoption of a panel report; under the new rules, all members would have to agree to a requested delay. And a new appellate review system was established, and members could appeal a decision to the appellate body. Again there were strict time limits on the time it took for an appeal to run its course. The process has some flexibility, but generally it takes about one year for a case to run its course or one and a quarter years if the panel's decision is appealed.

The new dispute settlement mechanism represented a fundamental change, moving the organization from a system of consensus to a much more legalistic mechanism for resolving disputes.

The GATT Becomes the WTO

Near the end of the Uruguay Round, the negotiators agreed to another provision that had enormous implications: to make the whole package a

increased, and the FMV system infuriated consumers of semiconductors—particularly computer makers such as Hewlett-Packard, NCR, and Compaq—and in fact threatened their competitiveness because their Japanese competitors could obtain semiconductors at low prices. At the time I worked for the largest U.S. technology trade association, the American Electronics Association, and both the large semiconductor and computer companies were important members. We formed a task force of the CEOs of the major companies and worked with Commerce to gradually reform the FMV system.

single undertaking. As noted above, in earlier rounds members could decide whether or not to adhere to the codes of conduct, such as the agreements on technical barriers to trade, trade-related investment measures, customs valuation, and import licensing.

The negotiators from the United States, Europe, and some other counties were concerned that this enabled some members to be "free riders," that is, to benefit from access to markets of countries that agreed to these codes while not having to undertake comparable responsibilities themselves. Additionally, negotiators felt that to the greatest extent possible, common rules that applied to trade with all countries greatly facilitated trade because exporters would have a uniform set of rules around the world. Accordingly, it was decided that all members would have to accept the responsibilities of all the agreements or drop out of the organization. (The Government Procurement Code and the Civil Aircraft Code were exceptions to the "single undertaking" and remain as plurilateral agreements.)

Because these new agreements on agriculture, services, intellectual property protection, and a binding dispute settlement mechanism fundamentally expanded the scope of the GATT, the negotiators decided to change the body's name from the General Agreement on Tariffs and Trade to the World Trade Organization. The approximately sixty agreements reached in the Uruguay Round and previous rounds since the original GATT agreement of some 65 pages now covered some 550 pages, not including the voluminous schedules of commitments by each country appended to the agreement.[15]

Although not part of the Uruguay Round, a plurilateral agreement to completely eliminate tariffs on information technology products—the Information Technology Agreement—was reached in December 1996. Originally, twenty-nine countries signed on, and by April 2013 the number had grown to seventy-four; these economies account for 97 percent of world trade in information technology products. This plurilateral agreement is now also part of the WTO.

Establishment of the WTO, while applauded by industry and the free trade community, enormously heightened fears of globalization among

---

15. The number of pages of the GATT and of the WTO, of course, depends on whether the document is printed in Microsoft Word or PDF, in English or some other language, and the size of the font used. When I printed these documents in Word, this was the number of pages of each, and these numbers are given here simply to indicate the magnitude of the change from the GATT to the WTO.

some in the general public. The agreements on intellectual property and services represented an enormous change. Previously, the GATT had applied to goods traded at the border, with the minor exception of the government procurement agreement. Intellectual property protection and many services, however, were areas subject to domestic regulation and reached way inside markets. Many environmentalists and others were concerned that this could restrict the ability of governments to pursue other socially desirable objectives, such as protecting the environment.

And developing countries were surprised and confused by the last-minute agreement that the new WTO would be a "single undertaking." Suddenly, they were committed to a number of agreements that previously had not been mandatory and that many developing countries really did not understand, such as the agreements on customs valuation, trade-related investment measures, and intellectual property protection. They would also soon learn that compliance with these agreements would be very expensive. (These concerns will be considered in chapter 6.)

Under the WTO's dispute settlement procedures, developed countries could no longer ignore international rulings on trade practices, and this limited the ability of governments to protect domestic industries. Weakening Section 301 to take away the right of unilateral action and the prohibition on using voluntary restraint agreements concerned many U.S. industries. However, WTO rules did continue to allow some forms of import protection that had been set out in the GATT, the most important being antidumping duties, countervailing duties, and safeguard actions.[16]

Import Protection under the WTO

The fundamental purpose of the GATT/WTO is to open markets to international trade in order to promote the efficient global production of goods and services. The basic rules of the GATT and WTO were developed in accordance with economic theory, as understood at the time the rules were developed, tempered by the limits of what could be negotiated internationally, and approved domestically.

---

16. The WTO/GATT also recognizes some other circumstances when protection against imports is justified, particularly the right of members to protect the health and safety of the populace or for reasons of national security.

The founders of the GATT recognized that some practices could distort the market and result in new inefficiencies. Two such practices were "dumping" and the subsidization of exported products, and the rules provided mechanisms whereby countries could offset the adverse impact of these two practices. A rationale for these rules was to reestablish a level playing field that would be in accordance with the intended impact of the law of comparative advantage.

Further, the founders recognized that on rare occasions, trade liberalization could lead to a flood of imports, which in turn could cause substantial injury to a domestic industry, and they provided a mechanism to allow countries to take temporary relief. Such a "safeguard" action, of course, is a temporary step away from efficient global production.

In agreeing to the original GATT and the results of the subsequent rounds of multilateral negotiations, the contracting parties considered the provisions on dumping, subsidies, and safeguards as integral to the balanced package. For the United States, the existence of these provisions was also necessary to gain a domestic political consensus sufficient to obtain approval of each trade round. Without assurance that they would be protected against unfair competition, a number of industries would have opposed the agreement. And some industries and labor organizations demanded the provisions allowing temporary relief to prevent serious disruption of an industry.

"Dumping," in GATT/WTO terminology, occurs when a company exports its products "at a price lower than the price it normally charges on its own home market."[17] Often, dumping may be a normal business practice; for example, at the end of the year, if a toy manufacturer has excess inventory of a product that will no longer be continued, it may well decide to clear out its warehouse and make room for next year's product by selling the remaining toys at less than it cost to manufacture them. A company may "dump" its products in its domestic market or in an export market.

Sometimes, however, dumping can be anticompetitive. For example, a large company may decide to squeeze out a less-well-financed competitor by selling below cost until the competitor leaves the market, where-

---

17. If the price charged in the home market cannot be used, governments may use the price for the like product exported to other markets, or they may have to determine if there is dumping based on the cost of production. The WTO Web site describes antidumping provisions: http://www.wto.org/english/tratop_e/adp_e/adp _e.htm.

upon the large company can raise prices. Even if this is not the case, dumping can cause material injury to other companies, either in the domestic market or in its export markets. Though dumping can cause injury to firms competing with the dumped product, the lower prices can be a boon to consumers, who are able to buy the product at a lower price, although the lower price may be temporary.

Under the GATT/WTO, contracting parties may impose antidumping duties to prevent material injury or the threat of material injury, provided that the duties are no greater than the margin of dumping. The rules only pertain to dumped products that are exported; each member is free to deal with dumping in its domestic market as it wishes.

In the United States, the EU member states, and many other countries, dumping as such is not illegal. However, predatory business practices are subject to laws on competition policy, and companies violating antitrust laws can be subject to substantial fines and also ordered to cease and desist. However, the WTO does not have rules governing competition policy.

Antidumping duties are specific; that is, they apply to imports of the specified product from a specified producer. Accordingly, imports from a foreign company found to be dumping are priced higher than imports from other companies, including companies from the same country. Antidumping duties are additional to the regular MFN duty. The rationale is that this is intended to restore a "level playing field" in which companies gain or lose market share based on their competitiveness, or to remove the injury to the domestic industry, whichever is the lesser amount.

The WTO Agreement on Subsidies and Countervailing Measures is somewhat different from the Agreement on Antidumping.[18] Unlike dumping, which is an action taken by a company, a subsidy is an action taken by a government. Because the WTO cannot set rules for companies, which is the responsibility of each contracting party, the Anti-Dumping Agreement only addresses actions that countries may take to offset dumping (i.e., impose antidumping duties), and it does not prohibit the actual dumping itself. However, the Agreement on Subsidies and Countervailing Measures dictates what governments are allowed to do with regard to subsidies and also defines what countervailing actions countries may take to offset injurious subsidies.

---

18. A good explanation of the Agreement on Subsidies and Countervailing Measures is available at http://www.wto.org/english/tratop_e/scm_e/subs_e.htm.

Under this agreement, subsidies that directly benefit exports and subsidies that favor the use of domestic content over imported products ("local content subsidies") are prohibited. These two categories of subsidy are subject to rapid dispute settlement procedures.

Other types of subsidies are defined as "actionable." If a contracting party believes its exports are being injured in a third market or in the market of the subsidizing country, it can bring a complaint under the regular WTO dispute settlement procedures. If it believes it is being injured in its home market, it can either bring a dispute settlement case or impose a countervailing duty to offset the injury, which cannot be greater than the amount of the subsidy. The imposition of countervailing duties and antidumping duties requires a transparent process to determine the amount of subsidy or dumping margin and whether there is material injury. Countervailing duties are imposed on all the imports of the specified product from the subsidizing country.

The Agreement on Safeguards provides the opportunity for a member to impose temporary relief in the form of increased tariffs or quotas to restrict imports that cause, or threaten to cause, serious injury to a domestic industry.[19] The term "serious injury" is defined as "significant impairment in the position of a domestic industry." "Serious injury" is considered to be a higher threshold than the "material injury" test for antidumping or countervailing duties, which is defined as an "important . . . deterioration in the operating performance of the domestic industry."

A safeguard action does not require a finding of "unfair," but it does need to be applied to all WTO members universally, consistent with MFN, although in practice in some circumstances it may be applied in a manner that has an impact on specific countries that are the source of the increased imports.[20] It has to be time limited—no more than four years, with a possible four-year extension. And it may require that the member taking a safeguard action provide compensation to those countries adversely affected by the action or face possible retaliation.

19. A good explanation of the Agreement on Safeguards is available at http://www.wto.org/english/tratop_e/safeg_e/safeint.htm.
20. It is often possible to design an action to impact some countries and not others. In the early 1980s, when the United States imposed high duties on imported motorcycles to deal with a surge of imports from Japan, it specified that the duties would apply only to motorcycles with large engines, not the smaller engines used on European motorcycles, thereby exempting those bikes from high tariffs.

Negotiations without End: The Doha Round

When the Uruguay Round negotiations ended, it was recognized that there was still much more that needed to be done, particularly in the areas of agriculture and services. Accordingly, the Uruguay Round agreement committed the WTO members to begin negotiations on these two areas in 2000, whether or not a new round had been started by that time.

Additionally, the EU member states and several other countries pressed for new negotiations on investment, competition policy, government procurement, and customs procedures that restrict trade. However, developing countries strongly opposed negotiations on these issues. A compromise was reached at the 1996 WTO Ministerial Meeting to set up working groups to examine these four issues to see if a consensus could be reached to include them in the next round of trade negotiations.

A major effort to launch a new round was subsequently made at the WTO's Ministerial Meeting in Seattle in 1999 but, as noted in chapter 1, this ended in chaos and failure. Finally, at the November 2001 Ministerial Meeting in Doha, a new round was launched, and the negotiations on agriculture and services, which had started on schedule, were incorporated into the new negotiating mandate.

To gain developing countries' support for the new round, it was agreed that a primary objective of the negotiations would be to better enable developing countries to benefit from the growth of world trade. [21] The second paragraph of the Ministerial Declaration emphasized this point: "The majority of WTO Members are developing countries. We seek to place their needs and interests at the heart of the Work Programme adopted in this Declaration. . . . We shall continue to make positive efforts designed to ensure that developing countries, and especially the least-developed among them, secure a share in the growth of world trade commensurate with the needs of their economic development."

In addition to general language that Doha was to be a development round, negotiators had to address serious concerns raised by the developing countries that the TRIPS agreement was preventing many countries from obtaining the drugs necessary to deal with the AIDS crisis. Patented antiretroviral drugs used to help patients with AIDS are ex-

---

21. The Ministerial statement is available at http://www.wto.org/english/thewto_e/minist_e/min01_e/mindecl_e.doc.

tremely expensive and far beyond the reach of most people in developing countries. where incomes are often less than $1 a day. Though the TRIPS agreement allows for compulsory licensing in cases of national emergency (which the AIDS epidemic clearly is for many African nations), developed countries as a general matter were pressing developing countries not to use this provision to license inexpensive generic drugs. Additionally, TRIPS only allowed compulsory licensing for producing drugs for the domestic market, and many African countries facing an AIDS epidemic have far too small a market size to support a generic drug industry.

Accordingly, the trade ministers agreed to a separate Declaration on the TRIPS Agreement and Public Health, issued in parallel to the Doha Ministerial Declaration.[22] This declaration reaffirmed that the TRIPS agreement should be interpreted and implemented in a manner consistent with WTO members' right to protect public health and, in particular, to promote access to medicines for all. The ministers were unable to agree on how to address the concern of small countries with no domestic manufacturing base regarding compulsory licensing, but they recognized the issue and agreed to resolve it within two years.

At the Cancun Ministerial Meeting in September 2003, an agreement on compulsory licensing was reached. Under this agreement, countries that want to produce generic drugs for export must issue a compulsory license and notify the WTO's TRIPS Council regarding the quantities being shipped and to whom. Additionally, a WTO member that wants to import the generic drug has to notify the TRIPS Council of its intent to use the system and specify the name and quantity of the generic product. It also must have measures to prevent reexportation.

The Doha meeting took place just two months after the September 11, 2001, terrorist attacks on the World Trade Center and the Pentagon. U.S. policymakers believed that poor, unstable countries could become havens for terrorists, and accordingly there was support for the idea of helping the developing countries—and particularly the least-developed ones—grow economically. A new round focused on development made sense in this context. Politically, it was also a necessity if a new round was to be launched. The developing countries, which were feeling shortchanged by the results of the Uruguay Round and now constituted a ma-

---

22. Available at http://www.wto.org/english/thewto_e/minist_e/min01_e/mindecl _trips_e.htm.

jority of the WTO's membership, would not have agreed to launch new negotiations without this commitment.

Although the mandate agreed to at Doha in 2001 set out the broad parameters for the negotiations, a number of issues were still unresolved. In particular, the European Union wanted the negotiations to include investment, competition policy, government procurement, and customs procedures that restrict trade. In the face of strong opposition from the developing countries at the 2003 Ministerial Conference, however, it was agreed that only negotiations on improving customs procedures (called "trade facilitation") would be included in the Doha Round, and that investment, competition policy, and government procurement would be dropped from the agenda.

The initial deadline for completing the negotiations was to be January 1, 2005, but this was missed. A new deadline for completing the Doha Round in 2006 was also missed, intense work in 2007 and 2008 failed to produce an agreement, and today most observers consider the negotiations dead for all intents and purposes. Nonetheless, a great deal of work has been done, and the negotiators have developed a broad outline of a potential deal, although the political will to bring the round to a conclusion is lacking.

Even if the political will were there, however, the results would still be minimal. The developed countries would reduce tariffs on nonagricultural goods across the board by an agreed-on percentage. However, the advanced developing countries—including nations such as China, India, and Brazil—would reduce their bound rates by a smaller amount but would make virtually no cuts in their actual applied rates, because these are far below their bound rates. The least-developed countries would not have to make any cuts.

In the agricultural sector, the developed countries would cut tariffs by half or more, although products deemed sensitive would be cut less. The developing countries would make smaller cuts, and the least-developed countries would not have to make any cuts. Total trade-distorting subsidies would be capped, albeit at a level for the United States that is above its current level of subsidization. And in the services area, only a very small degree of improved access would be achieved, because countries would basically just agree to additional bindings on existing practices. The most progress has been in the customs area, where there is some consensus on an agreement to reduce customs procedures that increase the costs of trade (trade facilitation).

The Doha Development Round has already lasted longer than any previous round; as noted above, though the negotiations have not officially been declared over, most observers consider them to be virtually dead. (As of April 2013, negotiators are still hoping to salvage a few issues, particularly the trade facilitation package, to have a "small package" for approval at the December Ministerial Meeting in Bali.)

There are many reasons for the failure of the Doha Round, including the 2008 financial collapse and the deep global recession it caused; the enormous complexity of trying to reach an agreement on these broad issues among the more than 150 WTO member countries; the unwillingness by some advanced developing countries—particularly India, Brazil, and China—to make serious concessions in access for non-agricultural products or services; and the unwillingness of the United States, the EU, and Japan to make significant concessions in their agricultural programs.

Another reason for the Doha Round's failure is that from the beginning it did not address the most important trade issues, such as currency manipulation and the treatment of state-owned enterprises. Its focus on development was probably misplaced, because other international organizations, such as the World Bank, are more central players in promoting economic development. As a result, major economic interests in the United States were not deeply supportive of a successful outcome, and no major country felt that the package agreed to by 2008 was sufficiently attractive to justify making major concessions of its own.

The WTO's New Members

Even though the Doha Development Round has apparently failed, in another important respect the WTO has presided over significant trade liberalization since its launch on January 1, 1995. By the end of 2012, forty-five additional countries had joined the WTO. As part of this process, the new members have had to make significant changes to their laws and practices to conform to WTO rules, and they have had to substantially liberalize their trade regimes.

New members need to be approved by all WTO members. When a country applies for membership, a working party is established to review the country's trade rules and regulations, and its compliance with WTO rules. Applicants enter into bilateral market access agreements with any member that presses for this, and the results of these bilateral negotiations are implemented on an MFN basis. The United States and other members demand that new applicants conform to WTO rules and, if they have high trade barriers, that they substantially liberalize their market in accordance with their level of development.

Ukraine is a good example of how a prospective member country experiences the typical process of joining the WTO. According to Andrii Goncharuk, Ukraine's former minister of foreign economic relations and trade, his country submitted its formal application in November 1993 and was finally admitted in May 2008, fifteen years later.[23] The Working Party, which had seventeen formal meetings and many informal meetings, consisted of forty-two countries that had expressed interest. In this process, Ukraine passed more than twenty laws to change its practices to comply with WTO rules. The changes made included ending export subsidies on agricultural products, eliminating duties on information technology products, becoming a party to the telecommunications services agreement, bringing its standards practices into conformity with the Agreement on Technical Barriers to Trade, and passing legislation regarding the protection of intellectual property rights.

China, the world's second-largest economy behind the United States, is far and away the most important new WTO member in terms of the size of its gross domestic product, as can be seen in table 2.2. China's accession to the WTO began in 1986 and was completed fifteen years later in 2001; the bilateral negotiations on market access with the United States took six years and resulted in improved access for U.S. exporters in many industrial and agricultural goods and some services. It also contained a commitment by China to eliminate all export duties and restrictions on exports, other than some that were specifically noted in the agreement. Additionally, the agreement contained a bilateral safeguard provision, which is similar to the safeguard provision in Article XIX of the WTO/GATT, except that the injury test is "market disruption," a lower standard than the "serious injury" test in WTO Article XIX.

The United States–China WTO accession agreement also contained an unprecedented provision "that China bring its foreign exchange regime into conformity with the obligations of Article VIII of the IMF by

---

23. Ambassador Andrii Goncharuk, "The Path of Ukraine into the WTO," in *Opportunities and Obligations: New Perspectives on Global and US Trade Policy*, edited by Terence P. Stewart (Amsterdam: Kluwer Law International, 2009).

Table 2.2. Major New and Pending Members of the World Trade Organization

Country	Year Admitted	GDP (billions of dollars)[a]
United Arab Emirates	1996	360
China	2001	7,318
Taiwan	2002	466
Saudi Arabia	2005	577
Vietnam	2007	124
Ukraine	2008	165
Russia	2012	1,858
Iran	Pending	331
Algeria	Pending	189
Kazakhstan	Pending	186
Libya	Pending	62

[a]GDP data are for 2011, except for Iran and Libya, for which the data are from 2009.
Sources: WTO new and pending members are available at http://www.wto.org/english/thewto_e/whatis_e/tif_e/org6_e.htm. GDP data are available at http://data.worldbank.org/data-catalog, and GDP data for Taipei are available at http://www.wto.org/english/res_e/booksp_e/anrep_e/trade_profiles12_e.pdf.

an agreed date, and limited its rights to use foreign exchange restrictions in the future."[24] However, the International Monetary Fund objected strenuously to this on the grounds that exchange restrictions were the IMF's jurisdiction, and the provision was dropped from the final accession protocol. (As we will see, dropping this commitment has had extremely unfortunate consequences for the United States and for countries that compete with China in world markets.)

In addition to China and Ukraine, other new WTO members that are significant markets are Saudi Arabia; Taiwan; the United Arab Emirates; Vietnam; and Russia, the world's tenth-largest economy. Russia was finally approved for membership at the December 2011 WTO Ministerial Conference after eighteen years of negotiations with some sixty WTO member countries. In the process of these negotiations, Russia agreed to substantially liberalize its trade regime. Twenty-five countries have "observer" status in the WTO, which means they must start acces-

24. Independent Evaluation Office of the International Monetary Fund, *IMF Involvement in International Trade Policy Issues* (Washington, D.C.: International Monetary Fund, 2009), 59.

sion negotiations within five years of becoming an observer.[25] Because joining the WTO is a lengthy and arduous process, countries must carefully consider the costs and benefits. Obviously, however, countries that do join believe that undertaking the WTO commitments will help them develop economically over the long term. In the case of Ukraine, for example, Andrii Goncharuk describes the benefits as:

1. "strengthening domestic policies and institutions for international trade . . . ";
2. "improving the ease and security of access to major export markets";
3. "accessing a dispute settlement mechanism for trade issues"; and
4. "providing Ukraine with a 'seat at the table' as the WTO members establish the rules that govern much of global trade."[26]

Though not stated by Goncharuk, however, perhaps the major motive for Ukraine to join the WTO was to be eligible to enter into negotiations with the EU to establish an FTA, because the EU will only enter into an FTA with WTO member countries. (The United States also requires its potential FTA partners to be WTO members, which was a motivation for Jordan, Oman, and Panama to join the WTO.)

Although the accession of these new members resulted in a significant liberalization of global trade barriers, WTO membership for the communist countries also required a significant change by the United States. When the GATT was first launched in 1947, the United States had applied MFN treatment to non-GATT member countries; this was not required by the GATT, but was a statutory requirement of the 1934 Reciprocal Trade Agreements Act. However, in 1951, as the Cold War intensified, the U.S. Congress amended the law to deny MFN treatment to most communist countries.

---

25. The status and numbers of WTO members and observers are as of April 9, 2013. A listing of WTO members and observers is available at http://www.wto.org/english/thewto_e/whatis_e/tif_e/org6_e.htm. The one exception to the rule that observers have to start accession negotiations within five years is the Holy See, for which this rule has been waived, and there is no expectation that the Holy See will become a member.

26. Goncharuk, "The Path of Ukraine into the WTO," 256.

The 1974 Trade Act revised this treatment in a provision, known as the Jackson-Vanik Amendment, which is still in effect. Under this legislation, the president cannot grant MFN treatment to any nonmarket country that restricts emigration, a prohibition that was particularly aimed at the Soviet Union for imposing restrictions on Jews trying to emigrate from Russia. However, this law allowed MFN treatment to be granted on a temporary basis if the United States negotiated a trade agreement with the country (which had to be extended every three years) and the president determined that the country did not restrict emigration, or by a presidential waiver. This waiver, however, had to be renewed annually and was subject to congressional override. Beginning in the late 1970s, the president also used this waiver authority to grant MFN treatment to the People's Republic of China.

Granting MFN treatment on a year-to-year basis is inconsistent with the obligation to provide MFN treatment unconditionally under GATT Article 1.[27] As the USSR dissolved and its former constituent states joined the WTO, the United States had to change how it treated these countries. To make it more palatable politically to grant a communist nation MFN treatment in the United States, MFN treatment was renamed "permanent normal trade relations" in 1998 legislation.

Today the only two countries that do not receive MFN treatment from the United States are Cuba and North Korea. Imports from these two nations face the original Smoot-Hawley high tariffs in the United States, such as a 70 percent duty on toys and an 80 percent duty on sundry plastic articles.

Exchange Rates: The Big Gap in Trade Rules

Although the GATT/WTO has made enormous progress in reducing barriers and distortions to trade in nonagricultural goods, there are still a number of gaps, such as the lack of rules governing competition policy and the loopholes in the TRIMs agreement. However, far and away the biggest gap is in the treatment of exchange rates.

27. An exception to the requirement to provide unconditional MFN is in Article XIII of the WTO/GATT, which allows a member to deny MFN status to a newly acceding country if it notifies the WTO/GATT accordingly. In such a case, the new member is not required to extend MFN treatment to that member. In fact, for the memberships of Mongolia, Kyrgyz Republic, and Georgia, the United States temporarily invoked Article XIII until permanent normal trade relations could be approved.

It has long been recognized that countries could use exchange rate policy as a trade distortion: an undervalued currency acts as a subsidy for the country's exports and a barrier to imports. The founders of the postwar institutions envisioned that the GATT would address trade issues and that exchange rate issues would be addressed by the International Monetary Fund.

GATT/WTO Article XV states that "Contracting Parties shall not, by exchange action, frustrate the intent of the provisions of this Agreement, nor, by trade action, the intent of the provisions of the Articles of Agreement of the International Monetary Fund." If there are problems, the WTO is to seek cooperation with the IMF "to pursue a co-ordinated policy with regard to exchange questions within the jurisdiction of the Fund." The WTO is then required to "accept all findings of statistical and other facts presented by the Fund relating to foreign exchange, monetary reserves and balances of payments, and shall accept the determination of the Fund as to whether action by a contracting party in exchange matters is in accordance with" the IMF rules.

The IMF does have rules on exchange rate manipulation, but unfortunately the IMF has proven to be very weak in its ability to address foreign exchange issues. In fact, the IMF has never concluded that a member was out of compliance with its obligations in this regard. Even if the IMF did conclude that a country was manipulating its exchange rate to take unfair advantage of the trade system, it has no leverage to deal with this issue, and it lacks a dispute settlement mechanism.[28]

Because the founders of the postwar institutions envisioned that the IMF would address this issue, WTO rules are inadequate to deal with the problem of deliberate currency manipulation. There have never been any WTO dispute settlement cases regarding Article XV's prohibition of exchange rate manipulation. And the subsidies / countervailing duty code is not useful, because it defines prohibited subsidies as being industry specific, not across the board, as is the impact of currency manipulation.

Another issue for the WTO is that its rules only address specific actions by governments, and a country's exchange rate is often affected by market forces, such as changes in economic competitiveness or global

28. The IMF does have enormous leverage over countries that run into severe balance-of-payments problems caused by deficits through its lending programs, but this leverage does not work vis-à-vis countries that have a surplus on their current account.

capital flooding into a "safe haven" in times of global crisis. However, an undervalued exchange rate can also be driven by government policy, such as deliberate and consistent central bank intervention in the foreign exchange market.

FTAs and the WTO

The founders of the postwar institutions envisioned a world where trade would be largely based on economic fundamentals and where nations would trade with one another on a basically equal level. The GATT, it was hoped, would set the structure that would enable that vision to become reality.

As noted, the first article of the GATT set out the requirement for MFN treatment under which discrimination was permitted in only two circumstances. One of those instances was the formation of customs unions and free trade areas (Article XXIV of the GATT). In a customs union, the participating countries eliminate all barriers to trade between themselves and adopt a common external tariff. In a free trade area (i.e., an FTA), all internal barriers to trade are eliminated, but each member country maintains its own external tariff that applies to nonmembers of the agreement.

This exception to the GATT was intended to allow Europe—and in particular France and Germany, the two historic enemies—to join together in a customs union where they would become economically linked and, it was expected, would live together in peace. Some recent analysis suggests that some American policymakers also wanted to allow the option for a future FTA between the United States and Canada.

For both political and economic reasons, however, policymakers envisioned such blocs as the exception to MFN status. Politically, it was believed that trading blocs could lead to friction and possibly even war, and economically that they could cause injury to nonmembers. According to economic theory, the members of a preferential trade bloc could benefit from the creation of new trade opportunities, while nonmembers might be hurt by loss of sales to a less-efficient member that only gains the sale because of the tariff preference.

Accordingly, GATT Article XXIV, which is now part of the WTO, was intended to minimize these risks. This article required that customs unions and free trade area agreements be notified to all members of the GATT and that all GATT members have the right to consult with the members of the agreement. To maximize the potential economic gains of a trade bloc and minimize the potential injury to nonmembers, Article XXIV required that trade barriers be removed on "substantially all" trade between the partners. And if the members of the bloc were forming a customs union with a common external tariff, nonmembers could be entitled to compensation where tariffs were increased as the common external tariff was formed.

Unfortunately, these rules have been almost totally ineffective, and today preferential trade is almost the rule, not the exception. The WTO reports that 354 agreements have been notified and are in force as of January 2013. FTAs account for more than 90 percent of these notified agreements, and customs unions make up fewer than 10 percent.[29] In addition to these agreements that have been notified to the WTO/GATT, there are others that have not been notified or are in a very early stage of negotiation.

The European Union, the most important of these agreements, consists of twenty-seven nations that have formed a customs and economic union and now constitute the world's largest trading bloc. Another agreement is the European Free Trade Area, which today consists of Iceland, Liechtenstein, Norway, and Switzerland.[30]

Most U.S. trade competitors are aggressively negotiating FTAs. For example, the EU has negotiated or is negotiating agreements with Albania, Algeria, Canada, Chile, Egypt, India, Israel, Jordan, South Korea, Lebanon, Mexico, Morocco, Tunisia, Turkey, and Ukraine.[31]

Developing countries also have formed many free trade arrangements among themselves, for example MERCOSUR (official members are Ar-

29. The WTO Web site on "regional trade agreements" is available at http://www.wto.org/english/tratop_e/region_e/region_e.htm.

30. The European Free Trade Area (EFTA) was originally established in 1960 by seven countries—Austria, Denmark, Norway, Portugal, Sweden, Switzerland, and the United Kingdom—that were not willing to join the European Community at that time and felt they needed their own trade bloc to protect their interests. Subsequently, however, as circumstances changed, the United Kingdom, Austria, Denmark, Portugal, and Sweden all joined the EU, while Liechtenstein and Iceland joined EFTA.

31. Bilateral and regional free trade agreements that have been notified to the WTO are listed on the Web site noted in n. 29.

gentina, Brazil, Paraguay, Uruguay, and Venezuela), and the East Africa Community (Kenya, Rwanda, Tanzania, and Uganda).

Whenever a country applies different tariff rates depending on the country of export, it needs to have a methodology for defining the origin of the product, known as "rules of origin." Rules of origin are very important in free trade area arrangements where members accord duty free treatment to one another. All members of the FTA must apply the same rules of origin, because once a product has cleared customs in one member, it can be transshipped free of duty to any other FTA member country.

Rules of origin can be very liberal and allow products to be shipped between members with a great deal of parts and material produced in a nonmember; or they can be very restrictive, at the extreme even requiring that 100 percent of the product be produced within the area, thereby excluding any foreign value added. They can also be used to nullify the market opening ostensibly granted by the duty elimination by requiring more local content than the partner country can economically produce.

The 1947 GATT did not have any specific rules for how countries should determine the origin of products, which was viewed as a technical exercise left to each country's discretion. At that time, the production process for goods was far more straightforward than it is today. Generally something was grown or mined in a country and either processed there or shipped raw for processing in another country, where it was "transformed" into a new product.

Today, the situation is radically different. Many goods are shipped repeatedly across borders, and part of the production occurs in many countries. For example, silicon for a semiconductor may come from one country, be processed in another, and then cross several borders while it is fabricated and developed, and then finally packaged in a different country. Automobiles today are assembled from parts produced in multiple countries. Multinational corporations have "value chains" for production that involve parts and components from many nations. Identifying origin is arbitrary.

As the GATT/WTO has eliminated various forms of protectionism during the past sixty years, countries have sometimes looked for imaginative new ways to protect their domestic industries, and thus they sometimes have used rules of origin.[32] The United States, EU member states,

32. In 1972, I was new to trade policy and my first assignment was to analyze the EC-EFTA trade agreement to see if it complied with GATT rules and if the United

the member states of the European Free Trade Area, Japan, and other countries all have different systems for determining rules of origin. Even where protectionism is not deliberate, the sheer diversity and complexity of these rules may reduce potential trade gains. For example, a product produced in Chile may qualify for duty-free trade under the U.S. rule of origin but not under the EU rule, even though the product is ostensibly duty free.

America's FTAs

America's FTAs all build on the WTO rules and often reiterate them in the agreement, although they also go beyond WTO rules in a number of areas. The U.S. agreements have evolved from a short and straightforward 1985 agreement with Israel to more complex and far-reaching recent agreements.

NAFTA provides the basic model for the subsequent U.S. FTAs, although this model has evolved considerably. Basically, U.S. negotiators use standard concepts in the negotiations, although these may be modified in minor respects to fit the needs of a U.S. trade partner or U.S political requirements. However, U.S. negotiators insist that all major areas of the model be covered.

U.S. negotiators sometimes refer to this model as the "gold standard." As the Government Accountability Office reports: "Taking products, sectors, or issues off the table, particularly ones such as intellectual property rights that are considered to provide a U.S. competitive advantage, generally precludes or creates an impasse in negotiations."[33]

One of the most important elements of America's FTAs is the elimination of tariff and nontariff barriers to trade. In general, under the U.S. agreements, both the United States and its trade partner eliminate duties

States might be owed compensation. After carefully reviewing the agreement and finding nothing, I came to the huge annex defining the rules of origin for the agreement. Initially, I thought this was just "technical," but then looked at it carefully to find it was highly protectionist—e.g., one rule stated that an electronic product would only qualify for duty free treatment if it contained less than 3 percent of semiconductors sourced from non-EC-EFTA countries. The United States launched a GATT Article XXII consultation, which led to some changes in the EC-EFTA rules.

33. U.S. Government Accountability Office, *An Analysis of Free Trade Agreements and Congressional and Private Sector Consultations under Trade Promotion Authority*, Report GAO-08-59 (Washington, D.C.: U.S. Government Printing Office, 2007), 18.

over a ten-year schedule to allow domestic producers time to adjust to the new competition, although there are many exceptions to this.

Agricultural liberalization generally lags that of nonagricultural goods. The United States–Israel agreement exempted the agricultural sector initially, although the two partner countries subsequently negotiated an agreement on trade in agricultural products, but this only opened trade on about a hundred items.

In subsequent agreements, the United States has insisted that trade barriers on agricultural products be significantly reduced or eliminated. However, the United States has refused to limit its domestic agricultural subsidies, and as a result some countries have been unwilling to conclude an FTA with the United States. For example, this was a major sticking point with Brazil in the negotiations with the United States for a free trade area of the Americas.

The rules of origin in America's FTAs, like those of other developed countries, are lengthy, complex, and sometimes designed to sharply limit incorporation of nonmember parts and materials. For example, the rules of origin in the United States–Singapore agreement are 260 pages long.

One chapter of U.S. FTAs pertains to government procurement. This section commits the parties to the agreement to publicize their procedures and opportunities to bid on projects, and for covered entities it generally has a lower threshold for allowing bids from companies in U.S. partner countries. For example, under the WTO government procurement agreement, signatories must allow bids from other signatories valued at more than $169,000 for covered entities for both goods and services to compete. In the agreements with Mexico, Singapore, and Chile, however, the threshold is $56,190, thereby providing more opportunities for competition. Additionally, some of the agreements open up additional state and federal agencies under the procurement coverage.

The Treatment of Investment, Services, and Intellectual Property Protection

In addition to the provisions regarding the traditional trade issues of market access for goods, NAFTA and all subsequent U.S. FTAs go beyond WTO rules for investment, services, and the protection of intellectual property rights. The chapter on *investment* in these agreements requires the parties to give treatment to investors from its partner that is no less favorable than it gives to its own domestic investors (national treatment) or to investors from any other nonparty (MFN treatment). This covers such areas as the right to establish or expand a subsidiary or to acquire a company. These rules also specify that investors from the partner country can appoint managers without regard to nationality.

The rules also spell out the right of investors from the partner country to transfer capital into its investment and to repatriate profits, dividends, proceeds from the sale of any part of the covered investment, and so forth. U.S. agreements define investment very broadly to include both foreign direct investments and short-term portfolio investment flows.

The investment chapter also builds on the WTO agreement on TRIMs —for example, by including some practices not spelled out in that agreement, such as a prohibition on requirements to transfer technology. The expropriation, either direct or indirect, of a covered investment is prohibited unless for a public purpose and provided that it is done in a nondiscriminatory manner and with full compensation.

The investment rules also contain a controversial "Investor-State Dispute Settlement" mechanism, under which a foreign investor from an FTA partner country can submit a claim against the partner government to an arbitration panel. Within specified time limits, the arbitration panel then issues a binding ruling on the dispute, which could include a requirement that the government provide monetary damages or restitution of property in the event the claimant prevails. Under this provision, investors have brought suits against governments (for the United States, this includes state governments) for environmental regulations, which, the investors argue, are a "taking" of the investment's value. (This argument is considered more fully in chapter 7, on trade and the environment.)

The investment rules in U.S. FTAs incorporate provisions of the bilateral investment treaties that the United States and its partner country already had in place before the FTA. By and large, the FTA investment provisions extend only to a marginal degree commitments already in place in these bilateral investment treaties.

The approach taken to *services* liberalization in U.S. FTAs subsequent to NAFTA is different from the structure in the WTO agreement in two important respects.[34] First, in the GATS, countries list the services

34. The 1985 U.S. trade agreement with Israel covered cross-border trade in services but not investment, and the provisions on services were not legally binding. The

that are to be covered (the "positive list" approach), whereas in U.S. FTAs after NAFTA, all services are covered unless specifically listed as an exemption (the "negative list" approach). In theory, the negative list approach would logically seem to result in greater liberalization than the GATS approach, but in practice most observers believe the results are fairly similar.

Secondly, the GATS covers the supply of services through four distinct modes of supply, whereas NAFTA's approach is to have a chapter on cross-border services (GATS Modes 1 and 2) and a separate chapter on investment (Mode 3). The significance of this is that the rules on investment in U.S. trade agreements apply equally to all subject areas, including both goods and services. Additionally, NAFTA and the Chile and Singapore agreements have a separate chapter on temporary entry for businesspersons (Mode 4); however, the other agreements do not have any provisions for the temporary entry of businesspersons. Additionally, a number of U.S. FTAs provide for greater market access in specific service sectors than is covered under WTO commitments.

U.S. trade negotiators often refer to the *intellectual property protection* provisions in its FTAs as "TRIPS Plus" because they go somewhat farther than the provisions in the WTO. As noted above, the WTO rules represent a balance between countries whose companies have substantial intellectual property that they want to protect for as long as possible and countries that do not have significant intellectual property and want access to the protected goods at lower prices. U.S. companies, of course, have substantial intellectual property, and thus not surprisingly U.S. negotiators have pressed for extensive protection.

In the WTO negotiations, there was more or less a balance of countries that were net holders of intellectual property and net consumers of intellectual property. However, in its FTA negotiations, the United States wields enormous power, and it has used this power to press for protection in excess of that accorded by the WTO.

The following are examples of areas where TRIPS Plus provisions go farther than the WTO's TRIPS agreement in protecting intellectual property:

agreement with Jordan signed in 2000 did not have separate chapters on cross-border supply and investment, but it did cover these areas in articles in the agreement. All subsequent U.S. FTAs have separate chapters on cross-border trade and investment.

- Under the TRIPS agreement, patents are protected for twenty years, and then the intellectual property is publicly available and can be freely used. However, U.S. FTAs provide for additional years of protection for pharmaceuticals if there are unreasonable delays in the filing of a patent or in marketing approval. Such delays are common in developing countries, where the capacity to analyze a patent application is generally weak.
- TRIPS Plus requires FTA partners to provide at least a seventy-year term of copyright protection, compared with fifty years in TRIPS.
- In the United States, pharmaceutical companies must submit their test data regarding the safety of a drug to the Food and Drug Administration in order to gain approval to market the drug. The TRIPS agreement requires members to protect these undisclosed data, but it does not require governments to grant exclusive rights to these data. Accordingly, some countries may require that these test data be made available to applicants seeking to market a generic drug, thereby speeding the approval process of the generic. However, under U.S. FTAs, applicants to market a generic pharmaceutical of a patented product are not allowed to use these test data for five years, which means that to produce a generic drug in one of the U.S. partner countries, an applicant must either replicate these data or wait for five years.
- Under U.S. FTAs, America's partner governments are required to inform a patent holder if a generic company has applied for marketing approval of its drug. The TRIPS agreement has no such requirement.

Not surprisingly, these TRIPS Plus provisions were highly contentious in many U.S. bilateral negotiations, and may have played a significant role in the failure of U.S. efforts to negotiate agreements with the Southern African Customs Union and Thailand.

The Trans-Pacific Partnership and Trans-Atlantic Trade and Investment Partnership

With the failure of the WTO Doha Development Round, the United States has turned its attention to two major regional negotiations that could have far-reaching impacts on the world trade system if they are successful. The farthest along are the negotiations for a Trans-Pacific Partnership (TPP) agreement that would eliminate trade barriers between twelve Asian-Pacific countries. The second are prospective negotiations with the European Union to establish a Trans-Atlantic Trade and Investment Partnership agreement to establish free trade between the United States and the EU.

The countries negotiating for the TPP agreement are Australia, Brunei, Canada, Chile, Japan, Malaysia, Mexico, New Zealand, Peru, Singapore, the United States, and Vietnam. These countries are highly diverse, both commercially and in terms of their economic structures. For example, Australia and the United States are wealthy nations, whereas Malaysia and Vietnam are lower-middle-income countries; Vietnam has a relatively protected market, while the others are more open.

Negotiators in the TPP are pursuing a comprehensive agreement that would include areas covered in most other U.S. bilateral trade agreements, such as trade in goods and services, intellectual property protection, government procurement, customs valuation, technical barriers to trade, sanitary and phytosanitary measures, trade remedies, and dispute settlement. In addition, the United States is also proposing several new areas. One of these is cross-border data flows, which has become an important issue in the Internet age, where data are sent around the world with the click of a computer's mouse and stored in data servers that may be located anywhere. A second area is "regulatory coherence," which aims to reduce the trade-distorting impact of different country regulations.

A TPP agreement has been seen from the beginning as a potential template to attract other economies belonging to the Asia-Pacific Economic Cooperation (APEC) forum, a group of twenty-one Pacific Rim economies such as China, Hong Kong, Indonesia, and Russia.[35]

Negotiations between the United States and the EU are not nearly as far along as the TPP negotiations, but they are addressing basically the same issues. However, the approaches taken in the TPP and the EU negotiations on some of these issues may be different. For example, in the approach to reducing the trade impact of differing regulations, the negotia-

35. The twenty-one members of APEC are Australia, Brunei, Canada, Chile, China, Hong Kong, Indonesia, Japan, South Korea, Malaysia, Mexico, New Zealand, Papua New Guinea, Peru, the Philippines, Russia, Singapore, Taiwan, Thailand, the United States, and Vietnam.

tions with the EU may consider the possibility of actual convergence, whereas the TPP negotiations will likely address only procedural changes.

Conclusion

Since the Reciprocal Trade Agreements Act of 1934, U.S. policy toward trade agreements has been based on the concept of reciprocity—that is, the United States would make concessions roughly equal to the concessions made by its trade partners. (As noted, however, there have been two exceptions to this. First, for a short period immediately after World War II, the United States deliberately opened its market to a greater extent than demanded of its trade partners in order to facilitate economic recovery in Europe and Japan. Second, the U.S. approach and the multilateral trade rules of the GATT/WTO allow developing countries to provide less market opening than developed countries.)

In the eight rounds of multilateral trade negotiations since the GATT was launched in 1947, the intent of trade negotiators has been to reduce trade barriers to promote economic growth. Though most trade barriers on nonagricultural goods have been removed, progress on trade liberalization in the agricultural area and services areas has been limited. Additionally, a huge hole in the trade rules remains with regard to the potential for the manipulation of exchange rates, and loopholes in other rules still provide room for a neomercantilist country to gain an unfair trade advantage.

One of the fundamental principles of the original GATT is the concept of MFN trade treatment, which requires all members of the GATT/WTO to provide all other members with the same treatment with regard to access to their market, although more favorable treatment can be given to developing countries. A second exception to MFN is that countries are allowed to negotiate FTAs with one or more countries, provided these agreements remove substantially all barriers to trade among the partners. Though originally this exception was envisioned as being very limited, the reality today is that almost all members of the WTO have negotiated these agreements and today there are 354 of them. These agreements discriminate against nonmembers and distort trade; the MFN principle is now almost the exception rather than the rule.

Although most barriers to trade in nonagricultural goods have been removed, the GATT/WTO rules do allow countries to impose temporary import restraints in order to give domestic industries an opportunity to adjust to global competition under specified conditions. They also permit member countries to impose antidumping and countervailing duties to offset foreign dumping or subsidy practices that distort trade so as to restore a *level playing field*, provided specified procedures are followed.

Efforts to conclude a new round of multilateral negotiations in the Doha Development Round have stalemated. In an attempt to spur the multilateral negotiations and to make progress on trade liberalization, the United States has increasingly turned to negotiating bilateral and regional agreements, and it now has agreements with twenty other nations. These agreements eliminate almost all barriers to trade between the United States and its partners, except in the agricultural area, where some high U.S. tariffs remain and the United States continues to give large subsidies to producers of specified products. Additionally, the rules in many of these agreements go farther than the multilateral rules, particularly with regard to services, investment, and intellectual property. The major U.S. negotiations today are the TPP negotiations with eleven other Asia-Pacific countries, and the Trans-Atlantic Trade and Investment Partnership negotiations with the European Union to further open trade between the EU and the United States.

Chapter 3

Trade Agreements and Economic Theory

Economists have had an enormous impact on trade policy, and they provide a strong rationale for free trade and for removal of trade barriers. Although the objective of a trade agreement is to liberalize trade, the actual provisions are heavily shaped by domestic and international political realities. The world has changed enormously from the time when David Ricardo proposed the law of comparative advantage, and in recent decades economists have modified their theories to account for trade in factors of production, such as capital and labor, the growth of supply chains that today dominate much of world trade, and the success of neomercantilist countries in achieving rapid growth.

Almost all Western economists today believe in the desirability of free trade, and this is the philosophy advocated by international institutions such as the World Bank, the International Monetary Fund, and the World Trade Organization (WTO). And this was the view after World War II, when Western leaders launched the General Agreement on Tariffs and Trade (GATT) in 1947.

However, economic theory has evolved substantially since the time of Adam Smith, and it has evolved rapidly since the GATT was founded. To understand U.S. trade agreements and how they should proceed in the future, it is important to review economic theory and see how it has evolved and where it is today.

In the seventeenth and eighteenth centuries, the predominant thinking was that a successful nation should export more than it imports and that the trade surplus should be used to expand the nation's treasure, primarily gold and silver. This would allow the country to have a bigger and more powerful army and navy and more colonies.

One of the better-known advocates of this philosophy, known as mercantilism, was Thomas Mun, a director of the British East India Company. In a letter written in the 1630s to his son, he said: "The ordinary means therefore to increase our wealth and treasure is by Foreign Trade, wherein wee must ever observe this rule; to sell more to strangers yearly than wee consume of theirs in value. . . . By this order duly kept in our trading, . . . that part of our stock which is not returned to us in wares must necessarily be brought home in treasure."[1]

Mercantilists believed that governments should promote exports and that governments should control economic activity and place restrictions on imports if needed to ensure an export surplus. Obviously, not all nations could have an export surplus, but mercantilists believed this was the goal and that successful nations would gain at the expense of those less successful. Ideally, under mercantilist theory, a nation would export finished goods and import raw materials, thereby maximizing domestic employment.

Then Adam Smith challenged this prevailing thinking in *The Wealth of Nations* published in 1776.[2] Smith argued that when one nation is more efficient than another country in producing a product, while the other nation is more efficient at producing another product, then both nations could benefit through trade. This would enable each nation to specialize in producing the product where it had an absolute advantage, and thereby increase total production over what it would be without trade. This insight implied very different policies than mercantilism. It implied less government involvement in the economy and a reduction of barriers to trade.

The Theory of Comparative Advantage

Forty-one years after *The Wealth of Nations* was published, David Ricardo introduced an extremely important modification to the theory in

1. Thomas Mun, in a letter written to his son in the 1630s, available at http://socserv.mcmaster.ca/econ/ugcm/3ll3/mun/treasure.txt.
2. William Bernstein notes that Smith was not the first to advocate the advantages of free trade. He says, "By far the most remarkable early free-trader was Henry Martyn, whose *Considerations upon the East India Trade* preceded by seventy-five years Adam Smith's *Wealth of Nations*." William J. Bernstein, *A Splendid Exchange: How Trade Shaped the World* (New York: Grove Press, 2008), 258.

his *On the Principles of Political Economy and Taxation*, published in 1817.[3] Ricardo observed that trade will occur between nations even where one country has an absolute advantage in producing all the products traded.

Ricardo showed that what was important was the *comparative advantage* of each nation in production. The theory of comparative advantage holds that even if one nation can produce all goods more cheaply than another nation, both nations can still trade under conditions where each benefits. Under this theory, what matters is relative efficiency.

Economists sometimes compare this to the situation where even though a lawyer might be more proficient at both law and typing than the secretary, it would still pay the lawyer to have the secretary handle the typing to allow more time for the higher-paying legal work. Similarly, if each country specializes in the products where it is comparatively more efficient, total production will be higher and consumers will have more goods to utilize.

Smith and Ricardo considered only labor as a "factor of production." In the early 1900s, this theory was further developed by two Swedish economists, Eli Heckscher and Bertil Ohlin, who considered several factors of production.[4] The so-called Heckscher-Ohlin theory basically holds that a country will export those commodities that are produced by the factor that it has in relative abundance, and that it will import products whose production requires factors of production where it has relatively less abundance. This situation is often portrayed in economics textbooks as a simplified model of two countries (England and Portugal) and two products (textiles and wine). In this simplified portrayal, England has relatively abundant capital and Portugal has relatively abundant labor, and textiles are relatively capital intensive whereas wine is relatively labor intensive. With these conditions, both nations would be better off if they freely traded, and under such a situation of free trade, England would export textiles and import wine. This would maximize efficiency, resulting in more total production of textiles and wine and cheaper prices for consumers than would be the case without trade. Through empirical studies and mathematical models, economists almost

3. David Ricardo, *On the Principles of Political Economy and Taxation* (London: John Murray, 1817).

4. Bertil Ohlin actually published this theory in 1933. A brief explanation of the Heckscher-Ohlin theory is available at http://nobelprize.org/educational_games/economics/trade/ohlin.html.

universally believe that this model holds equally well for multiple products and multiple countries.

In fact, economists consider this law of comparative advantage to be fundamental. As Dominick Salvatore says in his basic economics textbook *International Economics*, the law of comparative advantage remains "one of the most important and still unchallenged laws of economics. . . . The law of comparative advantage is the cornerstone of the pure theory of international trade."[5]

The law of comparative advantage also holds equally well for many factors of production. In addition to labor and capital, other factors of production include natural resources such as land and technology, and these can be subdivided. For example, land can be land for mining or land for farming, or technology for making cars or computer chips, or skilled and unskilled labor. Additionally, over time, factor endowments may change. For example, natural resources, such as coal reserves, may be used up, or a country's educational system may be improved, thereby providing a more highly skilled labor force.

Furthermore, some products do not utilize the same factors of production over their life cycle.[6] For example, when computers were first introduced, they were incredibly capital intensive and required highly skilled labor. Over time, as volume increased, costs came down and computers could be mass-produced. Initially, the United States had a comparative advantage in production; but today, when computers are mass-produced by relatively unskilled labor, the comparative advantage has shifted to countries with abundant cheap labor. And still other products may use different factors of production in different countries. For example, cotton production is highly mechanized in the United States but is very labor intensive in Africa. The fact that factors of production may change does not nullify the theory of comparative advantage; it just means that the mix of products that a nation can produce relatively more efficiently than its trade partners may change.

Traditional economic theories expounded by Ricardo and Heckscher-Ohlin are based on a number of important assumptions, such as perfect competition with no artificial barriers imposed by governments. A second assumption is that production occurs under diminishing or constant

---

5. Dominick Salvatore, *International Economics*, 8th ed. (Hoboken, N.J.: John Wiley & Sons, 2004), 15.

6. The concept of *product life cycle* was introduced by Raymond Vernon in 1966.

returns to scale, that is, the costs of producing each additional unit are the same or higher as production increases. For example, to increase his wheat crop, a farmer may be forced to use less-fertile land or pay more for laborers to harvest the wheat, thereby increasing the cost of each additional unit produced.

Another key assumption of traditional economic theory is that basic factors of production—such as land, labor, and capital—are not traded across borders. Although Ohlin believed that such basic factors of production were not traded, he argued that the relative returns to factors of production between countries would tend to be equalized as goods are traded between the countries. Subsequently, Samuelson argued that factor prices would in fact be equalized under free trade conditions, and this is known in economics as the factor price equalization theorem.[7] This might mean, for example, that international trade would cause wage rates for unskilled workers to fall in the high-wage country in relation to the rents available from capital and to the same level as wages in the low-wage country, and for wages to rise in relation to the rents available from capital in the low-wage country and equal to the level of the country where labor was less abundant. (The implications of this are important and are explored further in chapter 8.)

In static terms, the law of comparative advantage holds that all nations can benefit from free trade because of the increased output available for consumers as a result of more efficient production. James Jackson of the Congressional Research Service describes the benefits as follows: Trade liberalization, "by reducing foreign barriers to U.S. exports and by removing U.S. barriers to foreign goods and services, helps to strengthen those industries that are the most competitive and productive and to reinforce the shifting of labor and capital from less productive endeavors to more productive economic activities."[8]

Many economists, however, believe that the dynamic benefits of free trade may be greater than the static benefits. Dynamic benefits, for example, include the pressure on companies to be more efficient to meet foreign competition, the transfer of skills and knowledge, the introduction of new products, and the potential positive impact of the greater

7. A good explanation of this theorem, which shows a hypothetical trading relationship between two countries, is available at http://faculty.washington.edu/danby/bls324/trade/hos.html.

8. James K. Jackson, *Trade Agreements: Impact on the U.S. Economy* (Washington, D.C.: Congressional Research Service, 2006), 9.

adoption of commercial law. Thus trade can affect both what is produced (static effects) and how it is produced (dynamic effects).

Terms of Trade

Another important concept in international trade theory is the concept of "terms of trade." This refers to the amount of exports needed to obtain a given amount of imports, with the fewer amount of exports needed the better for the country. The terms of trade can shift, either benefiting a country or reducing its welfare.

Assume that the United States exports aircraft to Japan and imports televisions, and that one airplane can purchase 1,000 televisions. If one airplane now can purchase 2,000 televisions, the United States will be better off; alternatively, its welfare is diminished if it can only purchase 500 televisions with a single airplane.

A number of factors can affect the terms of trade, including changes in demand or supply, or government policy. In the example given just above, if Japanese demand for aircraft increases, the terms of trade will shift in the favor of the United States because it can demand more televisions for each airplane. Alternatively, if the Japanese begin producing aircraft, the terms of trade will shift in Japan's favor, because the supply of aircraft will now be larger and the Japanese will have alternative sources of supply.

Under certain conditions, improvements in a country's productivity can worsen its terms of trade. For example, if Japanese manufacturers of televisions become more efficient and reduce sale prices, Japan's terms of trade will worsen, as it will take more televisions to exchange for the airplane.

A country can also adopt a beggar-thy-neighbor stance by deliberately turning the terms of trade in its favor through the imposition of an *optimum tariff* or through currency manipulation. In his economics textbook, Dominick Salvatore defines an optimum tariff as

> that rate of tariff that maximizes the net benefit resulting from the improvement in the nation's terms of trade against the negative effect resulting from reduction in the volume of trade. . . . As the terms of trade of the nation imposing the tariff improve, those of the trade partner deteriorate, since they are the inverse. . . . Facing both a lower volume of trade and deteriorating terms of trade, the trade partner's

welfare definitely declines. As a result, the trade partner is likely to retaliate. . . . Note that even when the trade partner does not retaliate when one nation imposes the optimum tariff, the gains of the tariff-imposing nation are less than the losses of the trade partner, so that the world as a whole is worse off than under free trade. It is in this sense that free trade maximizes world welfare.[9]

If both countries play this game, both will be worse off. However, if only one country pursues this strategy, it can gain at its partner's expense.

The Economic Effects of Trade Liberalization

The objective of reducing barriers to trade, of course, is to increase the level of trade, which is expected to improve economic well-being. Economists often measure economic well-being in terms of the share of total output of goods and services (i.e., gross domestic product, GDP) that the country produces per person on average. GDP is the best measurement of economic well-being available, but it has significant conceptual difficulties. As Joseph Stiglitz notes, the measurement of GDP fails "to capture some of the factors that make a difference in people's lives and contribute to their happiness, such as security, leisure, income distribution and a clean environment—including the kinds of factors which growth itself needs to be sustainable."[10] Moreover, GDP does not distinguish between "good growth" and "bad growth"; for example, if a company dumps waste in a river as a by-product of its manufacturing, both the manufacturing and the subsequent cleaning up of the river contribute to the measurement of GDP.

As the result of a multilateral round of trade negotiations under the GATT/WTO, tariffs are reduced during a transition period but are not completely eliminated. In U.S. bilateral or regional free trade agreements (FTAs), however, parties to the agreement completely eliminate almost all tariffs on trade with each other, generally over a transition period, which may be five to ten years.

Although reducing barriers to trade generally represents a move toward free trade, there are situations when reducing a tariff can actually

9. Salvatore, *International Economics,* 255.
10. Stiglitz, "Progress, What Progress?" *OECD Observer,* no. 272, April 2009.

increase the effective rate of protection for a domestic industry. Jacob Viner gives an example: "Let us suppose that there are import duties both on wool and on woolen cloth, but that no wool is produced at home despite the duty. Removing the duty on wool while leaving the duty unchanged on the woolen cloth results in increased protection for the cloth industry while having no significance for wool-raising."[11]

This happens for some products as a result of multilateral trade negotiations. For example, a country often reduces tariffs on products that are not import sensitive—often because they are not produced in that country—to a greater extent than it reduces tariffs on import-sensitive products. In an FTA, where the end result is zero tariffs, this would not be an effect when the agreement is fully implemented. However, during the transition period it could well be relevant for some products. Other than this exception, however, reducing tariffs or other barriers to trade increases trade in the product, and this is the intent of the trade agreement.

The benefits to an economy from expanded exports as a trade partner improves market access are clear and indisputable. If the U.S. trade partner reduces barriers as a result of a trade agreement, U.S. exports will likely increase, which expands U.S. production and GDP. And suppliers to a firm that gains additional sales through exports will likely also increase their sales to that firm, thereby increasing GDP further.

The firms gaining sales through this may well hire more workers and possibly increase dividends to stockholders. This money is distributed through the economy a number of times as a result of what economists call the *money multiplier effect*, which states that for every $1 an individual receives as income, a portion of it will be spent (i.e., consumption) and a portion will be saved. If individuals save 10 percent of their income, for every $1 earned as income, 90 cents will be spent and 10 cents will be saved. The 90 cents that is spent then becomes income for another individual, and once again 90 percent of this will be spent on consumption. This continues until there is nothing left from the original $1 amount.

In fact, expanded exports increase a nation's GDP by definition. One equation economists use for determining GDP is GDP = Domestic consumption (C) + Domestic gross investment (In) + Government spending (G) + [Exports (E)—Imports (I)], or

11. Jacob Viner, *The Customs Union Issue* (New York: Carnegie Endowment for International Peace, 1950), 48.

$$GDP = C + In + G + (E—I)$$

The impact of trade on GDP, therefore, is the net amount that exports exceed or are less than imports. However, this is a static measure. As noted above, expanded exports also have a dynamic effect as companies become more efficient as sales increase.

The economic impact of increased imports is different. By the economists' definition of GDP, of course, increased imports reduce GDP. A way of looking at this is that if a U.S. firm produces a product that suddenly loses out to increased imports, it will reduce its production and employment, and consequently its suppliers will also reduce production and employment, thereby reducing economic output.

This would suggest that the mercantilists were right, that a nation would be well advised to restrict imports. However, almost all economists today would reject that conclusion, and in fact most economists believe that reducing its trade barriers benefits a country whether or not the country's trade partners also reduce their barriers. Adam Smith and many economists after him argue that the objective of production is to produce goods for consumption. Stephen Cohen and his colleagues express this argument as follows: "The theories of comparative advantage (both classical and neoclassical) imply that liberalizing trade is always beneficial to consumers in any country, regardless of whether the country's trading partners reciprocate by reducing their own trade barriers. From this perspective, the emphasis on the reciprocal lowering of trade barriers in most actual trade liberalization efforts . . . is misplaced."[12]

The benefits of unilateral elimination of trade barriers are particularly obvious in those cases where the country does not produce the product; in these cases, eliminating trade barriers expands consumer choice. (As noted above, however, an exception to this occurs in situations where reducing a trade barrier on a raw material or component that is not produced by the country increases the effective rate of protection for the finished product.)

Even where the country does produce the product, increased competition from trade liberalization will likely lead to lower prices by the domestic firms. In this event, some of the consumer's savings will then be

---

12. Stephen D. Cohen, Robert A. Blecker, and Peter D. Whitney, *Fundamentals of U.S. Foreign Trade Policy: Economics, Politics, Laws, and Issues* (Boulder, Colo.: Westview Press, 2003), 57.

spent consuming other products. The amount spent consuming other products will have positive production effects, which will somewhat mitigate the loss in production by the firm competing with the imports.

Increased import competition also has dynamic benefits by forcing domestic producers to become more efficient in order to compete in the lower price environment. Lower prices also may have a positive impact on monetary policy; because import competition reduces the threat of inflation, central banks can pursue a more liberal monetary policy of lower interest rates than otherwise would be the case. These lower rates benefit investment, housing, and other productive sectors.

Economic Models

Economists have developed a number of sophisticated models designed to simulate the changes in economic conditions that could be expected from a trade agreement. These models, which are based on modern economic theories of trade, are helpful where the barriers to trade are quantifiable, although the results are highly sensitive to the assumptions used in establishing the parameters of the model.

One type of model used extensively by economists to estimate the economy-wide effects of trade policy changes, such as the results of a multilateral trade round, is the Applied General Equilibrium Model, also called the Computable General Equilibrium (CGE) Model.[13] James Jackson of the Congressional Research Service notes: "These models incorporate assumptions about consumer behavior, market structure and organization, production technology, investment, and capital flows in the form of foreign direct investment."[14]

CGE models may be used to estimate the impact of a trade agreement on trade flows, labor, production, economic welfare, or even the environment. They may consider the effects of the agreement on all countries involved, and are ex ante; that is, they attempt to forecast changes that would result from a trade agreement. General equilibrium models are based on input-output models, which track how the output of one indus-

13. A commonly used and publicly available CGE model and comprehensive data base is available from the Global Trade Analysis Project, which is housed in the Department of Agricultural Economics at Purdue University. The GTAP model and database are available at https://www.gtap.agecon.purdue.edu/default.asp.

14. Jackson, *Trade Agreements*, 12.

try is an input to other industries. General equilibrium models use enormous data inputs that reflect all the elements to be considered.[15]

One of the great strengths of these models is that they can show how the effects on industries flow through the entire economy. One of their disadvantages is that because of their complexity, the assumptions behind their projections are not always transparent. Economic models are useful to give a sense of what might happen as a result of a trade agreement. They give the appearance of being authoritative, but users need to be aware that economic models are not predictive of what will actually happen and that they have significant weaknesses.

First, the results of any model depend on the assumptions underlying it, such as the degree to which imported products and domestically produced products can be substituted for one another, or whether or not there is perfect or imperfect competition. Differing assumptions can produce a wide range of results, not only in magnitude but also sometimes even in the direction of projected changes.

Second, the economic data needed are often weak, not only for developing countries but even for the United States and other developed nations. For example, trade and economic data between countries, and even within countries, are not readily comparable. In the United States, the North American Industry Classification System (NAICS), which is used to collect statistical data describing the U.S. economy, is based on industries with similar processes to produce goods or services. In contrast, data on international trade in goods are collected on a commodity basis.[16] The U.S. partners in the North American Free Trade Agreement (NAFTA), Canada and Mexico, also use NAICS, but the European Union uses a system called Nomenclature of Economic Activities. Although there are concordances between these differing systems, these are far from exact.

15. A second type of model commonly used is a gravity model, which assumes that larger economies have a greater pull on trade flows than smaller economies, and that proximity is an important factor affecting trade flows. And still another common type is a partial equilibrium model, which estimates the impact of a trade policy action on a specific sector, not the general economy. Partial equilibrium models do not capture linkages with other sectors and accordingly are useful when spillover effects are expected to be negligible. However, partial equilibrium models are more transparent than CGE models and it is easier to see the impact of changed assumptions.

16. A good source for trade data and an explanation of the data systems used is the Foreign Trade Statistics Web site at the Census Bureau, www.census.gov/foreigntrade/index.html.

Nontariff barriers—such as import quotas, subsidies, standards, and regulations—must be converted to their tariff equivalents, and this is often difficult and unreliable. For new areas covered in trade negotiations —such as services, investment, and intellectual property—efforts to measure the impact of barriers is even more difficult.

Although measuring the impact of tariffs is more accurate than measuring nontariff barriers or services, it is not as straightforward as it would seem. For example, often economists use a weighted tariff by considering the proportion of imports entering under that tariff line. A problem with this approach is that a very high duty will completely block imports, resulting in the false conclusion that that tariff line is given no weight.

In view of the problems with trade models, some economists dismiss their usefulness. For example, Bhagwati says: "I consider many of the estimates of trade expansion and of gains from trade—produced at great expense by number-crunching at institutions such as the World Bank with the aid of huge computable models . . . as little more than flights of fancy in contrived flying machines."[17] Many economists would consider this criticism extreme, but nonetheless trade models do need to be viewed with a large degree of caution.

The Economic Theory of Trade Blocs

The drafters of the GATT believed that reducing barriers to trade should be on a multilateral basis to get the greatest benefits of expanded production based on comparative advantage. As noted above, they enshrined this concept in Article I of the GATT (most-favored-nation, MFN, treatment), which requires members to give equal treatment with regard to trade barriers to all GATT members.

However, they also recognized a role for regional integration that would allow the members of a trade bloc to eliminate barriers on trade among themselves, while maintaining a discriminatory tariff on imports from nonmembers.[18] Accordingly, Article XXIV of the GATT provides

17. Jagdish Bhagwati, *In Defense of Globalization*, Council on Foreign Relations Report (New York:, Oxford University Press, 2004), 230.

18. The drafters of the GATT probably were focused on the potential benefits of a European customs union that would promote integration. Some historians argue that the U.S. negotiators also envisioned a possible U.S.-Canadian free trade agreement that would eliminate barriers to trade in North America.

for a major exception to the MFN principle that allows countries to form customs unions or free trade areas that may discriminate against nonmembers of the bloc.[19] In a customs union, the members eliminate trade barriers among themselves but erect a common customs tariff on imports from nonmembers. Members of a free trade area also eliminate trade barriers among themselves, but they each retain their own schedule of tariffs on imports from nonmembers.

Customs unions and free trade area agreements may expand trade and global welfare or they may diminish welfare, depending on whether they create new trade patterns based on comparative advantage or simply divert trade from a more competitive nonmember to a member of the trade bloc. In 1950, the economist Jacob Viner defined trade creation as the situation where a member of a preferential trading bloc has a comparative advantage in producing a product and is now able to sell it to its free trade area partners because trade barriers have been removed.

Trade creation benefits the exporters in the member of the trade bloc that has a comparative advantage in producing a product, and it benefits consumers in the importing member who now can purchase the product at a lower price. Domestic producers competing with the lower-cost imports from its partner country lose, but their loss is less than the gains to the exporters and consumers. Trade creation enhances global welfare through this greater efficiency.

In the case of trade diversion, however, a member gains its sales at the expense of a more competitive producer in a country that is not a member of the bloc, simply because its products enter its partner's market duty free, while the more competitive nonmember producer faces a discriminatory duty.[20] Nonmember country exporters that would have a comparative advantage under equal competitive conditions lose from trade diversion.

Additionally, under trade diversion, the importing country loses the tariff revenue it had collected on those imports which now come in duty free from its bloc partner. The consumer in the importing partner does

---

19. Another major exception to the MFN rule pertains to preferences for developing countries. This exception is considered further in chapter 6 below.

20. In *The Customs Union Issue,* Viner notes a qualification to the rule that global welfare is diminished if trade diversion is greater than trade creation, and that is when unit costs decrease in an industry as output expands. In such a case, a small country may not have been able to develop an industry because its market size was too small, but is able to develop the industry within a customs union or free trade arrangement.

gain, because the imported good no longer has to bear the cost of the tariff; however, the consumer's gain is necessarily less than or equal to the lost customs revenue, so the nation as a whole is less well off. Thus, trade diversion hurts both the importing country and the rest of the world. These losses are greater than the gains to the bloc member that gains exports due to trade diversion.

If trade diversion is greater than trade creation, formation of the customs union or FTA would diminish world welfare. If trade creation is greater, then global welfare is enhanced.

In addition to trade diversion and trade creation, which are basically static effects, participants in free trade areas and customs unions are also seeking dynamic benefits, such as expanded production as firms take advantage of the increased size of the market to increase output, and improved efficiency as firms adapt to increased competition. Access to a larger market is particularly important for small countries whose economy is too small to justify large-scale production.

To minimize the potential adverse consequences of such trade blocs, GATT Article XXIV requires that the members of a customs union or an FTA must eliminate trade barriers on "substantially all" trade between them, and that all the members of GATT have the opportunity to review the agreement. In the event that a GATT member not a party to the customs union faces higher tariffs on some products as a customs union is formed, Article XXIV requires that that member be compensated for the lost trade. However, as noted in chapter 2, Article XXIV has proven to be totally ineffective in restricting the growth of trade blocs; as a result, trade patterns today are significantly distorted by these preferential schemes.

Trade Theory Meets New Realities

From the time of Adam Smith in 1776 to the launching of the GATT in 1947, economic theory of trade evolved fairly slowly. Since the GATT was launched in 1947, however, there have been a number of significant modifications to the traditional Western economic theory of international trade. These modifications largely update the basic theory of trade to reflect the new realities of industry and commerce.

In the times of Smith, Ricardo, and Hecksher-Ohlin, companies were generally small and most international trade was in agricultural or mineral products or produced by small-scale manufacturing. By 1947, however, large-scale manufacturing had evolved, and a great deal of trade was in manufactured products.

In 1979, the economist Paul Krugman noted that a great deal of trade was taking place between developed countries that had similar factors of production. For example, the United States and the nations of Europe have broadly similar factors of production, yet conduct an enormous amount of trade generally within the same industries. Thus, the United States will export automobiles and auto parts to Europe and at the same time import autos and auto parts from Europe.

The Heckscher-Ohlin model, which is good at projecting likely trade patterns between countries where factors of production are different, really did not explain this trade pattern. Krugman's theory is based on product differentiation and economies of scale. For example, a Jeep and a Volkswagen are both automobiles, but they are highly differentiated as seen by the consumer. And both benefit from economies of scale; that is, the larger the production, the more costs can be reduced within a broad range of volume. Unlike wheat, where costs increase as volume is expanded, the cost of each additional automobile produced declines as production is increased, although at a very large volume of production costs would likely start to increase. Goods such as automobiles require large, mechanized production runs and substantial capital investment, and it may be extremely difficult for a new entrant to compete with an established firm.

Under trade based on product differentiation and economies of scale, several countries may produce the same product broadly defined and trade parts and differentiated products with one another. Thus, the United States might specialize in producing Jeeps, and Europe might specialize in producing Volkswagens. Clearly, a great deal of production in modern developed-country economies is in industries that experience increasing returns to scale, and in these industries returns to factors of production would not tend to equalize as a result of international trade. In fact, returns to labor in a labor-scarce economy might well increase, rather than decrease, as would be predicted by the factor price equalization theory.

Western economic theory has also changed in recent years to account for the fact that world trade has increased so much more rapidly than overall economic growth since the early 1970s. In 1973, the ratio of exports to GDP was 4.9 percent for the United States, and by 2005 this had more than doubled to 10.2 percent. For the world as a whole, this ratio was 10.5 percent in 1973, increasing to 20.5 percent in 2005.

What caused exports to increase more rapidly than production is that companies evolved from being domestically oriented to becoming multinational, and now many have evolved to become global. The first six rounds of GATT trade negotiations had reduced developed-country tariffs on industrial goods from the average of 40 percent after World War II to less than half that level by the end of the Kennedy Round in 1967. Additionally, international communications and transportation had improved enormously (the first commercial jet crossed the Atlantic in 1958, and the first satellite for commercial telecommunications was launched in 1965.)

As a result, companies in some industries, such as electronics and chemicals, became multinational corporations and increasingly began to purchase and produce parts and materials in a number of countries. Each time these parts and materials cross a border, an international trade transaction has occurred; and then, when the final good is exported, another international trade transaction has occurred.

This trend has increased enormously during the past twenty-five years, and now this cross-border trade occurs in virtually all industries. Many products will have parts and materials from many countries; for example, a new suit may have cotton from West Africa that has been processed into fabric in Bangladesh and sewn into a suit in China, with buttons imported from India. And then the suit may be exported to the United States. Another example is the first Airbus jumbo jet 380, which had parts and components from more than 1,500 suppliers in twenty-seven countries. Many companies today have global supply chains, procuring parts and materials worldwide. Each specific part or material in the value chain is sourced from the country that can produce the part most cheaply, whether because of its endowment of factors of production or because of special incentives, such as tax holidays.

Kei-Mu Yi of the World Bank notes that standard economic models account very well for the increase in world trade through the mid-1970s but cannot explain the growth of trade since then.[21] However, a model that accounts for supply chains does explain the growth in trade, and he believes that such vertical specialization accounts for about 30 percent of world trade today.

---

21. Kei-Mu Yi, *Can Vertical Specialization Explain the Growth of World Trade?* (New York: Federal Reserve Bank of New York, 1999).

Yi notes that tariff reductions have a far greater impact on these global supply chains than they do on traditional trade. To take the suit example, assume that China, Bangladesh, and the United States each reduces its tariffs by 1 percent and that imported fabric and buttons account for half the cost of the suit made in China; then the cost of producing the suit in China will be reduced by 0.5 percent. Coupled with the 1 percent U.S. tariff reduction, the cost to the U.S. consumer would be reduced by 1.5 percent. If the suit had been wholly produced in China, the cost to the consumer would have been reduced by just the U.S. tariff reduction, or 1 percent.

The emergence of these extensive supply chains has enormous implications. It means that for many products the traditional concept of "country of origin" no longer applies, because many products have many countries of origin. This in turn means that standard trade statistics have limitations in how useful they are for understanding what is really happening in world trade.[22] It has an impact on how countries should approach economic development, because it means that developing countries must become part of these global supply chains as a way to increase the amount of value added in the parts and materials provided to these supply chains. And it has an impact on how companies see themselves—a firm selling globally and procuring its parts and materials globally sees itself as a "global" firm rather than as a "national" firm.

Trade in Factors of Production and Services

Traditional economic theory assumed that goods are traded between countries, but that factors of production (e.g., labor, capital, and technology) and services are not traded from country to country. However, recently capital, technology, and services have been increasingly flowing easily over national borders, and even labor is moving from country to country more frequently. Accordingly, in recent rounds of multilateral negotiations and in U.S. bilateral agreements, negotiators have sought to develop rules governing investment, intellectual property protection, services, and labor.

In economic theory, if factors of production were fully mobile, the costs of all factors of production that could move across borders would

22. WTO deputy director-general Alejandro Jara gave an interesting speech May 26, 2010, in which he outlined some of the implications of supply chains for how we think about international trade. His speech is available at www.wto.org/english/news_e/news10_e/devel_26may10_e.htm.

result in equal costs in all trading countries. This would mean that the basis of comparative advantage for trade between countries would diminish and there would ultimately be less international trade.

In reality, of course, there are reasons other than trade barriers why factors of production such as capital or labor may not move across borders, even when there are no barriers and higher returns could be gained in other markets. Workers, for example, are reluctant to leave their homelands and family and friends, and investors are reluctant to invest in other markets where they have less familiarity. As a result, even eliminating all governmentally imposed barriers to trade in capital and labor would not lead to the complete equalization of costs between counties.

Like trade in investment and capital, post–World War II economists did not conceive of trade in services. In fact, trade in services was almost considered an oxymoron by early economists, such as Adam Smith and David Ricardo, who assumed that services are not tradable. This was also the view of trade negotiators for three or more decades after the GATT was launched.

Geza Feketukuty, the lead U.S. negotiator on services in the Uruguay Round, gives a wonderful anecdote of early efforts to launch negotiations on trade in services: "The Swiss delegate . . . dismissed trade in services by pointing out how impossible it was for him to have his hair cut by a barber in another country. The chairman of the committee . . . replied that every woman in Germany had benefited enormously from French exports of hairdressing services, and she was confident that the delegate's wife would confirm the same was true in Switzerland."[23]

Not surprisingly, economic theory as it applies to services trade is still being developed. In general, economists today assume that the basic theory of comparative advantage as it applies to goods applies equally well to cross-border trade in services. As Geza Feketekuty says, "The theory of comparative advantage as a theoretical statement about economic relationships should be equally valid whether the products encompassed by the theory are tradable physical goods such as shoes and oranges, or tradable services such as insurance and engineering."[24]

Many types of services, such as telecommunications, are intimately interconnected to other economic activity. Trade liberalization in these

23. Geza Feketekuty, *International Trade in Services: An Overview and Blueprint for Negotiations* (Cambridge, Mass.: American Enterprise Institute/Ballinger, 1988), 2–3.
    24. Ibid., 100.

areas can have far-reaching economic effects. For example, lowering the costs and increasing the availability of telecommunications services can help manufacturers compete in global markets, it can enable farmers to learn the latest techniques, and it can help other services sectors, such as tourism, that can now reach the world market through the Internet. Liberalization of telecommunications services even facilitated the creation of a new form of enterprise, namely, "offshoring," where companies moved some of their basic operations such as telemarketing call centers to low-cost locations in other countries.

In contrast, liberalizing restrictions in some other sectors, such as tourism, may affect revenues and employment for the providers and the country but will have only a minimal impact on the competitiveness of other sectors within the country. In other words, the liberalization of some services may have multiplier effects throughout the economy, whereas in other sectors the benefits will largely flow only to the affected sector.

Creating Comparative Advantage

The classic Western model of trade was based on eighteenth-century economic realities. Factors of production were relatively fixed: Land was immobile (although its fertility or usage might change), and labor mobility was highly restricted by political constraints. For most of the century, the movement of capital across borders was limited by political barriers and a lack of knowledge of other markets. (However, by the middle of the nineteenth century both capital and labor were flowing more freely between Europe and the Americas.) Technology in the eighteenth century was relatively simple by today's standards and was relatively similar in all countries. Additionally, the production of most products at that time was subject to diminishing returns, which meant that as production increased, the costs of producing each additional unit increased.

In this world, the classic Ricardian model of trade provided a good explanation for trade patterns, such as which countries would produce what products. England would produce textiles based on its wool production and capital availability, and Portugal would produce wine based on its sunshine and fertile soil. If Portugal chose to impose barriers to the importation of British textiles, its own economy would be less well off, and it would still be in Britain's interest to allow the free importation of Portuguese wine.

However, the world economy began to change in the twentieth century, as some products could be produced under conditions of increasing returns to scale. As a company produced more steel, production could be automated and the costs of each additional unit could be significantly reduced. And the same was true for automobiles and a growing number of other more sophisticated products.

By the last twenty-five years of the twentieth century, the global economy was significantly different. Land and labor were still relatively fixed, although capital could again move more freely around the world. However, technology was highly differentiated among countries, with the United States leading in many areas.

An established company in an industry that required extensive capital investment and knowledge had an enormous advantage over potential competitors. Its production runs were large, enabling it to produce products at low marginal cost. And the capital investment for a new competitor would be large.

In this new world, the economic policies pursued by a nation could create a new comparative advantage. A country could promote education and change its labor force from unskilled to semiskilled or even highly skilled. Or it could provide subsidies for research and development to create new technologies. Or it could take policy actions to force transfer of technology or capital from another country, such as allowing its companies to pirate technology from competitors or imposing a requirement that foreign investors transfer technology.

Ralph Gomory and William Baumol describe this well:

> The underlying reason for these significant departures from the original model is that the modern free-trade world is so different from the original historical setting of the free trade models. Today there is no one uniquely determined best economic outcome based on natural national advantages. Today's global economy does not single out a single best outcome, arrived at by international competition in which each country serves the world's best interests by producing just those goods that it can naturally turn out most efficiently. Rather, there are many possible outcomes that depend on what countries actually choose to do, what capabilities, natural or human-made, they actually develop.[25]

25. Ralph Gomory and William Baumol, *Global Trade and Conflicting National Interests* (Cambridge, Mass.: MIT Press, 2000), 5.

In the world of the late twentieth century, a country might be dominant in an industry because of its innate comparative advantage, or it might be dominant because of a strong boost from government policy, or it might be dominant because of historical accident. For example, the U.S. dominance in aircraft was probably due to a strong educational system that produced highly competent engineers, a large domestic market with a dedicated customer (the U.S. military), and the historical accident that the aircraft industries of the major U.S. competitors—Japan, Germany, and England—had all been destroyed in World War II.

Once such an industry becomes dominant, it is extremely difficult for other countries' industries to compete. The capital costs of entry may be very large, and it is difficult for a new entrant to master the technology. Additionally, the industry normally has a web of suppliers that are critical to competitiveness, such as steel companies and tire manufacturers. However, if such an industry loses its dominance, it is equally difficult for it to reenter the market.

A country with such a dominant industry benefits enormously economically. Because of its dominant position, such an industry may pay high wages and provide a stable base of employment.

Access to other markets plays an important role in this economic model where comparative advantage can be created. Without such access, it becomes extremely costly for a government to subsidize a new entrant because the subsidy must be large enough both to overcome foreign trade barriers and to jump-start the domestic producer. The WTO and U.S. FTAs also play an important role by setting out rules that govern what actions a country may take in many areas to create comparative advantage; for example, the subsidies code limits the type of subsidies that governments may grant.

Gomory and Baumol note that because countries can create a comparative advantage in goods with decreasing costs of production, there are many possible outcomes to trade patterns: "These outcomes vary in their consequences for the economic well-being of the countries involved. Some of these outcomes are good for one country, some are good for the other, some are good for both. But it often is true that the outcomes that are the very best for one country tend to be poor outcomes for its trading partner."[26]

Although country policies can lead to creation of a dominant industry, such an industry may not be as efficient as if it had occurred in an-

26. Ibid., 5.

other country. An example given by Gomory and Baumol is Japan's steel industry. Japan has no domestic energy supplies and high wages; by contrast, China "has low labor costs and lots of coal."[27] In theory, China would be the efficient producer of steel, but in reality Japan is the dominant producer. (This example is less valid today, as China has become a major steel producer.)

Although there are many areas where government policies can create comparative advantage, there are still many areas where the classic assumptions of an inherent comparative advantage still hold. The key is whether the industry is subject to constant or increasing costs, such as wheat, or decreasing costs, such as autos, aircraft, or semiconductors.

Neomercantilism

The economic theory based on Ricardo's concept of comparative advantage dominates current thinking in the West and formed the intellectual basis for formation of the GATT/WTO. The doctrine of mercantilism, which dominated thinking up to the end of the eighteenth century, is generally rejected by Western economists today.

However, a number of countries—including Japan, South Korea, China, and some other countries in the Far East—have pursued a neomercantilism model in which they seek to grow through an aggressive expansion of exports, coupled with a very measured reduction of import barriers. These countries seek to develop powerful export industries by initially protecting their domestic industry from foreign competition and providing subsidies and other support to stimulate growth, often including currency manipulation.

The success of some countries in pursuing a neomercantilist strategy does not refute the law of comparative advantage. In fact, the reason these countries are successful is that they focus on industries where they have or can create a comparative advantage. Thus, Japan first focused on industries such as steel and autos, and later on electronics, where a policy of import protection and domestic subsidies could enable their domestic firms to compete in world markets, and particularly the U.S. market.

To succeed in a neomercantilist strategy, of course, a country needs access to other markets, which the progressive liberalization of trade barriers under the GATT/WTO provided. Neomercantilists generally

---

27. Ibid., 21.

focus on key industries selected by government, a strategy known as *industrial policy*. A successful industrial policy requires a farsighted government. Japan had an extremely competent group of government officials in the Ministry of Industry and Trade (MITI), which oversaw its industrial policy and was basically immune from political pressures. Although MITI had many successes, it also made some missteps. For example, in their planning to develop a world-class auto industry in the 1950s, MITI officials initially believed they had too many auto companies, and urged Honda to merge with another company. Instead, Honda elected to invest in the United States and went on to become a leading auto producer.

Countries pursuing the neomercantilist model have also generally promoted education and high domestic savings to finance their growing export industries. For example, the savings rate in Japan has often been more than 20 percent of GDP, and it approaches 40 percent of China's GDP today. (By contrast, the U.S. savings rate has been only about 2 percent over the past decade and in some years was actually negative.)

Many economists argue that a neomercantilist strategy may be successful for a while, but that over time such a strategy will not be effective. Basically this argument is that the complexities for governments in picking potential winners and identifying how to promote those industries are too great. For example, Japan was very successful with its neomercantilist strategy until the mid-1990s. However, since then the Japanese economy has been stagnating, and many economists believe that Japan will need to change its approach to stimulating domestic demand rather than focusing on export markets. During the past ten years, South Korea and China have also pursued neomercantilist policies, and it remains to be seen if these are effective over the long term.

Additionally, a number of economists argue that government intervention can be effective in promoting a specific sector but that industrial policies are not effective at the macro level of benefiting the economy as a whole. In any case, Western economists and policymakers today almost universally reject the idea that the United States should adopt an industrial policy that picks winners and losers. Opponents of a possible U.S. industrial policy argue that under the U.S. system, such a policy would be subject to political pressures that would ensure failure.

Instead, the real debate among economists and policymakers is whether the United States should respond to foreign neomercantilist practices, and if so, how. Stephen Cohen and his colleagues say:

Free trade advocates argue that imposing import barriers, even if other countries do so, is tantamount to shooting oneself in the foot. The advisability of turning the other cheek to other countries' trade barriers is based on an economic argument traceable to Adam Smith in the eighteenth century: Since consumption is the sole end of production, consumers' interests come before producers' interests, especially those of relatively inefficient producers. Carried to its logical conclusion, this strategy recommends that the U.S. government take no action to offset the de facto subsidies provided to domestic consumers when imports are sold at prices below fair value.[28]

Others argue that the objective of free trade is to promote competition based on comparative advantage, which maximizes global efficiency. Practices such as subsidies or currency manipulation are a movement away from such competition and can produce a result where the less efficient producer dominates trade, thereby reducing total welfare. In these circumstances, taking an offsetting action, such as imposing a countervailing duty, could restore "a level playing field" where trade based on comparative advantage can occur.

Unbalanced Trade

The theory of comparative advantage assumes a world where trade between countries is in balance or at least where countries have a trade surplus or deficit that it is cyclical and temporary.[29] Relaxing the assumption "that international trade among nations is balanced, could lead a nation with a trade deficit to import some commodities in which it would have a comparative advantage and it would in fact export with balanced trade," says Dominick Salvatore. However, he does not see this as a big problem, "since most trade imbalances are generally not very large in relation to GNP [gross national product]."[30]

28. Cohen, Blecker, and Whitney. *Fundamentals of U.S. Foreign Trade Policy*, 8–9.
29. See, e.g., ibid., 54: "The theory of comparative advantage assumes that trade is balanced (i.e., exports equal imports in value) and that labor is fully employed. . . . If trade is not balanced, the surplus country must be exporting some goods in which it does not have a 'true' comparative advantage."
30. Salvatore, *International Economics*, 167.

In analyzing the impact of a surplus or deficit, economists often consider "trade" very broadly in definition. Generally, economists do not consider the simple balance in merchandise trade as relevant as the "current account," which includes the balance of trade for goods and services, plus net international income receipts (remitted profits from overseas investments, royalty payments, interest, and dividends) and unilateral transfers (foreign aid and transfers abroad by private citizens). Except for unilateral transfers, all these elements are covered in our trade agreements.

To give a real picture of how the nation is doing, the current account is often measured as a percentage of GDP; as a country grows, a larger surplus or deficit in the current account is not a source of concern because the economy can more readily absorb the impact.

A surplus or deficit in the current account can be affected by the business cycle. Thus, if our economy grows rapidly, the demand for imports will expand as consumers can afford to buy more and businesses need parts and supplies for expansion. Similarly, U.S. exports are affected by economic growth in its trade partners. If it grows more rapidly than its trade partners, in short, that will have a negative impact on the U.S. current account balance. Conversely, if the U.S. trade partners are growing more rapidly, that will have a positive impact on its current account balance.

Economists are not concerned with such cyclical trade deficits or surpluses. Additionally, they are not concerned if a deficit occurs because the country is borrowing heavily from abroad to finance investment that will be paid back later. During the nineteenth century, in fact, the United States was in exactly this position when it borrowed heavily to build railroads across the continent, steel mills, and other long-term investments. However, that is not the U.S. situation today. Today, it is borrowing heavily from other countries to finance short-term consumption, such as the newest and largest HDTVs from Japan or South Korea, and these purchases do not generate income to repay its debt in the future.

A fundamental accounting concept in international economics is that a country's overall balance of payments, which consists of both the current account and the capital account, has to be in balance. This means that if the current account is in deficit, the country's capital account has to be in surplus by an equal amount. The capital account consists of purchases or sales of foreign exchange by the central bank or by private citizens. This fundamental accounting principle can be seen as:

Balance of Payments = Current Account + Capital Account = Zero

Two factors that may lead to a deficit or surplus in the current account balance are the level of a nation's savings and investment compared with consumption, and the exchange rate between its currency and that of its trade partners. The level of a country's savings and investment compared with its consumption is inversely related to its trade balance. Joseph Stiglitz puts the matter as follows: "Trade deficits and foreign borrowing are two sides of the same coin. If borrowing from abroad goes up, so too will the trade deficit. This means that if government borrowing goes up, unless private savings goes up commensurately (or private investment decreases commensurately), the country will have to borrow more abroad, and the trade deficit will increase. . . . The reserve country can be thought of as exporting T-bills" in exchange for the import of goods and services.[31]

The second factor that can have an impact on a country's current account balance is the exchange rate. The exchange rate refers to the amount of foreign currencies that can be purchased by a country's own currency. According to economic theory, if a nation is running a persistent trade deficit, its exchange rate would be expected to fall in relation to its trade partners—for example, if the United States runs a persistent deficit, the dollar should purchase less foreign exchange such as euros or yen. This would mean that imported products will cost more, because it would take more dollars for each unit of foreign currency, and this would cause imports to decline. Additionally, U.S. exports should expand, as foreigners can buy more of its products for each unit of their currency.

However, countries can prevent this mechanism from operating by aggressively intervening in the foreign exchange markets. For example, under economic theory, the value of the dollar should decline in relation to the renminbi because the United States has enormous deficits, while China experiences comparable trade surpluses. However, China has pegged the renminbi to the dollar and has prevented its exchange rate from rising and thereby restoring a trade balance. China does this by using the dollars it accumulates from its trade surplus to aggressively purchase U.S. currency in the form of Treasury bills. The result has been an

---

31. Joseph E. Stiglitz, *Making Globalization Work* (New York: W. W. Norton, 2006), 252–53.

overvalued dollar and an undervalued renminbi. (This is similar to what Japan did in the early 1980s when the yen was undervalued and the dollar was overvalued.) In economic theory, an "undervalued exchange rate is *both* an import tax and an export subsidy and is hence the most mercantilist policy imaginable."[32]

Conclusion

Most economists today consider the law of comparative advantage to be one of the fundamental principles of economics. However, several very important caveats to the law of comparative advantage are often overlooked or glossed over.

First, David Ricardo based his theory on the assumption that the costs of production increase as production expands; in other words, each additional unit produced costs more than the previous unit, and this is true for many products, such as wheat. This assumption implies that countries have a comparative advantage in certain goods because of their natural endowment. However, many products today are produced under conditions of decreasing costs; for example, the cost of producing each additional semiconductor or airplane decreases as production expands. The extremely important implication of this is that countries can create comparative advantage.

A second extremely important caveat is the so-called factor price equalization theorem, which holds that international trade will cause the relative returns to factors of production, such as unskilled labor, to equalize between countries under free trade conditions. This would mean that for a high-wage country such as the United States, wages for unskilled workers would fall, while wages in labor-abundant countries would rise. However, factor prices will not tend to equalize in industries that have decreasing costs of production.

Third, Ricardo and other early economists based their theories on trade in goods, and they did not consider trade in factors of production. Today, however, basic factors of production such as labor, capital, and technology are traded. The implication of trade in factors of production

32. Aaditya Mattoo and Arvind Subramanian, *Currency Undervaluation and Sovereign Wealth Funds: A New Role for the World Trade Organization* (Washington, D.C.: World Bank, 2008), 3.

is that factor equalization will occur completely in a shorter time period than would occur under trade in goods only.

Fourth, Western economic theory assumes that trade will be reasonably balanced over time. Where this is not the case, it indicates that the deficit country will be importing products where it would normally have a comparative advantage; if these products are in areas that experience decreasing costs of production, over time the industry may lose its ability to compete in global markets.

The world has changed since the time of Smith and Ricardo. Today, trade is no longer mostly between small producers and farmers but giant global corporations that buy parts and materials from around the world and sell globally. These giant supply chains were made possible by trade liberalization and technology changes, and they account for the fact that international trade has expanded far more rapidly than global economic growth since 1970. These global supply chains also have implications for strategies for developing countries in promoting economic growth.

Clearly, the United States benefits when its trade partners reduce their trade barriers, because its exports will increase, generating expanded production and employment. Most economists also believe that the United States benefits from reducing its own trade barriers, as consumers gain from reduced costs and producers are forced by international competition to improve efficiency. However, import liberalization has an impact on domestic labor and production that needs to be considered.

Multilateral trade liberalization, where all countries reduce their trade barriers in parallel, best promotes trade based on comparative advantage. However, countries can abuse the system by adopting beggar-thy-neighbor policies.

Chapter 4

Trade Agreements and U.S. Commercial Interests

Under the auspices of the General Agreement on Tariffs and Trade/World Trade Organization (GATT/WTO), the developed countries' tariffs on non-agricultural goods have fallen from an average of 40 percent after World War II to less than 4 percent today, and this has been a major driver of the enormous increase in world trade that has occurred during the past sixty years. Because of the weaknesses of economic data, however, it is difficult to estimate the impact of this lessening of tariffs on the U.S. economy, although most economists believe it has been significant. Other GATT/WTO agreements, such as services and government procurement, have probably only had a small impact, although the agreement on protection of intellectual property has undoubtedly been important.

Additionally, most economists believe the impact of the North American Free Trade Agreement (NAFTA) has been significant; the other U.S. agreements now in effect have all been either with small countries or with countries such as Australia and South Korea that are on the other side of the world, and accordingly these have had less economic impact on the United States. However, current negotiations for a Trans-Pacific Partnership and for a Trans-Atlantic Trade and Investment Partnership have potentially enormous commercial importance.

The U.S. trade balance shifted from surplus to deficit in 1971, and it has increased steadily until it accounted for almost 6 percent of U.S. gross domestic product (GDP) in 2008 before the global financial and economic crisis. This structural deficit has had an adverse impact on the U.S. economy.

International trade in goods and services has become far more important today to both the world economy and to the United States than was the case sixty years ago. In fact, since 1950 world trade has increased twenty-seven-fold in volume terms, according to the WTO, while the world economy has only increased eightfold during the same period.[1] In other words, world trade has grown more than three times as fast as has global GDP, and by 2007 for the first time international trade equaled more than half of global GDP.

In fact, in just the decade between 2000 and 2010 world trade more than doubled, as can be seen in table 4.1, rising from $8.5 trillion to just over $20 trillion. Trade in nonagricultural merchandise accounted for about three-quarters of total trade in goods and services in 2010, while trade in agricultural products accounted for under 7 percent, and services for just over 18 percent.

Some trade today takes place under the conditions of absolute advantage on which Adam Smith based his revolutionary theory of international trade in 1776. For example, the United States imports oil because its domestic energy sources are not sufficient to meet its needs, and it imports asparagus in the winter to satisfy the nation's demand for fresh vegetables.

Most trade, however, takes place under the conditions of comparative advantage, as set out by David Ricardo and Heckscher-Ohlin. This would include products and services subject to the classic assumption of increasing costs of return, whereby each additional unit produced is more expensive than the last. For example, a farmer will experience increasing costs of return if he expands wheat production by producing on less fertile land. And it includes products and services subject to decreasing costs of return, such as automobiles or semiconductors, where the cost of producing an additional unit falls as production can be more efficiently mechanized (past a certain size, of course, costs would no longer decrease as production expanded further).

Along with this enormous growth in world trade, the GATT/WTO, largely under U.S. leadership, has developed an extensive system of rules that govern a great deal of international trade in goods, services, and the protection of intellectual property. To enforce these rules, the WTO has

---

1. World Trade Organization, "The Trade Situation in 2009–10," in *World Trade Report, 2010: Trade in Natural Resources* (Geneva: World Trade Organization), 20–37.

Table 4.1. World Exports of Merchandise, Services, and Agriculture

Category	2000	2002	2004	2006	2008	2010
Value of merchandise (billions of dollars)	$6,456	$6,492	$9,218	$12,120	$16,132	$15,254
Percentage of total world trade	76.0	74.8	75.4	76.3	75.7	74.9
Value of commercial services (billions of dollars)	$1,485	$1,602	$2,232	$2,827	$3,834	$3,747
Percentage of total world trade	17.5	18.4	18.2	17/8	18.0	18.4
Value of agricultural products (billions of dollars)	$551	$585	$782	$944	$1,348	$1,362
Percentage of total world trade	6.5	6.7	6.4	5.9	6.3	6.7
Total world trade (billions of dollars)	$8,492	$8,678	$12,232	$15,891	$21,314	$20,363

Source: World Trade Organization, "International Trade Statistics, June 25, 2012," http://stat.wto.org/StatisticalProgram/WSDBStatProgramHome.aspx?Language=E.

a well-developed dispute settlement mechanism with the power to impose sanctions. (As noted, however, the rules have a number of extremely important loopholes.)

Tariffs and the GATT/WTO

The reduction of tariffs and related nontariff barriers such as quotas and import licensing that took place in the eight rounds of multilateral trade negotiations held under the GATT's auspices played a critical role in this increase in world trade. At the end of World War II, developed-country tariffs on industrial goods averaged approximately 40 percent; by the start of the Doha Round in 2001, average tariffs were down to less than 4 percent.[2]

Tariffs on industrial goods were cut by approximately 35 percent in the first five GATT trade rounds held between 1947 and 1961. Only twenty-three countries participated in the first of these rounds; and only

2. Daniel W. Drezner, *U.S. Trade Strategy: Free Versus Fair.* Critical Policy Choices Series (New York: Council on Foreign Relations, 2006), 89.

a few more, twenty-six countries in total, participated in the fifth, the Dillon Round.

By 1965, as the Kennedy Round was just getting under way, developed-country tariffs on industrial products were down to an average of about 25 percent. By 1977, when the Kennedy Round tariff reductions had been fully implemented, tariffs had fallen by about another 35 percent, to about 16 percent. These lower tariffs enabled multinational corporations to begin to develop global supply chains in which parts and raw materials were sourced wherever they could be purchased most economically and then sold globally. The global companies at the top of these supply chain pyramids purchase their parts and raw materials from the cheapest source, which may be determined on the basis of comparative advantage, special preferential treatment, government subsidies, currency manipulation, geographic location, or other factors. Spurred by these global supply chains, as well as by falling costs of international transportation and communications, trade has increased some two times as fast as economic growth since the end of the Kennedy Round.

The Tokyo Round, which began in 1973 and concluded in 1979, produced an additional 35 percent reduction in developed-country industrial tariffs when the cuts were fully implemented. As a result of the Tokyo Round, the average U.S. tariff on industrial products declined from 6.1 to 4.2 percent, and comparable reductions were made by all the nineteen major developed-country participants. As noted in chapter 2, many nontariff barriers, such as quotas and import licensing, were eliminated, along with the reduction in tariff rates. Then the Uruguay Round, which began in 1986 and concluded in 1994, further reduced developed-country industrial tariffs by an additional 35 percent when the cuts were fully implemented in 2005.

The number of countries participating in each round also steadily increased, from 62 in the Kennedy Round to 123 in the Uruguay Round. Most of these new participants were developing countries, and they made significantly fewer tariff reductions than did the developed countries, and the least-developed countries did not have to make any concessions. Additionally, as noted, few reductions in trade barriers were made, even by the developed countries, in the agricultural area.

Although developed-country tariffs on nonagricultural goods were reduced enormously on average in these rounds of negotiation, tariffs on some products remain high, and a few nontariff barriers still remain. For example, the United States still maintains high duties on textiles (the average U.S. tariff on textiles is 7.9 percent, although some specific textile tariff lines are as high as 40 percent).[3]

Given the way these negotiations were conducted, one would expect that developed-country tariffs on nonagricultural goods would be low and that their tariffs on agricultural products would be significantly higher. And one would expect developing-country tariffs to be significantly higher than the tariffs of developed countries.

As can be seen in table 4.2, this is basically the pattern of tariffs among countries. Since the implementation of the Uruguay Round agreement, U.S. tariffs on nonagricultural goods are just 3.3 percent, whereas Japan's are just 2.5 percent and the European Union's are just 3.9 percent, and almost all tariffs in each of these three blocs are bound. Tariffs on agricultural goods, however, are far higher. The average bound tariff on agricultural goods for the United States is 4.8 percent, for the European Union, 12.3 percent; and for Japan, 20.9 percent.

Developing-country tariffs are generally significantly higher for both agricultural and nonagricultural goods than are developed-country tariffs, as can be seen in table 4.2 for China, Mexico, India, and Brazil. For example, Mexico's average bound tariff on nonagricultural goods is 34.9 percent, and India's is 34.6 percent. However, the rates actually applied by many developing countries are far lower than their bound rates.

The enormous reduction in trade barriers on industrial goods that occurred from 1947 to the 1980s would not have happened without the eight rounds of multilateral trade negotiations held by the GATT. U.S. industry, as well as labor, would have bitterly resisted unilateral tariff reductions.[4] In the face of this opposition, Congress never would have

---

3. These data are available from World Trade Organization, "Tariff Profiles: United States," http://stat.wto.org/TariffProfile/WSDBTariffPFView.aspx?Language =E&Country=US.

4. During the mid-1970s, I was responsible for managing the industry advisory process for the Tokyo Round negotiations. The United States had twenty-seven advisory committees that were cochaired by the Commerce Department and the Office of the U.S. Trade Representative. Early in the negotiations, the United States submitted an offer that would have led to large reductions in U.S. tariffs while other countries might have made only minimal offers. All but one of the advisory committees—that of the retailers—were adamantly opposed to any such package and would have surely blocked its approval by Congress. The United States then advised its trade partners that it would withdraw its offer unless it received reciprocal

Table 4.2. Tariff Rates after Implementation of the Uruguay Round (percent)

Economy	Average Duty on Nonagricultural Goods (Bound)	Average Duty on Nonagricultural Goods (Applied)	Average Duty on Agricultural Goods (Bound)	Average Duty on Agricultural Goods (Applied)
European Union	3.9	4.0	12.3	12.8
United States	3.3	3.3	4.8	4.9
China	9.2	8.7	15.7	15.6
Japan	2.5	2.5	20.9	17.3
South Korea	10.2	6.6	55.9	48.5
Canada	5.3	2.6	16.7	11.3
Hong Kong	0.0	0.0	0.0	0.0
Mexico	34.9	7.1	44.2	21.5
Singapore	6.4	0.0	24.6	0.2
India	34.6	10.1	113.3	31.8

Source: World Trade Organization, "World Tariff Profiles 2011: Applied MFN Tariffs," http://www.wto.org/english/res_e/booksp_e/tariff_profiles11_e.pdf.

agreed to such a substantial reduction of U.S. tariffs. The United States and other developed countries were only willing to reduce their barriers in exchange for the prospect of gaining access to new markets.

Other Drivers of Trade Liberalization

To a lesser extent, trade liberalization has also been driven by other forces than GATT/WTO multilateral negotiations. Preferential systems to benefit developing countries, bilateral and regional free trade agreements (FTAs), and unilateral trade liberalization often driven by the International Monetary Fund have also played a significant role.

Preferential systems, which are a major derogation from the most-favored-nation (MFN) principle, were authorized by the GATT in 1971. Under this derogation, developed countries may give preferential tariff treatment to products imported from developing countries, and today all developed countries have such schemes in place, as do some of the ad-

concessions. By the end of the negotiations, the major U.S. trade partners had agreed to concessions similar to those made by the United States, and almost all twenty-seven advisory committees supported the package.

vanced developing countries. Under this provision, in 1976 the United States implemented its Generalized System of Preferences (GSP), whereby eligible countries could export products covered by the scheme duty free to the United States. Today there are 131 eligible countries and 4,800 covered products; excluded from coverage are a number of import-sensitive products such as textiles. Communist countries, countries on the U.S. State Department's list of countries that support terrorism, and countries that have been designated as failing to protect intellectual property are excluded from eligibility. If an eligible country develops and reaches the status of a high-income developing country, it is *graduated* from the program; that is, it is no longer eligible for preferential trade treatment.

The United States also has several preference schemes in place that build on the GSP system. The largest is the African Growth and Opportunity Act (AGOA), which was instituted in 2000. Sub-Saharan African countries are eligible to participate in AGOA provided they meet specific criteria, such as either being a market-based economy or making progress toward becoming one, eliminating barriers to U.S. trade and investment, protecting intellectual property rights, and protecting human rights and workers' rights. Countries can lose their eligibility if they fail to meet the criteria; some thirty-five countries have participated, although the participating countries have varied. Other U.S. preferential schemes include the Caribbean Basin Initiative, with eighteen beneficiary countries; and the Andean Act, which was enacted in 1991 to benefit Bolivia, Colombia, Ecuador, and Peru.[5]

The preference programs of the United States and other countries have several serious limitations. First, they are unilateral. This means that a beneficiary country can be dropped or the eligibility criteria can be changed at any time the United States or other providing country so chooses. These preference programs are also one-way; while the United States grants preferential treatment to the developing countries, they do not grant similar treatment to U.S. exporters. Second, these programs need to be periodically renewed by Congress, which creates business uncertainty. And third, these programs do not cover all goods; in fact, many of the products not covered are precisely those labor-intensive products where developing countries have a comparative advantage.

5. Information on U.S. preferential programs is available on the Office of the U.S. Trade Representative's Web site at http://www.ustr.gov/trade-topics/trade-development/preference-programs.

Trade liberalization has also been driven by the bilateral and regional FTAs that the United States and other countries have negotiated, as described in chapter 2. These were allowed under the original GATT, although it was not originally envisioned that such agreements would be very extensive. The first agreement for the United States, as previously noted, was the 1985 agreement with Israel, and today the United States has such agreements in place with twenty countries. Other countries and the European Union have many similar agreements, and today a significant portion of world trade takes place under these FTAs.

Under GATT/WTO rules, FTAs are supposed to eliminate substantially all barriers to trade in goods and services; a transitional period is allowed, during which barriers on nonsensitive products are eliminated immediately, while barriers on sensitive products may be reduced—and eventually eliminated—in annual increments, often over a ten-year span. Unlike preferential systems to benefit developing countries, which must be periodically renewed, FTAs are expected to be permanent—although they do contain provisions to allow them to be abrogated. And they are two-way; that is, U.S. exporters also benefit from free access to its partner country.

As a result of the U.S. trade agreements program, in 2012 just under 35 percent of U.S. imports entered under one of its bilateral or regional FTAs.[6] An additional 14 percent entered duty free under the GSP program and 2 percent under AGOA. However, the basic U.S. tariff rate structure set out in the Smoot-Hawley tariff is still in effect, but applies to only a minuscule percentage of total U.S. imports, basically imports from North Korea and Cuba.

Another driver of trade liberalization worldwide has been the International Monetary Fund. From 1980 to 2000, the IMF often required developing countries to unilaterally reduce their tariffs and other trade barriers as a condition for receiving its financial support. The IMF imposed requirements to reduce tariffs on fifteen middle-income countries and twenty-five low-income countries that were WTO members, and on three middle-income countries and seven low-income countries that were in the process of joining the WTO.

---

6. These data are from the U.S. International Trade Administration, "TradeStats Express," http://tse.export.gov/TSE/TSEhome.aspx.

However, the IMF's approach to reducing trade barriers was substantially different from the WTO's. The Independent Evaluation Office of the IMF says that

while both [the IMF and the WTO] are dedicated to a common vision of a liberal global trading system, their approaches to trade liberalization are fundamentally different. . . . The WTO's approach involves reciprocal liberalization through multilateral negotiations backed by a dispute settlement mechanism. The IMF aims to support best practices—trade policies (even if not the result of reciprocal bargaining) it views as bolstering efficiency and stability. Also, the WTO provides greater leeway for its developing country members to phase in global agreements, while the IMF aims to apply economic principles uniformly across its members, albeit with muscle linked to whether a country has a lending arrangement.[7]

Although the IMF demanded these unilateral tariff reductions, it did not require that they be bound under the WTO. Accordingly, these countries were free to later raise their duties back to higher levels.

The IMF's heavy-handed approach to trade liberalization raised substantial criticisms. The IMF's Independent Evaluation Office acknowledges that "the IMF's orientation toward unilateral trade liberalization has stoked the debates on whether such liberalization is always in a country's own interests and whether preferential trade agreements are harmful." In the face of widespread criticism, in 2000 the IMF scaled back its involvement in removing traditional barriers to trade.

The GATT/WTO's approach is a better approach than was the IMF's in several ways. First, bound tariff rates have the advantage of giving the business community certainty for making important decisions, while applied rates, which can be easily changed, do not. Second, the abrupt elimination of barriers required by the IMF did not provide an opportunity for orderly adjustment to increased competition, whereas the GATT/WTO's approach of phasing in tariff reductions over a number of years does. For example, with regard to Tanzania, the IMF's Indepen-

7. Independent Evaluation Office of the International Monetary Fund, *IMF Involvement in International Trade Policy Issues* (Washington, D.C.: International Monetary Fund, 2009), 6.

dent Evaluation Office notes that "the pace of tariff reform . . . was probably too ambitious. While it is not clear that slower phasing of the tariff
reform would have aroused less opposition from business groups, it
could arguably have allowed the authorities to deal better with the fiscal
implications of lower tariff rates."[8]

The Economic Impact of Trade Liberalization

What then has been the economic impact of this substantial reduction
in tariffs and related nontariff barriers, both from the eight rounds of
multilateral trade negotiations and from the extensive FTAs of the
United States and of other countries? Unfortunately, it is difficult to answer this question with any precision for a number of reasons:

• It is extremely difficult if not impossible to isolate the effects of trade
  agreements from the impact of changes in transportation and communications, exchange rate variations, geopolitical events, and other
  economic events. And often these other factors have a greater economic impact than do trade agreements.
• The necessary data to compare trade agreement partners with nonmembers are fairly sketchy.
• The major multilateral trade rounds have had transition periods of
  five to ten years, which complicates analysis. FTAs also have transition periods, and tariffs are eliminated over different time periods for
  different products, an even greater complication.
• Many factors besides tariff rates affect trade flows, such as geographic
  proximity, common versus different language, differing currencies,
  and historical accident.
• Many of the FTAs have not been in effect long enough to make rea-
  soned judgments.

Accordingly, it is not surprising that economists have differing views on
the impact of trade agreements. Here it is useful to highlight just a few.
    Daniel Drezner highlights a study by analysts at the Institute for In-
ternational Economics who attempted to measure the cumulative impact of trade liberalization since 1945 by using a Computable General

8. Ibid., 106.

Equilibrium model. Their estimate was that the economic benefits for the United States range between $800 billion to $1.45 trillion per year in additional output, which would be a benefit of between $2,800 and $5,000 per person.[9]

Theo Eicher and Christian Henn outline a sequence of conflicting studies by economists regarding the impact of the WTO: "Rose jump-started the literature when he documented the absence of WTO effects on bilateral trade volumes. After updating Rose's data set to include both de jure and de facto WTO membership, Tomz, Goldstein and Rivers . . . did find positive WTO trade effects. Alternatively, Subramanian and Wei . . . examined different groups of WTO members and reported positive WTO trade effects for industrialized countries only."[10] Eicher and Henn go on to conclude that they could not find trade effects of WTO membership, but that there were significant effects from preferential FTAs.

Actually, these conclusions are not inconsistent. First, developing countries have only marginally participated in the multilateral trade rounds, and consequently little trade effects would be expected. This would be consistent with Subramanian and Wei's finding of positive effects for industrialized countries only. Second, some analyses of the trade effects include agriculture along with industrial products; but as we have noted, tariff cuts on agricultural products in the trade rounds were minimal.

More fundamentally, however, the Institute for International Economics study looked at the cumulative impact of the GATT multilateral trade rounds. At the launch of the GATT, developed-country tariffs on industrial products averaged some 40 percent, and these were cut by roughly 35 percent in the first five trade rounds. Then they were cut an additional 35 to 40 percent in the Kennedy Round and another 35 to 40 percent in the Tokyo Round, and finally the Uruguay Round cut another 35 to 40 percent. Though the percentage reduction in each of these three rounds is similar, the amount cut was less in each subsequent round because the starting level was lower; consequently the trade effect was less with each round of tariff cuts.

9. Drezner, *U.S. Trade Strategy*, 16.
10. Theo S. Eicher and Christian Henn, *In Search of WTO Trade Effects: Preferential Trade Agreements Promote Trade Strongly, but Unevenly*, Working Paper 09/31 (Washington, D.C.: International Monetary Fund, 2009), 3.

It is hard to imagine that reducing developed-country tariffs over the past sixty years from an average of 40 percent to less than 5 percent today did not have an enormous impact, spurring global trade and promoting growth. However, it is also true that recent rounds have had less effect, and that the potential future gains from reducing developed-country tariffs on nonagricultural goods are relatively small. Potential gains to world welfare from trade liberalization in the agricultural sector and by developing countries, however, remain large.

The Impact of U.S. Bilateral Agreements

The U.S. preferential agreement that has had far and away the greatest impact on trade and the U.S. economy is NAFTA. The Congressional Research Service evaluated four studies on the impact of the agreement during its first decade—one by the Congressional Budget Office, the second by the World Bank, the third by the Carnegie Endowment for International Peace, and the fourth by the U.S. International Trade Commission. These studies indicate that NAFTA has had a modest positive impact on both the United States and Mexico.

For example, the Congressional Budget Office model estimated that NAFTA accounted for a 2 percent marginal growth rate in U.S. exports and imports in 1994, but that this rose to an 11 percent increase in U.S. exports and an 8 percent increase in U.S. imports in 2001. However, it concluded that other events, particularly the 1994 Mexican peso crisis, had a greater impact on trade trends than did the elimination of tariffs. It noted, however, that one of the important effects of the trade agreement was that Mexico raised tariffs against non-NAFTA countries during the peso crisis but not against its NAFTA partners, an example of how trade agreements can lock in trade rules and increase certainty for the business community.[11] The World Bank study estimated that Mexico's GDP per capita was 4 to 5 percent higher than it would have been without NAFTA by 2002.

Other than NAFTA with Canada and Mexico, the only U.S. trade partners of significant economic size have been Australia and South Korea, and each of these countries has an economy only about 5 percent as

11. J. F. Hornbeck, *NAFTA at Ten: Lessons from Recent Studies* (Washington, D.C.: Congressional Research Service, 2004), 2.

large as that of the United States. America's other bilateral and regional agreements have all been with small countries—ranging from the smallest, Nicaragua, which is less than 0.5 percent the size of the U.S. economy, to Chile, which is about 1.5 percent of the size of the U.S. economy, as can be seen in table 4.3. The trade generated by these agreements with small countries will not be significant enough to have a measurable impact on the U.S. economy, although some specific sectors may be affected by some of these other agreements.

Although Australia and South Korea are roughly the size of the Mexican economy, the economic impact on the United States will be far less than the impact of the U.S. FTA with Mexico. This is because these coun-

Table 4.3. U.S. Free Trade Agreements

Country	Gross Domestic Product (dollars)	Simple Average MFN Bound Agricultural Tariff (percent)	Simple Average MFN Bound Nonagricultural Tariff (percent)
Australia	1,371,763,885,599	4	11
Bahrain	22,945,456,867	39	34
Canada	1,736,050,505,051	18	5
Chile	248,585,243,788	26	25
Colombia	331,654,672,814	92	35
Costa Rica	41,006,959,585	43	43
Dominican Republic	55,611,245,616	39	33
El Salvador	23,054,100,000	43	36
Guatemala	46,900,000,257	51	40
Honduras	17,259,407,972	32	32
Israel	242,928,731,135	73	12
Jordan	28,840,197,019	24	15
Mexico	1,155,316,052,667	45	35
Morocco	100,221,001,988	54	39
Nicaragua	7,297,481,501	43	40
Oman	71,781,535,039	28	12
Panama	30,676,800,000	28	22
Peru	176,662,074,713	31	29
Singapore	239,699,598,462	27	6
South Korea	1,116,247,397,319	56	10
United States	15,094,000,000,000	5	3

Note: MFN = most favored nation.
Sources: GDP data are from World Bank, World Development Indicators, http://data
.worldbank.org/indicator/NY.GDP.MKTP.CD. Average MFN bound tariff rates are from
the WTO's Web site, http://stat.wto.org/TariffProfile/WSDBTariffPFReporter.aspx?Language
=E.

tries are literally on the other side of the Earth, while America shares a 2,000-mile border with Mexico. Geographic proximity means less costly transportation and more business familiarity.

Many U.S. bilateral agreements are with developing nations, which were able to export many products to the United States duty free under the U.S. Generalized System of Preferences or other preferential arrangement before the FTA went into effect. However, the FTA will provide almost completely duty-free access and greater assurance of access to the U.S. market for these countries.

In contrast, the United States is gaining substantially improved access to each of its partner countries except for Singapore, which already had basically zero duties on all imports from all countries. As can be seen in table 4.3, average tariffs in some U.S. partner countries are quite high, and accordingly this represents a significant advantage for U.S. exporters in competing in these markets vis-à-vis exporters that face the MFN duty.

Many U.S. partner countries have FTAs in place or are negotiating them, with some U.S. competitors, such as the EU and Canada, as can be seen in table 4.4. In these cases, U.S. agreements level the playing field with exporters from other countries that also have an FTA.

For example, Israel had negotiated an FTA with the EU before the U.S. agreement, and U.S. exporters had been losing share to European firms for several years earlier than the U.S. agreement because of trade diversion. The U.S. agreement with Israel put U.S. exporters on a competitive footing with EU exporters. Another example is Chile. Before the U.S. agreement, the United States had lost market share to Argentina, Brazil, and other nations that already had FTAs with Chile. However, after the agreement, U.S. exports to Chile increased by 365 percent, from $2.4 billion in 2003 to $11.4 billion in 2008, and the U.S. market share rose from 15 percent in 2003 to 19 percent in 2008.[12]

By 2011, U.S. tariffs had only been eliminated on imports from Israel, Canada, Mexico, and Jordan. U.S. duties are not fully eliminated on imports from Singapore until 2014, and its tariffs in the other agreements

---

12. This information is from the U.S. Government Accountability Office's report on the commercial impact of the Chile, Jordan, Morocco, and Singapore FTAs: U.S. Government Accountability Office, *An Analysis of Free Trade Agreements and Congressional and Private Sector Consultations under Trade Promotion Authority* (Washington, D.C.: U.S. Government Printing Office, 2007).

Table 4.4. U.S. Partners' Other Free Trade Agreements

U.S. Partner Country	U.S. Partner's Other FTAs
Australia	New Zealand, Chile, Papua New Guinea, Singapore
Bahrain	GCC, PAFTA
Canada	Chile, Colombia, Costa Rica, Israel, Peru, EFTA
Chile	Canada, El Salvador, China, Costa Rica, South Korea, EFTA, EU, Panama, Japan, Mexico, Peru, Turkey
Colombia	Mexico, Venezuela, Andean Community, Mercosur, Venezuela, CARICOM, Panama, Honduras, El Salvador, Costa Rica, Nicaragua, Guatemala, Canada, Chile, EFTA
Costa Rica	Canada, Chile, CARICOM, Dominican Republic, El Salvador, Guatemala, Honduras, Mexico, Nicaragua, Panama, CACM
Dominican Republic	CARICOM
El Salvador	Honduras, Taiwan, Panama, Mexico, Chile, CACM
Guatemala	Taiwan, Mexico, CACM
Honduras	El Salvador, Taiwan, Mexico, CACM, Chile
Israel	Canada, EFTA, EU, Mexico, Turkey
Jordan	EFTA, EU, Singapore, PAFTA, Turkey
South Korea	Singapore, Taiwan, El Salvador, Colombia, Dominican Republic, Mexico, Guatemala, Honduras, Nicaragua, Costa Rica
Mexico	Bolivia, Chile, Colombia, Costa Rica, El Salvador, Guatemala, Honduras, Israel, Nicaragua, Uruguay, Japan, Mercosur, EFTA, EU, Canada
Morocco	EFTA, EU, Turkey, PAFTA
Nicaragua	Mexico, Venezuela, Colombia, Panama, CACM
Oman	GCC, PAFTA
Panama	Chile, Costa Rica, El Salvador, Singapore, Taiwan
Peru	Canada, EFTA, Singapore, Thailand, Mercosur, Cuba, Chile, China, South Korea
Singapore	New Zealand, China, India, Japan, South Korea, EFTA, India, Jordan, Panama, Peru, Australia

Note: EFTA = European Free Trade Area; PAFTA = Pan-Arab Free Trade Area; CARICOM = Caribbean Community; CACM = Central American Common Market; GCC = Gulf Cooperation Council.
Source: World Trade Organization, "Regional Trade Agreements," http://www.wto.org/english/tratop_e/region_e/region_e.htm.

will not be fully eliminated until the middle of this decade, and not until 2023 on some agricultural imports from Australia. Accordingly, the economic impact from these FTAs will only be felt over a period of time.

Additionally, a number of the agreements allow the United States to maintain tariff rate quotas on a number of agricultural products; whereas imports at a level below the quota will be duty free, any imports above the quota may still face a very high duty. For example, the Caribbean region is a major sugar producer. However, under the Central American Free Trade Agreement–Dominican Republic (CAFTA-DR), the United States is increasing its tariff rate quota on sugar only to a slight extent, with prohibitive tariff rates in effect for imports over the quota. Accordingly, there will only be a minor increase in U.S. sugar imports from the Dominican Republic and the CAFTA countries.

The Commercial Potential of TPP and TTIP

In contrast, U.S. negotiations for a Trans-Pacific Partnership (TPP) and for a Trans-Atlantic Trade and Investment Partnership (TTIP) potentially have enormous commercial significance.

The United States is currently negotiating with eleven other countries to create a TPP free trade area. The United States already has an FTA with six of these countries: Australia, Canada, Chile, Mexico, Peru, and Singapore. Four of the five countries with which it does not have an agreement—Brunei, Malaysia, New Zealand, and Vietnam—are all relatively small economically; combined, their GDP is only $578 billion, which is less than 4 percent of the size of the U.S. GDP of $15 trillion, so gaining full access to these markets is not a high commercial priority. However, with a GDP of $5.8 trillion, Japan's participation greatly increases the commercial significance of these negotiations.

In addition to opening these new markets to U.S. exporters, however, a successful TPP negotiation could provide a mechanism for strengthening existing U.S. agreements with the six other countries. In particular, the 1994 NAFTA does not have a number of the features of the newer agreements, and the TPP negotiations provide a venue for upgrading this agreement. U.S. agreements with Australia, Chile, Peru, and Singapore could also be upgraded to some extent. Again, however, improving these six agreements is not a top commercial priority.

Instead, the main commercial importance of the TPP negotiations is that a successful TPP agreement could provide a template for future agreements with other Asia-Pacific Economic Cooperation (APEC) countries, such as Indonesia and China, and possibly for future multilateral WTO negotiations. As noted, current multilateral rules under the WTO have some very serious gaps that neomercantilist countries can exploit to gain a commercial advantage at their trade partner's expense. Major gaps include the lack of effective rules governing currency manipulation, the behavior of state-owned enterprises, forced transfers of technology, and anticompetitive behavior. To protect U.S. commercial interests and to achieve its potential as a template for other future agreements, the TPP needs to address these issues.

Although the negotiations with the European Union are in a very early stage, the commercial importance of a possible U.S-EU FTA is enormous. Whereas both the United States and the EU have low tariffs and relatively few nontariff trade barriers, the twenty-seven EU member nations constitute a huge market (the EU countries have a combined GDP of $17.5 trillion, compared with the $15 trillion U.S. economy), and accordingly there are substantial opportunities for market expansion.[13]

In both the TPP and TTIP, negotiators are discussing other avenues to expanding trade and promoting economic efficiency, particularly by reducing the trade-distorting aspects of differing regulations, which may be a greater barrier to expanded trade today than formal trade barriers. To get a sense of the potential of this, the United Nations Industrial Development Organization reports that the U.S. Food and Drug Administration and its EU and Japanese counterparts require a total of sixty-seven different tests for fish and shellfish products.[14] Qualifying under these standards requires testing and certification mechanisms within each country that are internationally recognized, and this is costly for both the regulators and businesses.

The Government Procurement Code's Impact

The forty-one WTO member countries that have signed onto the Government Procurement Code did so to open new markets for their firms and to make their own procurement systems more effective. The code requires that these countries publish procurement opportunities for goods

13. Croatia is expected to join the EU in July 2013, bringing the number of EU member nations to twenty-eight.
14. United Nations Industrial Development Organization, *Trade Capacity-Building Background Paper: Supply Side Constraints on the Trade Performance of African Countries*, Background Paper 1 (Vienna: United Nations Industrial Development Organization, 2006), 7.

and services over the threshold level for covered entities, as described in chapter 2.

To the extent that foreign suppliers can provide goods and services at a lower price than domestic firms and win procurement contracts covered by the code, the U.S. taxpayer will benefit as government procurement dollars purchase more for less. However, in competing for foreign procurement opportunities, most companies generally invest in the targeted country. The implication of this for the U.S. trade balance is complex. A U.S. firm investing overseas is probably more likely to source parts and raw materials from the United States than would a foreign firm, and similarly a foreign firm investing in the United States is more likely to source parts and raw materials from its home market than would a U.S. company. Accordingly, U.S. exports might increase to some extent if U.S. firms gain sales in other country procurement markets, and U.S. imports might increase to some extent as other national firms win procurement sales in America.

The larger impact on the balance of payments, however, would likely occur if firms investing overseas and winning new markets through government procurement repatriate profits to the home country. These profits might be used to expand investment in the home country or passed on to stockholders, thereby benefiting the economy. However, U.S. tax law discourages the repatriation of profits, thereby denying the U.S. economy these potential benefits. (This is discussed further in chapter 9.)

Article XIX:5 of the WTO's Government Procurement Agreement (GPA) requires signatories to collect and provide to the GPA Committee on an annual basis statistics on the number and estimated value of contracts awarded, broken down by entity and categories of products and services. To the extent possible, statistics must also be provided on the country of origin of products and services purchased by a party to the Government Procurement Code.

However, a number of the signatories do not provide data on the country of origin of the products and services purchased, including the United States and Canada, although a few, like the EU, do provide data on purchases by the country of origin. A number of other signatories have not reported any data, and others have not posted recent data. Accordingly, it is impossible to assess whether U.S. firms benefit to the same extent or a greater or lesser extent than other countries' firms under the WTO's GPA.

As noted in chapter 2, bilateral U.S. FTAs also commit the United States and its partners to open their government procurement markets beyond the requirements of the WTO. However, there are also no data on the extent to which these agreements have opened additional procurement.

Given the inadequacy of the data on actual procurement under the GPA, the only assessment that can be made is to consider the theoretical government procurement market opened up by the United States and other countries. This theoretical government procurement market excludes procurement under the threshold level, procurement by noncovered entities, employee compensation, and some specific carve-outs (e.g., the United States retains set-asides for small and minority businesses).

In a 2002 paper published by the Organization for Economic Cooperation and Development (OECD), Denis Audet estimated that OECD countries committed to allowing bids from other signatory companies valued at $1,795 billion, and non-OECD signatories committed to allowing bids on an additional $287 billion.[15] He estimated that this "contestable" procurement was equal to some 30 percent of 1998 world merchandise and commercial services exports, although obviously many foreign bidders for procurement contracts would not actually win their bids.

Liberalizing Trade in Services

The services sector today accounts for more than 60 percent of global production and employment, and it represents 20 percent of total trade on a balance-of-payments basis, according to the WTO.[16] International trade in services has been growing rapidly, with some economists estimating that it is growing at perhaps double the rate of goods trade.[17] Partly, of course, the increase in trade in services is due to the Internet

15. Denis Audet, "Government Procurement: A Synthesis Report," *OECD Journal on Budgeting* 2, no. 3 (2002): 149–94, at 151.

16. World Trade Organization, "The General Agreement on Trade in Services (GATS): Objectives, Coverage, and Disciplines," http://www.wto.org/english/tratop_e/serv_e/gatsqa_e.htm.

17. John Whalley, *Assessing the Benefits to Developing Countries of Liberalization in Services Trade*, NBER Working Paper 10181 (Cambridge, Mass.: National Bureau of Economic Research, 2003), 6.

and electronic commerce, although the major cause is probably the increasing importance of services in maturing economies.

By and large, services represent a larger element of the economy in developed countries than in developing countries, although there is a large variance between countries. The services sector accounts for 76.2 percent of the U.S. GDP, the third highest of OECD countries, with Luxembourg the highest, at 85.1 percent, and France second, at 77.3 percent.[18]

The financial sector is the largest service sector in the United States, with value added in 2010 just over $3 trillion, as can be seen in table 4.5. Business, professional, and technical services is the second-largest sector, followed by the distribution, health, construction, transportation, telecommunications, educational, and recreational sectors. In terms of employment, however, the ranking changes. The distribution sector employs the most, with just over 22 million workers; the health sector is second, with 15.9 million workers; business and professional is third, with 9.4 million workers; and construction is fourth, with 7.9 million workers. The financial sector is fifth, with 6.2 million workers.

The business services sector is the largest exporter of services, followed by the transportation and financial sectors. All sectors have a positive balance of payments except transportation, which has a deficit of $14 billion. Business and professional services has a large surplus of $39 billion. Data on trade in the distribution sector are not available, although some trade in the United States is certainly conducted by foreign-owned service providers, and a great deal of trade is in imported products or goods for export.

Generally, the delivery of services requires that the provider be close to the customer; for example, repair of equipment requires the mechanic to be on site to work on the equipment. Because of the need for proximity, many service providers—particularly large ones—invest in the markets they wish to serve. Additionally, almost all services are consumed as soon as provided and cannot be stored in inventory to be used later.

Because of the need for proximity, almost twice as much of the overseas sales by U.S. service providers is through foreign affiliates (Mode 3) as is exported across the border (Modes 1 and 2). U.S. Department of Commerce data show that by value, $806 billion of services sales to

18. Organization for Economic Cooperation and Development, "OECD in Figures 2008" (Paris: Organization for Economic Cooperation and Development, 2008), 16–17, http://www.oecd-ilibrary.org/economics/oecd-in-figures-2008_oif-2008-en.

Table 4.5. Selected U.S. Service Industries, 2010 (millions of dollars)

Industry	Value Added	U.S. Exports	U.S. Imports	Employment (thousands)
Business, professional, technical	1,782,837	107,675	68,763	9,383
Telecommunications	347,282	8,283	7,334	1,361
Construction	511,639	10,136	4,792	7,851
Distribution	1,682,225	N.A.	N.A.	22,101
Educational	163,101	15,732	4,523	3,047
Financial	3,007,185	68,552	61,689	6,194
Health-related	1,109,187	2,306	660	15,873
Recreational, cultural, sporting	80,387	15,661	1,719	2,068
Transportation	402,524	82,440	96,686	4,571

Note: Exports and imports are for 2007. N.A. = not available.
Sources: Bureau of Economic Analysis, www.bea.gov/industry/gdpbyind_data.htm (value added and employment); and www.bea.gov/international/xls/tab1a.xls (exports/imports)

foreign markets by American providers was through foreign affiliates in 2006, compared with just $415 billion in sales across the border. U.S. imports of services of $616 billion came through foreign affiliates established in the United States, compared with $314 billion imported across the border.[19] Most of services trade carried out through foreign affiliates is conducted by large corporations that can afford the overhead costs of a foreign office and can accept the risks of operating in a foreign environment.

A major problem in trying to assess the commercial impact of the services provisions in U.S. trade agreements is that the data on services barriers and trade are weak, although they are greatly improved from what were available during the Uruguay Round.

The United States compiles data on trade for the services sector in a different format than the WTO categories, and it is hard to reconcile U.S. data with the WTO categories. Furthermore, some traded services have historically been lumped into manufacturing statistics. Specifically, goods trade is often reported on a cost, insurance, and freight basis, which includes both insurance for the goods and the cost of freight (services), as well as the cost of the particular good being traded.

19. Jennifer Koncz and Anne Flatness, "U.S. International Services: Cross-Border Trade in 2007 and Services Supplied through Affiliates in 2006," U.S. Bureau of Economic Analysis, October 2008, 16, http://www.bea.gov/scb/pdf/2008/10 percent 20October/services _text.pdf.

An additional reason why data on services trade are weak is that trade in services is largely invisible; it comes across the computer, is purchased when traveling abroad, or is generated by a foreign investment in the country. Unlike goods trade, where customs receipts provide reasonably accurate data, services trade is not directly observable. Accordingly, data must be collected through government surveys, which are less reliable than customs receipts.[20]

In addition to the problems of collecting data, it is difficult to even identify barriers to services trade. As noted, determining the trade impact of a regulation often requires detailed knowledge of the industry, and judgments have to be made whether a regulation is protectionist or serves a legitimate purpose.

To get around the problem of the lack of good data on barriers to services trade, economists are trying a number of different approaches. Some examples of these approaches include:

- A direct approach, which may involve interviewing companies involved in the market; this, of course is resource intensive and often subjective.
- Indirectly, by inferring the presence of market barriers from other factors, such as price differentials between markets. However, it is hard to make comparisons based on price alone, because prices are influenced by quality, tax structure, currency changes, domestic regulations, and many other factors.
- A measurement of a country's openness based on its commitments to the WTO is being developed by Bernard Hoekman of the World Bank. He assigned a weight of zero to "unbound" commitments, a weight of 1 to full commitments, and a weight of 0.5 to commitments where restrictions were notified. As noted, however, most countries' practices are significantly more liberal than their WTO commitments, so at best this approach only estimates the degree of openness of WTO bound commitments.

---

20. It is easier to collect data on the export of services, because generally these are provided by large firms that can supply information on their sales. Import data are harder to compile and probably understate the actual amount because services are generally purchased by multiple consumers. The reliability of data for goods trade tends to be the opposite; import data are more reliable than export data because governments collect tariffs on imports and accordingly closely monitor imports coming into the country.

John Whalley suggests with some understatement that efforts to date to measure "barriers to service trade flows, while clearly defensible on the grounds that this is all there is, nonetheless encounter numerous pitfalls and must therefore be used with great care."[21]

Given all these problems, it should be no surprise that it is difficult to determine the actual economic impact of the WTO's General Agreement on Trade in Services (GATS) agreement or of the services provisions in U.S. preferential trade agreements, both in terms of trade expansion and economic effects. As noted, little actual liberalization occurred as a result of the GATS or the U.S. preferential trade agreements. Further, trade patterns are heavily influenced by many factors other than market access, such as currency changes, or differing rates of economic growth in foreign markets compared with the United States. These factors would have a far greater impact on trade patterns than would the small degree of liberalization resulting from U.S. trade agreements.

Although it is not possible to measure the precise impact of the services provisions in U.S. trade agreements, a number of specific effects can be noted. First, the importance of binding current practices should not be underestimated. For example, the Internet was just beginning to change communications in a fundamental way in 1995, and binding the existing level of openness at that time proved to be extremely important. Another example of the importance of commitments that freeze the status quo is provided by Japan's commitment not to discriminate in insurance. Today, Japan is in the process of privatizing its postal service, which has historically been a major provider of insurance, and this will have to be done in a manner consistent with its binding. A third example is the U.S. commitment to bind the number of H1-B visas, which allow temporary workers to enter the United States for work purposes, at the 1995 level under Mode 4, which pertains to the presence of natural persons. Later, in response to domestic political pressures, Congress wanted to reduce the number of H1-B visas below the U.S. bound level, but it was restrained by the U.S. GATS commitment. Binding practices in a public document notified to the WTO also provides greater transparency and gives service providers a better understanding of the rules of the road as they seek to expand business globally.

Another tangible benefit is that the GATS framework provides the basis for negotiating the accession of new WTO members. At the end of

---

21. Whalley, *Assessing the Benefits*, 29.

the Uruguay Round, there were 123 members, and by August 2012 there were 157. Each of these new members had to make concessions—often very extensive—to be admitted to the WTO. For example, as part of the price to be admitted to the WTO in 2001, China's commitments on financial services "were among the most radical ever negotiated in the context of the WTO."[22]

Regarding the impact of the services provisions in U.S. bilateral FTAs, the U.S. International Trade Commission (ITC) has analyzed the Chile, Singapore, Australia, Morocco, CAFTA-DR, and Bahrain agreements.[23] The ITC concluded that U.S. imports of services from its partner country are not expected to increase as a result of its preferential trade agreements, because the U.S. services market is already largely open. Additionally, the ITC concluded that U.S. exports of services are also not projected to increase significantly due to these agreements. Except for Australia, this is due in large measure to the small market size of the U.S. partner; and in the case of Chile, Singapore, and Australia, this prediction is also due to the existing openness of these markets. However, the ITC did project that several sectors, such as insurance and banking, will have minor gains.

The economic impact on the United States of export of services through either Modes 1 or 2 is the same as the export of goods; specifically, it creates revenue for the exporter that may be invested in the United States to expand the business or used to expand consumption or savings in the United States.

Expanded exports under Mode 3, where a U.S. firm invests in another country to deliver services, has less benefit for the U.S. economy. Basically, the major benefit to the U.S. economy from this mode of expanded services exports occurs if the firm repatriates profits to the United States, either to return to stockholders or to invest in the United States. Additionally there could be a small increase in employment in the home office of the company to support the overseas investment, or increased sourcing of parts from the United States for the new facility.

The economic impact of Mode 4, where foreign workers or students come to the United States, is more complex. The firm using such workers

22. Constantinos Stephanou, *Including Financial Services in Preferential Trade Agreements: Lessons of International Experience for China*, Policy Research Working Paper 4898 (Washington, D.C.: World Bank, 2009), 4.

23. The ITC studies considered here are those on Chile, Singapore, Australia, Morocco, CAFTA-DR, and Bahrain—all available on the ITC's Web site http://www.usitc.gov.

would presumably benefit and increase output, which would have a positive impact. However, the additional workers might displace American workers, thereby having a negative impact. The number of such temporary workers is currently capped by Congress at 65,000 and is limited to the highly skilled workers on which the technology industry and others say they depend, because a sufficient number of these workers are not otherwise available in the United States.[24]

Protecting Intellectual Property

Most economists believe that a core comparative advantage for the United States is its intellectual property, including the knowledge of how to produce something, the unique name of a company or product, a book or song, or a new computer program. Innovation in developing new products and techniques has driven development throughout much of U.S. history.

A major motivation for firms and individuals to develop new intellectual property is the chance it can give for profit. However, intellectual property loses much of its value if competitors can freely use the knowledge. Accordingly, one of the most important mechanisms by which the United States and other countries seek to encourage the development of intellectual property is by granting the developer an exclusive right to use the intellectual property for a defined period of time.

Principal examples of such protection are patents, trademarks, and copyrights. A patent in the United States may be given to a new and nonobvious process or article of manufacture, and it grants the holder the exclusive right to use that knowledge for twenty years. Often the patent holder will choose to make the patented intellectual property available to others, generally for a royalty fee.

A trademark is a word, phrase, or symbol that identifies a company, product, or other item from other similar items. Trademarks are important to many companies that want consumers to recognize and value their products over those of their competitors. Trademarks can be registered with the Trademark Office, but they are only enforceable through the court system, and they are only valid for as long as the product is in active commerce.

24. The program that provides temporary visas to highly skilled workers is known as the H1B program.

Copyrights apply to original works of authorship—such as books, articles, and music—and they give the author the exclusive right to the material, although copyright holders often license use of the material for a royalty fee. Material does not need to be registered to be protected by copyright law; but in the event of violations, the ability of the holder of the copyright to enforce his or her rights through the legal system is enhanced if the work has been registered with the U.S. Copyright Office.

Because many firms conduct business around the world, in addition to protecting their intellectual property in the United States, many firms and individuals also seek to protect their knowledge or product in other markets. Similarly, firms and individuals in other countries often seek to protect their intellectual property in the United States.

Although intellectual property is still a comparative advantage of the United States, its lead has been declining as other countries have actively sought to develop their own intellectual property. As an example of this, the U.S. patent office issued slightly more than 107,000 patents in 2010 to U.S. companies or individuals, but it issued slightly more patents to foreign inventors, just over 111,000. The major foreign recipients of U.S. patents in 2010 were Japan (44,814), Germany (12,363), South Korea (11,671), Taiwan (8,238), Canada (4,852), France (4,450), and the United Kingdom (4,302).[25]

Royalty payments to U.S. firms and individuals for the use of their intellectual property by foreigners in 2010 equaled $95.8 billion, up from $16.6 billion in 1990, whereas payments to foreign firms and individuals by U.S. entities for the use of their intellectual property equaled only $29.2 billion in 2010, up from $3.1 billion in 1990. This actually understates the value of U.S. intellectual property, because many firms and individuals do not license their intellectual property for royalty payments, but instead use it for themselves.

As noted in chapter 2, to better protect U.S. intellectual property, the Uruguay Round's trade negotiators developed the agreement on Trade-Related Intellectual Property (TRIPS). Intellectual property had already been protected at that time by a number of international agreements, most prominently the World Intellectual Property Organization (WIPO). However, WIPO had no enforcement mechanism, and some countries

---

25. Data on U.S. patents issued are available at the U.S. Patent and Trademark Office Web site, http://www.uspto.gov/web/offices/ac/ido/oeip/taf/cst_utl.htm.

had not adequately incorporated their WIPO obligations into their domestic laws.

Piracy of intellectual property was common; even where countries had laws to protect intellectual property, enforcement was often weak and ineffective. This, of course, meant that trying to enforce intellectual property rights in the courts of these countries was an exercise in futility. Piracy of U.S. intellectual property hurts U.S. exporters attempting to sell in the market where piracy occurs, and it hurts U.S. exporters in other markets, because pirated goods often find their way into the global trade system. By including the WIPO rules in the TRIPS agreement, WTO members were now compelled to abide by these provisions or be subject to the stringent WTO dispute settlement mechanism. This forced a number of countries to clamp down on piracy.

For example, before China joined the WTO, its laws protecting intellectual property were inadequate and there was virtually no enforcement of even the existing laws. As a result, many items—such as records, designer clothes, and books—were systematically pirated. As the price for joining the WTO, China was required to strengthen its laws and practices regarding intellectual property protection. However, enforcement is still very weak, and there is still enormous piracy of U.S. intellectual property in China.

Other countries also had to significantly strengthen their intellectual property protection. For example, a number of large developing countries—such as Argentina, Brazil, and India—had excluded pharmaceutical products from eligibility for patent protection, and vigorous industries developed in those countries that basically pirated brand drugs, costing U.S. pharmaceutical companies billions in profits.[26]

The TRIPS agreement also required the United States to extend the term of patent protection to twenty years from the seventeen years that had been in effect. This change was largely driven in the Uruguay Round negotiations by the EU and Japan and by the U.S. pharmaceutical industry, which faces high costs to develop new drugs and large risks that new drugs will not be approved by the regulatory authorities. Additionally, once the research has led to an approved new drug, the costs of pro-

26. See Carsten Fink and Kimberly Elliott, "Tripping over Health: U.S. Policy on Patents and Drug Access in Developing Countries," in *The White House and the World: A Global Development Agenda for the Next U.S. President*, edited by Nancy Birdsall (Washington, D.C.: Center for Global Development, 2008), 217.

duction are low, which makes it inexpensive to produce generics to compete. Accordingly, the industry was able to persuade negotiators that twenty years of patent protection was appropriate.

U.S. industry generally views the TRIPS agreement as an important tool in protecting its intellectual property. However, there is still an enormous amount of piracy of intellectual property globally. To a large extent, this is because the TRIPS agreement is relatively weak in ensuring that countries fully enforce their domestic laws.

The Impact of Import Relief Actions

As noted in chapter 2, the WTO allows three basic measures that can be taken to protect domestic industry against foreign competition, namely, duties that can be imposed on products deemed to be "dumped" in the market (antidumping duties), countervailing duty actions against foreign subsidies, and broad import relief that can be imposed against imports of a specific product from all nations (safeguards).

By far, the most frequently used of these actions are the antidumping provisions. Since January 1, 1995, when the WTO went into effect, and June 30, 2010, an investigation was initiated by a WTO member on 3,752 occasions to see if an imported product was being dumped in the market. By comparison, only 250 countervailing duty actions and 216 safeguard actions were initiated.

Before the conclusion of the Uruguay Round, the United States and the EU were the major practitioners of the antidumping provisions. In the Kennedy, Tokyo, and Uruguay rounds, countries with export interests, such as Japan and South Korea, pressed for provisions that would make it more difficult to impose antidumping duties. The United States, as a major user of these rules, was largely on the defensive.

However, since the Uruguay Round, other countries, such as India, have become major users of the antidumping provisions. As can be seen in table 4.6, the United States has initiated the second-highest number of actions, at 442, followed by the EU and Argentina. The United States is the major user of countervailing duties, having initiated 104 cases, followed by the EU with 56, while India is the major user of the safeguard provisions, with 26 initiations.

China has most often been the target of dumping complaints (764 instances), followed by South Korea (268 instances); however, the United

Table 4.6. Import Relief Actions: Top Five Initiators of Antidumping, Countervailing Duty, and Safeguard Actions under the World Trade Organization, January 1, 1995–June 30, 2010

Antidumping Actions		Countervailing Duty Actions		Safeguard Actions	
India	613	United States	104	India	26
United States	442	European Union	56	Turkey	15
European Union	414	Canada	24	Jordan	15
Argentina	277	South Africa	13	Chile	12
Australia/South	212	Australia	11	United States	10
Africa (tie)		All users	250	All users	216
All users	3,752				

Sources: Data on antidumping initiations are from the WTO Web site, http://www.wto.org/english/tratop_e/adp_e/adp_e.htm. Data on countervailing duty initiations are from the WTO's Web site, http://www.wto.org/english/tratop_e/scm_e/scm_e.htm. Data on safeguards initiations are from the WTO's Web site, http://www.wto.org/english/tratop_e/safeg_e/safeg_e.htm.

States has been targeted 210 times during this period. With regard to countervailing duty actions, India has been targeted the most (48 instances), followed by China (40) and South Korea (17); the United States has been targeted 12 times. (Safeguard actions, as noted, are implemented against imports from all countries and are not country specific). Base metals are the most frequent target for antidumping and countervailing duty cases; second is the chemicals sector, third are resins and plastics, and prepared foodstuffs and beverages are fourth.

A number of economists support the usage of countervailing duties; as Stephen Cohen notes, "Because subsidies are considered an interference with free markets to begin with, countervailing duties that offset foreign subsidies are seen as restoring the market to its natural equilibrium, and thus as making international markets work more efficiently."[27] However, other economists believe that countries are best off ignoring foreign subsidies or dumping, even when they might injure domestic industry, because the consumer benefits from the cheaper goods.

However, the commercial impact is more complex. Antidumping duties are often criticized as protectionist, because dumping can be a legitimate business reaction to dispose of excess inventory. As Daniel Ikenson

27. Stephen D. Cohen, Robert A. Blecker, and Peter D. Whitney, *Fundamentals of U.S. Foreign Trade Policy: Economies, Politics, Laws, and Issues* (Boulder, Colo.: Westview Press, 2003), 64.

notes, "Many firms—particularly those operating in high-fixed-cost industries—drop their prices below the full costs of production when facing reduced demand for seasonal or cyclical reasons. As long as the price charged is high enough to cover the firm's variable costs, any price above variable cost contributes toward coverage of the firm's fixed costs."[28]

Conversely, dumping can be a legitimate cause of concern, and antidumping duties can be entirely appropriate if a dominant firm is dumping its products in a foreign market in order to weaken its competitors, or if its actions have the effect of destroying competition even if this is not the intent. In his study of antidumping activity, Douglas Irwin notes that there are more frequent petitions for antidumping duties when tariffs are low, when unemployment is high, when the exchange rates do not reflect commercial conditions, or when import penetration is high.

Unlike countervailing or antidumping duties, safeguard actions are inherently protectionist in nature. The intent of a safeguard action is to give a domestic industry "breathing room" to enable it to regroup and either become competitive in the future or phase down in an orderly fashion to give workers and capital an opportunity to redeploy.

Safeguard rules have a number of features designed to ensure that any action is limited. First, a country adopting a safeguard measure generally compensates its trade partners that are injured by the action. Thus, while the safeguard is protectionist, a balance of trade advantages is maintained.

Second, in theory, antidumping duties are supposed to be temporary, but many remain in effect for many years, while safeguard actions cannot exceed eight years and need to be progressively reduced and phased out during that period. Third, in applying antidumping and countervailing duties, the government is not allowed to take into account the impact on consuming interests such as retailers; in considering a safeguard action, however, these interests may be taken into account, and the remedy can often be tailored to minimize peripheral damage.

However, perhaps the most important advantage of safeguards over antidumping is that the government can require the domestic industry to take specific actions as a condition for receiving temporary protection. These specific actions may be designed to help the industry adjust to

28. Daniel Ikenson, *Protection Made to Order: Domestic Industry's Capture and Reconfiguration of U.S. Antidumping Policy* (Washington, D.C.: Cato Institute, 2010), 8.

global competition, or they may be designed to encourage an orderly phase-out.

An example of an effective safeguard action was the U.S. action on motorcycles in 1984. At that time there was only one U.S. producer— Harley Davidson—and that company submitted an action plan as to how it intended to regain competitiveness if import relief was granted; that plan was monitored annually to ensure that it was fulfilling its commitments. Additionally, injury to Harley Davidson was only caused by motorcycles with large engines, and so smaller bikes were exempted from the import duties. Harley Davidson was given five years of relief, but after four years the company had regained competitiveness and requested that the import duties imposed under the safeguard action be removed. As a result of this safeguard action, Harley Davidson is still in business today.

Though safeguards are a mechanism allowed by the WTO and have advantages over other forms of import protection, they were last used by the United States in 2001. Other countries, however, use this mechanism. For example, the EU imposed safeguards in 2002, 2003, 2004, 2005, and 2010, and Canada had two safeguard actions in 2005.

It is impossible to assess the impact of these import relief measures on world trade. Safeguard actions obviously temporarily lessen the gains to the world economy from trade liberalization, although they may promote competition in the long run if they enable an industry to survive that otherwise would be severely injured by an event outside its control. Antidumping and countervailing duty actions promote trade based on comparative advantage in theory provided they exactly offset the subsidy or extent of dumping; but in practice, both have protectionist elements, making any overall assessment difficult and unreliable.

The U.S. Trade Deficit

In general one can conclude that this enormous reduction in tariffs and other trade barriers as a result of U.S. trade agreements has had a strong positive impact on its broad economy, although some industries and workers have been injured. However, special note must be taken of the huge structural U.S. trade deficit. As noted in chapter 3, economists generally assume that trade deficits are not structural, and thus not something to worry about. Unfortunately, as can be seen in table 4.7, the

U.S. trade deficit is structural and has been deteriorating, and equaled some 5 percent of U.S. GDP between 2005 and 2008.

The U.S. trade deficit creates two major problems. First, most economists believe there will come a point when U.S. creditors will no longer be willing or able to lend America money to continue funding its consumption. In that event, the value of the dollar will fall and interest rates will rise, which will likely precipitate a severe recession or even a depression.

The second problem, however, is that the U.S. trade deficit is a drag on its economy, and its structural deficit means that the United States is importing some products where it actually has a comparative advantage and that it is not exporting other products that would be exported if the market were working correctly. Joseph Stiglitz notes that "just as exports create jobs, imports destroy them, and when imports exceed exports there is a real risk of insufficiency of aggregate demand. Aggregate demand that would have been translated into jobs at home is translated into demand for goods produced abroad."[29]

The Department of Commerce estimates that every $1 billion in exports created 4,926 jobs in 2012.[30] In theory, this would mean that there would have been an additional 2.8 million jobs in the United States if it had eliminated its $560 billion trade deficit through increased exports. However, reality is more complicated than this. Many factors contribute to the employment level, such as the stage of the business cycle and the age of the population, although trade is a significant factor. Nonetheless, over the long term the U.S. employment rate and standard of living would have been higher if its trade was better balanced between imports and exports.[31]

29. Joseph E. Stiglitz, *Making Globalization Work* (New York: W. W. Norton, 2006), 253.

30. Martin Johnson and Chris Rasmussen, *Jobs Supported by Exports 2012: An Update* (Washington, D.C.: International Trade Administration, U.S. Department of Commerce, 2013).

31. Some economists argue that the U.S. deficits should be of little concern. E.g., Daniel Griswold at the Cato Institute examined data on the U.S. current account deficit and GDP growth between 1980 and 2006. He concluded that "economic growth has been more than twice as fast, on average, in years in which the current account deficit grew sharply compared to those years in which it actually declined. . . . Trade deficits tend to be pro-cyclical, growing when the economy expands and contracting when the economy slows or slips into recession." Daniel Griswold, "Are Trade Deficits a Drag on U.S. Economic Growth?" Cato Institute, March 27, 2007.

Table 4.7. U.S. Trade Balance, 1970–2012

Year	Net Trade Balance in Goods and Services (billions of dollars)	U.S. Gross Domestic Product (GDP, in billions of dollars)	Trade Balance as Percentage of GDP
1970	4	1,038	0.004
1975	16	1,638	0.01
1980	−13.0	2,788	−0.005
1985	−115.2	4,218	−0.027
1990	−77.6	5,801	−0.013
1995	−90.7	7,415	−0.012
2000	−382.1	9,952	−0.038
2005	−722.7	12,623	−0.057
2006	−769.3	13,377	−0.058
2007	−713.1	14,029	−0.051
2008	−709.7	14,292	−0.050
2009	−388.8	13,974	−0.028
2010	−511.7	14,499	−0.035
2011	−568.1	15,076	−0.038
2012	−560.0	15,685*	−0.036

Source: Bureau of Economic Analysis, U.S. Department of Commerce, "National Income and Product Accounts Tables," http://www.bea.gov/iTable/iTable.cfm?ReqID=9&step=1.
*GDP figures may vary slightly according to source.

So what has caused the U.S. current account deficit, and what role have its trade agreements played in this? First, its current account deficit is driven by its deficit in goods trade. The United States has a positive trade balance in services, although its surplus is only about 10 percent the size of its deficit in goods trade. Remittances on U.S. investments in other countries and remittances from the United States to foreign investors are roughly in balance, so that is not a factor, and the other elements of the current account are small.

The United States consistently ran a surplus in trade in goods until 1971, when it shifted into deficit, and its deficits have increased fairly steadily since that time, although with some variation due to the business cycle. The huge U.S. trade deficit in goods equaled $738 billion in 2011, and of this $25 billion was in oil and $295 billion was in its bilateral trade deficit with China.

This is true, but the real issue is cause and effect. Trade deficits do not cause economic growth; instead, if the United States is growing more rapidly than its trade partners, that will tend to lead to a trade deficit. The real issue with U.S. deficits is that they are structural and too large.

The easiest part to explain regarding the U.S. trade deficit is its dependence on imported oil, which is largely due to its failure to develop an energy policy, even though it has known since the 1970s that its dependence on imported oil was not in its economic or national security interest. A 2010 study by the Congressional Research Service notes that the United States has the largest energy reserves of any country, although its oil reserves are relatively small, equal to only about seven years of current consumption. Some analysts are projecting that the United States will be a net exporter of fossil fuel energy within several years.

The other causes of the structural trade deficit of the United States are more difficult to explain. There is some difference of views among economists as to the primary cause of the enormous U.S. deficits with China and other countries in non-oil products. Some economists argue that the U.S. trade deficit is driven by capital flows, as described in chapter 3. The argument behind this view is complex, but (to oversimplify) it is based on the fact that by definition every nation's balance of payments must be in exact balance; the balance of payments consists of the current account, where the United States has a huge deficit, and the capital account, where it has an equally huge surplus.

What is happening in trade today is that the United States is importing substantially more goods and services than it exports, and it pays for these imports largely by issuing Treasury bills, which in essence are IOUs for future payment. It is the purchase of these Treasury bills by the Chinese and others that underlies the huge surplus in the U.S. capital account. The problem is that producing and exporting real goods and services increase employment and the nation's productive capability; producing Treasury bills only requires the click of a computer's mouse. So the United States is losing out in terms of economic benefit to the broad economy; in essence, it is borrowing from tomorrow to pay for consumption today.

The debate among economists is whether these capital flows drive the U.S. trade deficit or whether the trade deficit drives the surplus on its capital account. Is the reality that the Chinese and others want to purchase U.S. Treasury bills as a good investment, which then requires a U.S. trade deficit of equal size, or is it that America does not produce as much as it wants to consume and therefore must borrow money from the rest of the world?

Most likely, both these elements are at play. The U.S. capital markets are the world's safe haven, and other countries' investors seek refuge in

Treasury bills or other U.S. financial assets to balance their portfolios or as a place to hide in uncertain times. This causes a surplus in the U.S. capital account and a mirror-image deficit in the current account.

Coupled with this, the United States has a very low rate of savings as a nation, primarily driven by its persistent federal budget deficits and extensive borrowing by households. To finance its consumption that exceeds its savings, it eagerly borrows from abroad and, as noted, other countries so far have been ready to lend it money. However, when the global economic uncertainty that has rocked world markets since 2008 subsides, investors may invest in markets other than the United States because of concerns that the United States will be repaying its debts in sharply devalued dollars.

Two other factors also play an important role in the U.S.trade deficits. The most significant is the deliberate neomercantilist strategies for economic development pursued by some countries, most notably China today, but also by Japan in the 1970s and 1980s. Under this strategy, the Chinese government deliberately pegs its currency, the renminbi, at an artificially low exchange rate to the dollar. The resulting undervalued currency acts both as a subsidy for Chinese exports and as a trade barrier for U.S. exports into China. Rather than trying to accumulate gold, as mercantilists did in Thomas Muns's day, China is trying to increase employment and reduce its enormous level of poverty through rapidly expanding exports.

It needs to be noted, however, that the 2011 $295 billion U.S. trade deficit with China overstates the real bilateral imbalance with that country. Global business has changed from the way it was when the U.S. system of collecting trade statistics was developed; today, many products are produced by companies that have huge global supply chains, compared with the older model of firms generally producing a finished product with raw materials from the same nation. Many U.S. imports from China are goods that have been produced with raw materials and components that have been sourced from around the world.

What this means is that standard trade nomenclature overinflates the size of the U.S. trade deficit with China. If statistics were able to more accurately track these complex transactions, we would see that some of the deficit that America now attributes to China is actually spread out among a number of countries. However, China's undervalued renminbi is a particular concern, because it forces many of its neighbors to also maintain undervalued currencies in order to compete in global markets.

What this analysis indicates is that the WTO/GATT and the U.S. trade agreements did not cause the U.S. trade imbalance. Much of the U.S. trade deficit is due to its own policies, particularly the federal budget deficit, its low savings rate, and its overreliance on foreign petroleum. However, there are large gaps in the trade rules, most notably the lack of effective rules governing currency manipulation, and this does play a significant role by allowing neomercantilist countries to pursue beggar-thy-neighbor policies that do cause the U.S. economy real harm.

Conclusion

Developed-country tariffs on industrial goods have been reduced from an average of approximately 40 percent to less than 4 percent today, although trade barriers and distortions in the agricultural sector remain high. Developing-country tariffs have also been reduced, although they are significantly higher than developed-country tariffs. Additionally, nontariff barriers to trade have been enormously reduced. This trade liberalization has been a major cause of the twenty-seven-fold increase in volume in world trade since 1950, which is more than three times the increase in the world economy. Because trade is only one of many factors that have had an impact on economic growth and because of the weaknesses of economic data, it is difficult to estimate the actual effect of trade liberalization, and the range of opinions on the impact is wide, although most economists believe the impact has been significant.

It is impossible to estimate the impact of the WTO's Government Procurement Agreement, because the United States and a number of other code signatories do not provide data on the level of purchases by the country of origin. Under the services agreement, the United States and other signatories basically just bound the level of current barriers to trade. Though bindings are important and have prevented the imposition of new barriers, it is doubtful if this agreement has led to a significant increase in services trade.

A core competitive advantage for the United States is its intellectual property, and the TRIPS agreement has had a significant impact in strengthening the protection of its intellectual property in many countries, including China, India, and Brazil. Though more still needs to be done to better protect U.S. intellectual property, particularly with regard to enforcement, this agreement has undoubtedly led to an increase in U.S. exports and in the royalty payments received by U.S. holders of intellectual property.

Except for the FTAs with Canada, Mexico, South Korea, and Australia, U.S. FTAs have all been with countries that are less than 5 percent the size of the U.S. economy, and these agreements have had almost no impact on the U.S. economy. The South Korean and Australian agreements will have some impact, but it will be lessened due to the distance between them and America. However, according to the Congressional Budget Office, NAFTA may have led to an 11 percent increase in U.S. exports and an 8 percent increase in U.S. imports in 2001.

Current U.S. negotiations—the Trans-Pacific Partnership and the Trans-Atlantic Trade and Investment Partnership—may produce agreements that will have an enormous impact, both on the U.S. economy and on the world trade system.

The U.S. trade balance in goods turned from surplus to deficit in 1971, has grown relatively steadily since, and has ballooned to an unsustainable level since 2000. America's deficit is caused by its fiscal policies, its dependence on foreign oil, and the neomercantilist trade policies pursued by some of its trade partners, particularly China, which include currency manipulation and trade distortions that take advantage of gaps in the international trade rules. The huge U.S. structural trade deficit equaled almost 6 percent of its GDP before the recent global financial and economic crisis, and leads to a substantial loss of production and jobs.

Chapter 5

Foreign Policy: The Other Driver

*Trade agreements were seen as an important foreign policy tool immedi-
ately after World War II, when U.S. policymakers negotiated trade agreements that were designed to promote economic development in Europe and
Japan. After 1971, when the U.S. trade balance in goods swung into deficit,
foreign policy objectives took a back seat to promoting its commercial interests, although foreign policy concerns were important in negotiating a free
trade agreement (FTA) with Israel. After the terror attacks of September
2001, foreign policy concerns were again important as U.S. policymakers
came to believe that promoting democracy and economic development was
important in the "war on terrorism" and that trade agreements were an important tool for promoting democracy and development. The U.S. trade
agreements were extremely successful immediately after World War II;
however, the foreign policy impact since 9/11 has been far more mixed.*

U.S. trade policy immediately after World War II was based on the
foreign policy objective of promoting strong democracies in Europe
and Japan to block the spread of communism. Negotiating trade agreements to reduce trade barriers multilaterally was seen by policymakers
as necessary to promote economic growth in Europe, Japan, and other
Western-oriented countries. To this end, the United States pressed for
the formation of the General Agreement on Tariffs and Trade (GATT)
in 1947 and for several rounds of multilateral trade negotiations in
which the United States was willing to sacrifice commercial interests by
reducing its trade barriers to a greater extent than required of other
participants.

Whereas foreign policy concerns dominated U.S. trade policy through the Kennedy Round (1964–67), by the early 1970s commercial concerns rose to the fore, as the U.S. trade balance swung into deficit and Japan and the European Communities became economically competitive. Although commercial concerns dominated U.S. trade policy in this period, promoting freer trade was also seen as supportive of its foreign policy interests. Accordingly, the United States pressed for a successful conclusion to both the Tokyo Round (1973–79) and the Uruguay Round (1986–94), but it insisted that its developed-country trade partners open their markets to the same extent as it was doing.

Then came the September 11, 2001, terrorist attacks on the United States, and foreign policy concerns gained renewed urgency. Policymakers in the Bush administration came to believe that failed states such as Afghanistan and the closed states in the Middle East were breeding grounds for terrorists, and that economic development could be an important tool in the antiterrorism campaign. As an element of the U.S. strategy of the "war on terrorism," the president announced plans for a Middle East Free Trade Area. And in the wake of the 9/11 attack, a new round of multilateral trade negotiations—the Doha Round—was launched in November 2001 with the stated objective of promoting development in the poorest countries. U.S. foreign policy objectives also influenced the U.S. decision to negotiate FTAs with several other countries.

The United States, of course, has many tools to achieve its foreign policy objectives, including hard power, such as military force, and soft power, such as diplomacy and foreign aid. Furthermore, trade agreements are only one element of trade policy, which has a range of tools including sticks, such as trade sanctions, and carrots, such as preferential trade treatment, export financing, and bilateral investment treaties. However, FTAs can be viewed as the ultimate carrot, as such an agreement is the farthest ranging and the deepest form of trade relationship.

An FTA can promote foreign policy objectives in a number of ways. There is the immediate symbolism of entering into negotiations and announcing an agreement that says to the world "we are partners." The agreement provides a forum for ongoing discussion and the resolution of commercial disputes that might otherwise fester or become foreign policy problems. And perhaps most important is that the trade agreement is expected to foster economic growth in the U.S. partner country, and this economic growth is considered important for promoting democracy, for removing safe havens for terrorists, and even for reducing the flow of narcotics and illegal immigration into the United States.

Trade Agreements and Foreign Policy: World War II through 9/11

As World War II was ending and policymakers began to consider how to develop the postwar global architecture, they were determined not to repeat the economic policy failures of the prewar period. Many felt that the high tariffs enacted by the United States in the Tariff Act of 1930, commonly known as the Smoot-Hawley Act, along with retaliation from its trading partners, had contributed to the severity of the Great Depression.[1] Additionally, many felt that restrictive trade agreements, such as Nazi Germany's trade and exchange controls and Britain's system of imperial preferences, had been contributing factors to the war.

As Robert Pollard and Samuel Wells described the post–World War II consensus, "a common set of beliefs, attitudes, and experiences informed the American prescriptions for world peace and prosperity. Almost every official concerned with economic diplomacy believed that the high tariffs, currency instability, and autarky which so many nations had practiced during the 1930s had set the stage for global depression and war."[2]

As the war ended, Europe and Japan were flat on their backs economically, and world trade had largely dried up. Policymakers felt that barriers to trade with America's allies had to be reduced to help jumpstart economic growth. At the conference in Bretton Woods, New Hampshire, in July 1944, the postwar planners recognized the need for expanded trade, and they envisioned an organization to oversee the trade system. In the words of Cordell Hull, U.S. secretary of state at the time of the Bretton Woods conference, "Unhampered trade dovetailed with peace; high tariffs, trade barriers, and unfair economic competi-

---

1. It should be noted that scholars disagree about the extent to which the Tariff Act of 1930 raised tariffs and contributed to the Depression.
2. Robert A. Pollard and Samuel F. Wells Jr., "1945–1960: The Era of American Economic Hegemony," in *Economics and World Power*, edited by William Becker and Samuel F. Wells Jr. (New York: Columbia University Press, 1984), 334–35.

tion, with war. . . . If we could get a freer flow of trade, . . . so that one country would not be deadly jealous of another and the living standards of all countries might rise, thereby eliminating the economic dissatisfaction that breeds war, we might have a reasonable chance of lasting peace."[3]

To help Europe and Japan recover economically, the United States launched the Marshall Plan in 1948, and by 1952 it had channeled more than $13 billion in aid to Europe. In addition to foreign aid, the United States used trade to spur economic growth in its allies. Presidents Truman and Eisenhower supported five additional GATT trade rounds to reduce tariffs among GATT members.[4] Both presidents saw trade policy as an integral part of U.S. foreign policy. As President Eisenhower wrote in his memoirs, "A legislative matter of utmost importance to our economy and to the conduct of our foreign relations was the extension of the Trade Agreements Act," which provided the authority for the conduct of three of those five trade rounds.[5]

U.S. support for more open trade, of course, did not extend to its commercial dealings with the USSR. In response to Soviet aggression in Europe, President Truman adopted a "containment" strategy in March 1947, which promised to "support free peoples who are resisting attempted subjugation."[6] Under this strategy, the United States and Western Europe created NATO in 1949. And the United States maintained tariffs at their high Smoot-Hawley rates on imports from the Soviet Union and its Warsaw Pact allies.

By the early 1960s, the world had changed. In 1961 and 1962, the United States–USSR Cold War was at one of its hottest points: The Berlin Wall went up in 1961, separating East and West Berlin; the Vietnam situation was escalating; and the October 1962 Cuban missile crisis almost led to a nuclear exchange. And Fidel Castro, who had seized power in Cuba in 1959, was forging constantly closer relations with

3. Cordell Hull, *The Memoirs of Cordell Hull, Volume 1*, edited by Andrew Henry Thomas Berding (New York: Macmillan, 1948), 81.

4. The five trade rounds were Geneva (1947), Annecy (1949), Torquay (1950), Geneva (1956), and Dillon (1960–61).

5. Dwight D. Eisenhower, *Mandate for Change, The White House Years, 1953–1956* (New York: Doubleday, 1963), 208.

6. "President Harry S. Truman's Address Before a Joint Session of Congress, March 12, 1947," last modified 2008, Yale Law School, Avalon Project, http://avalon .law.yale.edu/20th_centure/trudoc.asp.

Moscow and challenging the United States throughout Central and South America.

At the same time, Europe had regained significant economic strength. The European Economic Community (EEC) was in the process of establishing a customs union between Belgium, France, Germany, Italy, Luxembourg, and the Netherlands, and by 1962 it had established a highly protectionist Common Agricultural Policy that discriminated against American farm exports. Furthermore, the United Kingdom, Denmark, Ireland, and Norway were in an initial process of seeking membership in the EEC. From the beginning of the postwar period, the United States had supported formation of the EEC and had seen it as a bulwark against the Soviet Union. Now, however, the United States faced a potentially severe economic challenge as Europe moved to a customs union with high duties on imports of U.S. products, while European firms traded in the large, tariff-free EEC market.

Arizona congressman Morris Udall expressed this dilemma succinctly:

> I am convinced that the success of the Common Market has been one of the greatest disappointments the Communists have suffered in post-war years. The Kremlin's plan for world domination called for the capitalist economies of Europe to stagnate and, eventually, to collapse. . . . Today, Khrushchev sees the Common Market and its expansion as the most formidable barrier to communism, not because it is directed against the Soviet Union but because it strengthens the whole Free World. . . . But while economic integration represents new sources of strength for the Atlantic Alliance, the keystone of our Cold War strategy, the Common Market also has within it a potential for divisive economic rivalry. The heart of the matter lies in the fact that, while tearing down tariff walls against goods exchanged among themselves, Europeans are preserving barriers against the goods of outsiders, including ourselves.[7]

To reconcile the competing U.S. commercial and foreign policy interests, President Kennedy sought and obtained new legislation, the Trade Expansion Act of 1962, which provided the authority for negotiation of

7. See the report by Congressman Morris K. Udall: "The Trade Expansion Act of 1962: A Bold New Instrument of American Policy," University of Arizona, http://www.library.arizona.edu/exhibits/udall/congrept/87th/620517.html.

the Kennedy Round from 1964 to 1967. The intent of this legislation was to support the continued integration of Europe as a shield against the spread of communism, while reducing the commercial impact by negotiating reductions in the external tariffs imposed by the EEC and thereby reducing the margin of preference U.S. exporters would have to overcome to sell in Europe.

Foreign policy objectives were explicit in the 1962 Trade Expansion Act. The purposes of that act, which were to be achieved "through trade agreements affording mutual trade benefits," were

1. "to stimulate the economic growth of the United States and maintain and enlarge foreign markets for the products of United States agriculture, industry, mining, and commerce;
2. to strengthen economic relations with foreign countries through the development of open and nondiscriminatory trading in the free world; and
3. to prevent communist economic penetration."[8]

In signing the act on October 11, 1962, President Kennedy said, "A vital expanding economy in the free world is a strong counter to the threat of the world communist movement. This act is, therefore, an important new weapon to advance the cause of freedom."[9]

And in light of Castro's challenge to the rest of Latin America, President Kennedy noted that "we're particularly concerned that the countries of Latin America shall have an opportunity to participate in this period of economic growth particularly as it affects the Common Market as well as our own United States. We will use the specific authorities designed to widen markets for the raw materials and manufactures of the less-developed nations whose economic growth is so important to us all and to strengthen our efforts to end discriminatory and preferential arrangements which in the long run can only make everyone poorer and the free world less united."[10]

By the early 1970s, commercial concerns had risen to the forefront. In 1971, for the first time since the end of World War II, the U.S. trade bal-

8. Public Law 87-794, Oct. 11, 1962, Sec. 102, Statement of Purposes.
9. John F. Kennedy, "Remarks upon Signing the Trade Expansion Act," Executive Office of the President, October 11, 1962, http://www.jfklink.com/speeches/jfk/publicpapers/1962/jfk449_62.html.
10. Ibid.

ance in goods shifted into deficit, the labor movement moved from supporting free trade to concerns with job displacement, and a number of industries faced greater competition in world markets. In this phase, which lasted until the 9/11 terrorist attacks, the United States continued to seek trade liberalization and believed that expanded trade promoted its own economic growth. In the two multilateral trade rounds of this period, the Tokyo Round and the Uruguay Round, commercial interests dominated the U.S. negotiating approach, although foreign policy interests were still relevant and the secretary of state could be counted on to testify in support of the negotiations. However, no longer were the trade agreements seen as critical foreign policy tools in which the United States would agree to greater trade liberalization than that of its developed-country trade partners.

Negotiation of the first U.S. postwar FTA with Israel in 1985, however, was primarily driven by foreign policy objectives. Israel was the close U.S. ally in the Middle East, and in 1985 it was facing massive inflation of more than 400 percent a year. An FTA was seen as a way to help stabilize this U.S. ally.

As Edward Hudgins of the Heritage Foundation put it in support of the negotiations, "Israel is America's closest ally in the Middle East, sharing this country's commitment to freedom and democracy, and American opposition to Soviet expansion. An economically strong Israel is better able to defend itself and thus protect both its own and U.S. interests. And its increasing prosperity, assisted by free trade, would provide a powerful example for the citizens of Arab countries who have grown tired of continuing poverty brought on by statist economic policies and military opposition to Israel. Thus a free trade area with Israel would advance the economic and political goals of both countries."[11]

There was also a commercial interest for the United States in negotiating an FTA with Israel. At that time, Israel and the EEC were negotiating an FTA and the United States was concerned that its exporters would be put at a commercial disadvantage. An FTA where U.S. exporters would also have duty-free access to the Israeli market would level the playing field.

Similarly, while the major U.S. objective in negotiating the North American Free Trade Agreement (NAFTA) was commercial, foreign

---

11. Edward Hudgins, "Executive Memorandum 53: The Case for a U.S.-Israel Free Trade Area," Heritage Foundation, May 22, 1984, http://www.heritage.org/ Research/TradeandForeignAid/EM53.cfm.

policy interests were also significant. U.S. policymakers saw an FTA with Mexico as a way to promote democracy and to slow down the flow of illegal immigrants and narcotics into the United States. As President Bill Clinton said in his November 3, 1993, letter to Congress supporting NAFTA, "Our commitment to more free and more fair world trade has encouraged democracy and human rights in nations that trade with us. With the end of the Cold War, and the growing significance of the global economy, trade agreements that lower barriers to American exports rise in importance. The North American Free Trade Agreement is the first trade expansion measure of this new era. . . . NAFTA will also provide strong incentives for cooperation on illegal immigration and drug interdiction."[12]

9/11 and the Resurgence of Foreign Policy Objectives

With the terrorist attacks of September 11, 2001, foreign policy objectives returned to a preeminent role in setting the direction of U.S. policy regarding trade agreements. U.S. policymakers came to see the closed societies in the Middle East as breeding grounds for terrorists, and the belief that democracies made the world safer gained renewed credence. Trade agreements were seen as a potential tool to promote the rule of law and to help U.S. partners in the agreements grow economically and move toward more solid democratic government.

As Secretary of State Condoleezza Rice said, "Then came the attacks of September 11, 2001. As in the aftermath of the attack on Pearl Harbor in 1941, the United States was swept into a fundamentally different world. . . . This new reality has led us to some significant changes in our policy. We recognize that democratic state building is now an urgent component of our national interest. And in the broader Middle East, we recognize that freedom and democracy are the only ideas that can, over time, lead to just and lasting stability."[13]

The Bush administration came to see democracies as more responsible and peaceful than authoritarian governments: "The world has a clear interest in the spread of democratic values, because stable and free na-

12. William Clinton, "Message to the Congress, Transmitting Proposed Legislation to Implement the North American Free Trade Agreement," Executive Office of the President, November 3, 1993.

13. Condoleezza Rice, "Rethinking the National Interest," *Foreign Affairs*, July–August 2008, 2, 3.

tions do not breed the ideologies of murder. They encourage the peaceful pursuit of a better life."[14] The 2006 National Security Strategy of the United States presented democracy promotion in soaring rhetoric: "Because democracies are the most responsible members of the international system, promoting democracy is the most effective long-term measure for strengthening international stability; reducing regional conflicts; countering terrorism and terror-supporting extremism; and extending peace and prosperity."[15]

The administration's National Security Strategy committed to using all political, economic, diplomatic, and other tools "in the cause of ending tyranny and promoting effective democracy." Thirteen specific tools were listed, including "concluding free trade agreements (FTAs) that encourage countries to enhance the rule of law, fight corruption, and further democratic accountability."[16]

Just months after the 9/11 attacks, the administration successfully pressed U.S. trade partners to agree to launch a new round of multilateral trade negotiations. At their November 2001 Ministerial Meeting held in Doha, the members of the World Trade Organization (WTO) agreed to a negotiating mandate that emphasized economic development and particularly the need to ensure that the least-developed countries benefit from expanded trade. From a foreign policy perspective, the United States believed that expanded trade resulting from reductions in trade barriers and distortions would promote economic development, which in turn would advance U.S. interests in promoting democracy and freedom.

However, it was not in the multilateral arena where trade policy became integral to U.S. foreign policy but in the realm of U.S. bilateral and regional FTAs. At the end of 2001, the United States only had bilateral agreements with Israel and Jordan, as well as NAFTA. However, parallel to the launch of the Doha Round, the United States launched negotiations with several countries for bilateral FTAs, and by 2004 the free trade spigot was fully open. First came agreements with Chile and Singapore, then Australia, Morocco, the Central American Free Trade

14. George W. Bush, "Statement of the President," Executive Office of the President, February 26, 2003, 3, http://www.whitehouse.gov/news/releases/2003/02/20030226-11.html.
15. "The National Security Strategy of the United States of America," March 2006, 3, http://www.whitehouse.gov/nsc/nss/2006/.
16. Ibid., 6, 7.

Agreement (CAFTA-DR, including the Dominican Republic), Bahrain, Oman, and Peru.

In its public statements supporting FTAs, including the "letter of intent" to negotiate an agreement, the administration often presented a number of reasons why a specific negotiation would be in the U.S. foreign policy interest. Promoting democracy and American values has been cited for most agreements. For example, in his letter of intent to Congress to enter into an FTA with Costa Rica, El Salvador, Honduras, Guatemala, and Nicaragua, the president stated: "This agreement will write a new page of our history with Central America—one that depicts sustained engagement in support of democracy, peaceful regional integration, economic opportunity, and hope."[17]

Other justifications have included assisting in the "war on terrorism," limiting the flow of narcotics and illegal immigration to the United States, promoting peace in the Middle East, and advancing U.S. objectives of broader regional agreements, including the Middle East Free Trade Area, the Free Trade Area of the Americas, and an Asian-Pacific trade area.

U.S. Trade Agreements and the Promotion of Democracy

Trade agreements can promote democracy in a number of ways. First, in the negotiations for an agreement, U.S. negotiators encourage their counterparts to consult with their private sector—including labor, business, and civil society representatives—and the U.S. Agency for International Development often provides funding to developing countries negotiating with the United States to establish such a consultative system. For many developing countries, this represents their first experience in systematically seeking private-sector input on a major policy issue.

Second, trade agreements are based on the rule of law. The WTO requires countries to notify their tariff schedule and restricts arbitrary increases in duties. Other elements of trade agreements—including intellectual property protection, the imposition of standards, and limitations on subsidies for products and services—are also governed by specific rules. To ensure adherence, both U.S. agreements and the WTO include

17. Available at http://www.whitehouse.gov/news/releases/2004/02/20040220-10 .html.

robust dispute settlement provisions. For some developing countries, a trade agreement represents the first major adoption of laws governing commerce.

Most important, however, advocates of the importance of trade agreements for the promotion of democracy and the prevention of terror argue that trade agreements stimulate economic growth. In "Rethinking the National Interest," Condoleezza Rice says:

> Ultimately, one of the best ways to support the growth of democratic institutions and civil society is to expand free and fair trade and investment. The very process of implementing a trade agreement or a bilateral investment treaty helps to hasten and consolidate democratic development. Legal and political institutions that can enforce property rights are better able to protect human rights and the rule of law. Independent courts that can resolve commercial disputes can better resolve civil and political disputes. The transparency needed to fight corporate corruption makes it harder for political corruption to go unnoticed and unpunished. A rising middle class also creates new centers of social power for political movements and parties. Trade is a divisive issue in our country right now, but we must not forget that it is essential not only for the health of our domestic economy but also for the success of our foreign policy.[18]

U.S. trade representative Robert Zoellick, in testimony on March 5, 2003, before the Senate Finance Committee, compared the post-9/11 policy to that immediately following World War II: "Just as U.S. economic policy after World War II helped establish democracy in Western Europe and Japan, today's free trade agenda will both open new markets for the United States and strengthen fragile democracies in Central and South America, Africa, and Asia."[19]

The Bush administration came to see economic development as a key component in the war on terrorism. Underdeveloped, unstable countries were seen as safe havens for terrorists, and impoverished people were seen as potential recruits for terror organizations. Democracy was seen as providing a peaceful alternative to terrorism for countries to address

---

18. Rice, "Rethinking," 12.
19. "Statement of Robert B. Zoellick, U.S. Trade Representative, before the Committee on Finance, U.S. Senate," March 5, 2003, 19.

grievances. In the Bush administration's view, trade promoted economic development, and economic development promoted democracy. Thus, trade and economic development were keys to the war on terrorism through the promotion of democracy.

Bush's trade representative, Robert Zoellick, put the issue this way: "Trade promotes freedom by supporting the development of the private sector, encouraging the rule of law, spurring economic liberty, and increasing freedom of choice. Trade also services our security interests in the campaign against terrorism by helping to tackle the global challenges of poverty and privation. Poverty does not cause terrorism, but there is little doubt that poor, fragmented societies can become havens in which terrorists can thrive."[20]

In addition to viewing expanded trade as a long-term tool in promoting economic growth and limiting potential havens for terrorists, the administration argued that agreements with countries that supported us in the "war on terror" should be supported. Specifically, this argument was advanced for FTAs with Morocco, Malaysia, and Thailand.

Have the U.S. FTAs been effective in promoting democracy in its trade partners? It is not possible to answer this question at this time by examining U.S. bilateral agreements, because the sample size is small (the United States has FTAs with only twenty countries). Furthermore, most of these agreements are so recent that it is premature to attempt to draw any conclusions of the agreement's impact on democracy (all but four went into effect in 2004 or more recently).

Additionally, the trade agreement with the United States is only one of many factors influencing the extent to which its partner country moves toward or away from democracy. Other factors, such as the geopolitical situation affecting the country, are far more important. Additionally, it is not clear if opening trade contributes to democracy or if a country first moves toward democracy and then opens up its trade system.

Economists and political scientists are split on the role that trade and economic development play in strengthening democracy. Quan Li and Rafael Reuveny conclude that there is a negative relationship between trade openness and democracy, as do Francisco Rodriguez and Dani Rodrik.[21] However, studies by Ernesto Lopez-Cordova and Christopher

20. Ibid., 17.
21. Quan Li and Rafael Reuveny, "Economic Globalization and Democracy: An Empirical Analysis," *British Journal of Political Science* 33 (2003): 29–54; Fran-

Meissner and by Daniel Griswold have found a positive correlation between trade openness and democracy.[22]

Often, economic development can be very destabilizing. As Eva Bellin notes, "Rapid democratization carries with it the danger of tipping deeply divided countries into sectarian civil war, fueling radicalism rather than moderation, and empowering forces that are deeply anti-American. But this is not equally true in every country; in many cases, a process of political opening, properly calibrated, would enhance stability and advance the process of moderation."[23]

The reality is that encouraging democracy requires patience, and the desire for democracy needs to grow from within the country. The United States cannot force democratization on an unwilling partner country. John Sewell, former president of the Overseas Development Council and a scholar at the Woodrow Wilson Center, warns: "The history of Europe and the United States in the 19th and 20th centuries should remind policymakers that achieving stable open markets and open societies was neither easy nor automatic. Indeed, . . . policymakers ignore the links between political and economic reform in countries where neither is established at their peril."[24]

The Middle East

As noted above, the United States implemented a bilateral FTA with Israel in 1985, primarily for foreign policy reasons. Eight years later, in 1993, Israel and the Palestine Liberation Organization signed the Oslo Accords, which were intended to be a framework for future relations between Israel and Palestine; and in 1994, Israel signed a peace treaty with

cisco Rodriguez and Dani Rodrik, *Trade Policy and Economic Growth: A Skeptic's Guide to Cross-National Evidence*, NBER Working Paper W7081 (Cambridge, Mass.: National Bureau of Economic Research, 1999).

22. Ernesto Lopez-Cordova and Christopher Meissner, *The Globalization of Trade and Democracy, 1870–2000*, NBER Working Paper 11117 (Cambridge, Mass.: National Bureau of Economic Research, 2012), http://www.nber.org/papers/w11117; Daniel T. Griswold, "Trading Tyranny for Freedom: How Open Markets Till the Soil for Democracy," Cato Institute, http:cato.org/pubs/tpa/tpa-026.pdf.

23. Eva Bellin, "Democratization and Its Discontents: Should America Push Political Reform in the Middle East?" *Foreign Affairs*, July–August 2008, 112–19, at 119.

24. John Sewell, "The New Realism: Globalization, Development and American National Interests," unpublished paper, August 21, 2004, 6.

Jordan, making that country the second Arab nation after Egypt to recognize the State of Israel. To encourage the peace process, in 1996 the United States amended the Israeli FTA to also provide duty-free treatment to exports from the West Bank, Gaza, and any subsequent Qualified Industrial Zones (QIZ) that might be created in Jordan and Egypt. President Clinton and many members of Congress felt that it was important to promote the peace process by encouraging economic development through expanded trade.

The QIZ program was designed to further Arab-Israeli economic cooperation. Goods produced in a qualified zone in Jordan or Egypt could qualify for duty-free treatment when exported to the United States, provided that they contained input from Israel and included at least 35 percent added value in the QIZ. Jordan immediately implemented the program; and building on this, the United States and Jordan began negotiations for a bilateral FTA. The United States–Jordan FTA was signed on October 24, 2000, setting the stage for Jordan to become the third U.S. FTA after Israel and NAFTA.

Then, following the terrorist attacks of September 11, 2001, and as part of the "war on terror," President Bush announced the Middle East Free Trade Initiative in May 2003, with the objective of bringing the Middle Eastern countries into the global economy as an important foundation for promoting peace in the region. Because the Middle Eastern countries are at various stages of integration into the global economy, the initiative envisioned several graduated steps for Middle Eastern nations to increase trade and investment.[25] The first step in this plan was to encourage and assist Middle Eastern countries that are not currently members of the WTO to become members; the announced focus here was on Lebanon, Algeria, and Yemen. The second step was to have bilateral investment treaties and trade and investment framework action plans with interested Middle Eastern countries.[26] Along with this, the United States committed to improve its Generalized System of Preferences to better benefit Middle Eastern countries.

25. USTR, press release, http://www.ustr.gov/Trade_Agreements/Regional/MEFTA/Section_Index.html.

26. As of February 2, 2012, the United States has bilateral investment treaties, which are designed to protect private investment and promote market-oriented policies, with forty countries. The United States has trade and investment framework agreements with thirty-nine countries, and these provide an avenue for mutual and regular discussions of trade and investment issues.

The final step would be to negotiate bilateral FTAs with the Middle Eastern countries, leading to the creation of a Middle East Free Trade Area (MEFTA) by 2013. These agreements would build on the FTAs that the United States already had with Israel and Jordan at that time. U.S. policymakers envisioned that these agreements might come in clusters, perhaps with the countries of the Maghreb and with the Gulf Cooperation Council, and that these might then be joined into the full MEFTA.[27]

A White House fact sheet describing this initiative quotes President Bush as stating: "Across the globe, free markets and trade have helped defeat poverty, and taught men and women the habits of liberty. So I propose the establishment of a United States–Middle East free trade area within a decade."[28] In a May 2003 Commencement Address at the University of South Carolina, he added: "In an age of global terror and weapons of mass destruction what happens in the Middle East greatly matters to America. The bitterness of that region can bring violence and suffering to our own cities. The advance of freedom and peace in the Middle East would drain this bitterness and increase our own security."[29]

Morocco became the first Middle Eastern country to complete a free trade area negotiation with the United States as part of the MEFTA strategy, and the agreement was implemented on January 1, 2006. Negotiations between the United States and Morocco were launched in 2003, when King Mohammad of Morocco visited President Bush. Morocco was a logical early target, because it was among the first Islamic states to denounce the September 11, 2001, terrorist attacks and declare solidarity with the American people in the war against terrorism. Additionally, Morocco is a relatively stable and liberalizing Arab Muslim nation.

Next, the FTA with Bahrain was implemented in August 2006. Again, there were a number of reasons for negotiating an agreement with Bahrain. Bahrain and the United States signed a Defense Cooperation Agreement in October 1991, granting U.S. forces access to Bahraini facilities, and Bahrain was the headquarters of the U.S. Navy's Fifth Fleet.

27. The Maghreb countries are generally considered to include Algeria, Morocco, and Tunisia, and the Gulf Cooperation Council countries are Bahrain, Kuwait, Oman, Qatar, Saudi Arabia, and UAE.
28. "Proposed Middle East Initiatives," White House Fact Sheet, May 9, 2003.
29. "Remarks by President Bush at the Commencement Address at the University of South Carolina," May 9, 2003.

An FTA with Oman was signed in January 2006. Like Bahrain, there were important defense reasons to select Oman as a trade partner; for example, Oman hosts three Air Force pre-positioning sites, and Omani airbases have been essential to the U.S. efforts in both Iraq and Afghanistan.

The United States also entered into negotiations for a free trade area with the United Arab Emirates (UAE), and again there were important reasons for the UAE to be an early target for an FTA. The UAE is a significant military ally of the United States; in 2006, U.S. naval vessels made more than 600 visits to UAE ports, more than to any other country outside the United States. The FTA negotiations, however, were not successful, primarily because the UAE was unwilling to open its services and oil sector to 100 percent foreign ownership, as demanded by the United States. This issue was not a stumbling block with Oman and Bahrain, primarily because the oil sector is less important in those countries and because those countries were already more open to foreign ownership.

The United States had also considered negotiating an FTA with Egypt. As a first step, in December 2004 the United States and Egypt signed an agreement to create QIZs that would allow for duty-free export to the United States of Egyptian goods that contained Israeli inputs. In announcing this agreement, the U.S. trade representative, Robert Zoellick, described it as "a concrete, practical result of President Bush's plan to promote closer U.S. trade ties with the Middle East so as to strengthen development, openness, and peaceful economic links between Israel and its neighbors."[30]

However, in 2005 parliamentary elections the opposition party made an unexpectedly strong showing. Egyptian president Hosni Mubarek then postponed the next scheduled elections for two years and imprisoned the opposition presidential candidate, Ayman Nour. As a consequence, the United States dropped efforts to negotiate an FTA with Egypt.

The concept of a Middle East Free Trade Area actually has extensive roots in the Arab world. In 1997, the seventeen members of the Arab League agreed on a project to create a Greater Arab Free Trade Area (GAFTA). The seventeen GAFTA countries are slightly different from

---

30. USTR, press release, December 10, 2004, http://www.ustr.gov/about-us/press-office/press-releases/archives/2004/december/united-states-egypt-and-isreal-launch-hi.

the MEFTA proposed by the Bush administration, as can be seen in table 5.1. GAFTA would include Sudan, which MEFTA would not, and MEFTA would include Algeria, Cyprus, and Israel, which would not be in GAFTA.

The Arab League has made some progress in forming GAFTA, but substantial trade barriers to intraregional trade remain. Reducing these trade barriers in the Middle East could be important, because intraregional trade currently is minimal; only 7.6 percent of overall exports are within the region, even less than the intraregional trade in Africa.[31] Obviously, the fact that many Middle Eastern countries concentrate on oil production that is exported to the developed countries is a cause of the low level of intraregional trade, but another major factor is the high level of trade barriers to intraregional trade still maintained by each country.

The Americas

Achieving a free trade area of the Americas has been a U.S. objective at least since President George H. W. Bush announced the Enterprise of the Americas Initiative in June 1990.[32] To expand trade, he announced that the United States "stands ready to enter into free trade agreements with other markets in Latin America and the Caribbean. . . . We look forward to the day when not only are the Americas the first fully free, democratic hemisphere but when all are equal partners in a free trade zone stretching from the port of Anchorage to the Tierra del Fuego."[33]

31. Bessma Momani, "A Middle East Free Trade Area: Economic Interdependence and Peace Considered," *World Economy* 30, no. 11 (November 2007): 1682–1700.

32. U.S. concerns with South and Central America, of course, go back at least to President Monroe's 1823 address to Congress, when he warned European powers not to interfere in the affairs of the newly independent Latin American states. More recently, prior to the fall of the Berlin Wall, U.S. interests in South and Central America centered on containing communism. In 1961, President Kennedy announced the Alliance for Progress to establish economic cooperation between North and South America. The ten-year plan "to build a hemisphere where all men can hope for a suitable standard of living and all can live out their lives in dignity and in freedom" was intended to counter the emerging communist threat from Cuba. Though the Alliance for Progress did not envision trade liberalization, it did call for a substantial increase in U.S. foreign aid, which unfortunately was not forthcoming as the Vietnam War heated up.

33. President Bush's remarks are available at http://www.presidency.ucsb.edu/ws/index.php?pid=18644.

Table 5.1. Proposed MEFTA and GAFTA Memberships

Country	MEFTA	GAFTA	WTO
Algeria*	Yes	No	Nonmember
Bahrain	Yes	Yes	Member
Cyprus	Yes	No	Member
Egypt	Yes	Yes	Member
Iran	Yes	No	Nonmember
Iraq	Yes	Yes	Observer
Israel	Yes	No	Member
Jordan	Yes	Yes	Member
Kuwait	Yes	Yes	Member
Lebanon*	Yes	Yes	Negotiating accession
Libya	Yes	Yes	Negotiating accession
Morocco	Yes	Yes	Member
Oman	Yes	Yes	Member
Palestine**	Yes	Yes	Observer
Qatar	Yes	Yes	Member
Saudi Arabia	Yes	Yes	Member
Sudan	No	Yes	Negotiating accession
Syria	Yes	Yes	Nonmember
Tunisia	Yes	Yes	Member
Yemen*	Yes	Yes	Negotiating accession
UAE	Yes	Yes	Member

Note: MEFTA = Middle East Free Trade Area; GAFTA = Greater Arab Free Trade Area.
* The United States is supporting WTO membership.
** The Palestine Authority participates in the United States–Israel FTA.
Sources: For MEFTA, http//www.accessmylibrary.com/coms2/summary_0286-18446067_ITM; for GAFTA, http://www.mit.gov.jo/Default.aspx?tabid=732; for WTO, http://www.wto.org/english/thewto_e/whatis_e/tif_e/org6_e.htm.

Actual negotiations to construct a Free Trade Area of the Americas (FTAA) were subsequently launched at the First Summit of the Americas held in Miami in December 1994. The objective of these negotiations was to eliminate barriers to trade and investment among the thirty-four democracies in the Americas. In their Declaration of Principles, the heads of state of the participating countries said that "free trade and increased economic integration are key factors for raising standards of living, improving the working conditions of people in the Americas and better protecting the environment."[34]

U.S. trade negotiators saw an FTAA both in commercial and in foreign policy terms. In his letter of intent to negotiate the trade agreement,

34. Declaration of Principles, http://www.ftaa-alca.org/summits/miami/declara_e.asp.

U.S. trade representative Robert Zoellick said: "By reducing and then eliminating hemispheric trade barriers, the FTAA will provide substantial and growing foreign markets for U.S. goods and services. The FTAA agreement will also strengthen the rule of law, solidify economic reform throughout the hemisphere, and reinforce the democratic principles that unite FTAA countries."[35]

All countries in South, Central, and North America were participants in the FTAA negotiations except Cuba, which was considered by the United States to be the only nondemocratic nation in the Americas. Logically, of course, if trade promotes economic growth and this in turn promotes democracy, it would have made sense to include Cuba in the proposed FTAA. However, U.S. negotiators no doubt felt that this would place too great a political burden on the negotiations. The United States has maintained an economic, commercial, and financial embargo against Cuba since 1962, when Congress passed the "Cuban Democracy Act" with the stated purpose of promoting democracy in Cuba. By 1994, of course, it was clear that the approach of embargoing trade had failed to promote democracy in Cuba. However, opponents of opening up trade with Cuba had substantial political clout, and they would have greatly complicated the negotiations.

To achieve an FTAA, the Bush administration pursued a two-pronged strategy, with the first prong being direct negotiations among the thirty-four North and South American democracies. Parallel to this, the United States also sought to negotiate FTAs with individual countries in the Americas "to create competition among countries for liberalization in the Western Hemisphere, thus furthering our efforts to establish a Free Trade Area of the Americas."[36] This strategy, originally called "competitive liberalization" and later "complementary liberalization," was also pursued in other regions to generate pressure for other regional agreements as well as to successfully conclude the multilateral Doha Round. Interest in generating momentum for the FTAA was specifically stated as a U.S. objective in negotiations with Chile, the Dominican Republic, Bolivia, Colombia, Ecuador, Peru, and Panama.

35. "Letter of Intent to Negotiate a Free Trade Area of the Americas from the USTR Robert Zoellick," October 1, 2002, http://www.ustr.gov/assets/Document_Library/Press_Releases/2002/October/asset_upload_file166_1908.pdf.

36. "Letter of Intent to Negotiate an FTA with Chile, from Robert Zoellick," October 1, 2002.

Negotiations for the FTAA were far advanced by April 2001, when the Summit of the Americas was held in Quebec. The thirty-four nations participating in the negotiations were negotiating in nine separate groups: market access, agriculture, services, investment, intellectual property rights, government procurement, subsidies and antidumping, competition policy, and dispute settlement. In February 2003, the United States made a far-reaching offer to eliminate duties and open up trade, and the outlook for the negotiations looked promising.

However, by the time of the fourth summit held in 2005, it was becoming clear that negotiations were at an impasse. In the Summit Declaration, the difference in view between the countries was apparent, as some members called for continued negotiations, while "other member states maintain that the necessary conditions are not yet in place for achieving a balanced and equitable free trade agreement with effective access to markets free from subsidies and trade-distorting practices."[37]

The primary cause of the impasse was disagreement on handling trade in agricultural products. In particular, Brazil was unwilling to open its market to U.S. goods and services unless the United States limited its agricultural subsidies and reduced its agricultural trade barriers significantly. Both Brazil and the United States recognized that the only way politically the United States could cut agricultural subsidies was in the multilateral Doha Round, where all countries, and particularly the EU, would also reduce their subsidies. Accordingly, it was clear at that time that further progress on the FTAA would have to wait for progress in the Doha negotiations.

A minor factor in the collapse of the FTAA negotiations was the growing influence of Venezuela's Hugo Chávez, who had long been a critic of the FTAA, which he saw as an extension of U.S. imperialism. In place of the FTAA, Chávez advocated the Bolivarian Alternative for the Americas (Bolivariana para los Pueblos de Nuestra América), which was based on a socialist model and had been launched in 2004 by Cuba and Venezuela. At the 2005 summit, Chavez organized a countermeeting which he called the "Summit of the People."

In the face of the FTAA impasse, the United States redoubled its focus on bilateral FTA negotiations already under way in the Americas. In

37. "Summit Declaration," http://www.summit-americas.org/Documents%20 for%20Argentina%20Summit%202005/IV%20Summit/Declaracion/Declaracion% 20IV%20Cumbre-eng%20nov5%209pm%20rev.1.pdf.

November 2003, the U.S. trade representative had notified Congress of his intent to negotiate agreements with Columbia, Peru, Ecuador, and Bolivia, which were members of the Andean Pact, along with Venezuela. (Venezuela announced its intent to pull out of the Andean Pact in 2006.) In addition to gaining access for U.S. exporters, the letter of intent noted that an FTA with the Andean countries would "enhance our efforts to strengthen democracy," "advance our goals of helping the Andean countries to combat narcotrafficking," and "lend momentum to concluding the Free Trade Area of the Americas."[38]

The Office of the U.S. Trade Representative (USTR) also notified Congress of the intent to negotiate with Panama in November 2003. Stated reasons were that an "FTA with Panama will contribute to our efforts to strengthen democracy and support for fundamental values throughout the region. . . . Panama is a valued partner in the achievement of other important U.S. interests as well, including the fight against narcotrafficking, terrorism, and money laundering. Indeed, an FTA will serve to strengthen not only economic ties but also political and security ones."[39]

In February 2004, the USTR had notified Congress of his intent to negotiate agreements with Costa Rica, El Salvador, Honduras, Guatemala, Nicaragua, and the Dominican Republic. A Department of State press release described these agreements as being "about much more than trade." "U.S. security is connected to development in the hemisphere. Criminal gangs, drug trafficking, even trafficking in persons create dangerous transnational networks. The CAFTA-DR offers a way to treat the cause of the problem, rather than just the symptoms."[40]

Asia

Foreign policy objectives are not as important in shaping U.S. FTA negotiations with Asian countries as was the case for its Middle Eastern agreements. The impetus for its trade agreements with the Asian countries is primarily to promote its commercial interests.

38. Letter to the Senate from the U.S. trade representative, Robert Zoellick, November 18, 2003.
39. Ibid.
40. U.S. Department of State, "CAFTA-DR: Strengthening Freedom, Democracy, and Security," press release [n.d.].

In October 2002, President Bush announced the Enterprise for ASEAN Initiative, which set out the U.S. objective of entering into FTAs with the individual member countries of the Association of Southeast Asian Nations (ASEAN) that are also members of the WTO. To date, the United States has negotiated an FTA with Singapore and had been in negotiations for an FTA with Malaysia and Thailand. The letter of intent to negotiate with Singapore does not mention any foreign policy objectives, whereas the letters of intent to negotiate with Malaysia and Thailand only briefly note that the countries have been partners in the global war on terrorism.

The letter of intent to negotiate an agreement with Australia notes that the agreement would "further deepen the ties between our societies and strengthen the foundation of our security alliance."[41] The letter of intent for South Korea also emphasizes commercial interests, but notes that "we are partners in the global war on terrorism, and the extensive ties between the U.S. and Korean armed forces bolster U.S. strategic interests in the region."[42]

U.S. insistence on including the investor-state dispute settlement provisions created problems for both the Australian and South Korean negotiations. Australia refused to include these provisions in the U.S.-Australian FTA. The South Korean negotiators resisted their inclusion but finally agreed. However, when the government sought approval of the agreement from the South Korean Parliament, the opposition party refused to support the agreement unless the investor-state dispute settlement provisions were removed, and the government ultimately had to ram the agreement through on a straight party-line vote.

U.S. negotiations for a Trans-Pacific Partnership (TPP) agreement do have an extremely important foreign policy aspect. China represents the major geopolitical challenge for the United States today, and China's neomercantilist policies are damaging the U.S. economy. The United States needs to find a way to persuade China to adopt economic policies that do not injure its trade partners, and a successful TPP that limits the scope for neomercantilist policies could be important in this regard. If

41. Letter from Robert B. Zoellick, U.S. trade representative, "Intent to Initiate Free Trade Negotiations with Australia," to U.S. House of Representatives, November 13, 2002.

42. "U.S. Trade Representative Letter to Hon. Ted Stevens, President Pro Tempore, U.S. Senate, on 'Free Trade Agreement—Republic of Korea,'" *Congressional Record* 152, no. 11 (February 2, 2006): S504.

the TPP has been constructed to limit potential damage from neomercantilist policies, this could be an approach to encourage China to end its beggar-thy-neighbor policies and refocus its economic policies on domestic consumption rather than exports.

Conclusion

Trade agreements were seen as an important foreign policy tool immediately after World War II and again after the terrorist attacks of September 11, 2001. After 9/11, U.S. policymakers came to believe that promoting democracy and economic development were important in the "war on terror" and that trade agreements were an important tool for promoting democracy and development.

The argument that a properly constructed trade agreement can promote democracy does seem to have some merit. A trade agreement can promote a greater reliance on the rule of law and greater private-sector involvement in policy; a trade agreement can also encourage economic growth, which many feel is important if a country is to become more democratic. There are many more direct tools for promoting democracy than trade agreements, of course, such as foreign assistance to civil society groups working for democracy, sanctions against countries that rig elections, and public condemnation of nondemocratic acts, but the impact of a trade agreement would seem to be more long term than these other tools.

If U.S. trade agreements are to be an effective foreign policy tool, however, the United States should be prepared to be more flexible in the future, rather than insisting on a one-size-fits-all model. Its demands to include the investor-state dispute mechanism complicated negotiations with a number of countries, and insisting on full investment access was a nonstarter with the UAE.

Today, negotiations for the TPP have important foreign policy implications. China's neomercantilist trade policies are a threat to the stability of the world trade system. The United States needs to address these policies, but it must do so in a way that does not make China an enemy. If a successful TPP agreement can be negotiated that closes the loopholes in the current trade rules—particularly regarding currency manipulation, state-owned enterprises, and forced technology transfer—and attracts other countries to join, it could be an important mechanism to encourage China to change its approach. The long-term objective of the TPP negotiations needs to be the creation of a broad agreement that other countries belonging to the Asia-Pacific Economic Cooperation forum—such as China, South Korea, and Indonesia—will want to join.

Promoting the economic development of U.S. trade partners is critical to assisting in a gradual strengthening of democratic forces and to achieving other U.S. objectives, such as curbing illegal immigration and narcotics flows to the United States. Therefore, it is imperative that agreements negotiated for foreign policy reasons be constructed to support economic development in U.S. trade partners. This issue is considered in the next chapter.

Chapter 6

Economic Development:
A Missed Opportunity

U.S. policymakers have long argued that helping poor countries develop economically is not only the moral thing to do but that it is also in the U.S. national interest, assuming that those poor countries are not antagonistic to U.S. security. As poor countries grow, they become bigger markets for U.S. exports, and economic growth may strengthen democracy and make these countries less likely to provide safe havens for terrorists.

Economic theories regarding the role of trade and development have changed over the past fifty years, although U.S. policymakers today generally argue that improving access to the U.S. market for poor countries can be an important tool to help them develop, and that these countries can also help themselves by reducing their own barriers to imports and building their capacity to export. To benefit from trade, however, developing countries need to have the right policies and infrastructure.

The General Agreement on Tariffs and Trade's (GATT's) treatment of developing countries also has evolved, becoming progressively more responsive to developing countries' concerns. The World Trade Organization (WTO), which was launched in 1995 as a result of the Uruguay Round, promoted developing-country interests in some respects, but in others greatly exacerbated the developed country / developing country divide. The latest round of multilateral trade negotiations, the Doha Round, was launched with great fanfare as a "development" round in the wake of the terrorist attacks on September 11, 2001. The reality, however, is that developed-country negotiators approached the actual negotiations as a traditional trade round.

A number of U.S. free trade agreements (FTAs) with developing countries were undertaken for foreign policy reasons. So that the United States can fulfill its foreign policy objectives, it is critical that these agreements help to promote economic development in America's developing-country partners; however, U.S. agreements include features that may have a negative impact on development in U.S. partner countries.

The role of economic development in U.S. trade policy took on increased significance in the wake of the September 11, 2001, terrorist attacks on the United States, as noted in chapter 5. After 9/11, policymakers argued that impoverished nations could be havens for terrorists and could be breeding grounds for dissatisfaction and potential new terrorists. And they believed that economic development would help create more democratic governments.

Trade expansion was seen as an important tool to promote economic development, and the rules in trade agreements were seen as useful in promoting the rule of law in developing countries. Accordingly, promoting economic development became an important objective of the U.S. trade agreements program.

From a commercial perspective, it is also in the long-run interest of the United States for poor countries to develop economically. Poor countries cannot afford to buy many U.S. products, such as Boeing aircraft or Ford cars. As developing countries become prosperous, however, U.S. exporters find new and growing markets.

After 9/11 the United States pushed trade agreements as a tool for economic development, both in U.S. bilateral FTAs and in the WTO. Bilateral and regional negotiations were launched with a number of poor countries in the Americas, the Middle East, and Africa, and the United States pressed for a new round of multilateral trade negotiations in the WTO. This new round was launched in November 2011, with a vow by WTO members "to make positive efforts designed to ensure that developing countries, and especially the least-developed among them, secure a share in the growth of world trade commensurate with the needs of their economic development."[1] The round was dubbed the Doha Development Round.

---

1. WTO Ministerial Declaration, November 2001, paragraph 2, http://www.wto .org/english/thewto_e/minist_e/min01_e/mindecl_e.htm.

Changing Theories of Trade and Development

Economic theories regarding how trade policy can promote development have changed radically over the past fifty years, as have the actual practices of developing countries. To a significant extent, trade theory has driven policies adopted by newly independent countries, and to a significant extent the actual real world results of different trade policies have then shaped economic theory.

In the early 1960s and the 1970s, as Europe's former colonies gained their independence, the dominant view among economists was that the best way to promote economic development was through a policy of *import substitution*, which called for high trade barriers, often coupled with subsidies and preferred treatment for domestic industries. One of the most well-known advocates of this policy was Raul Prebisch, an influential Argentine economist. Although Prebisch was mainly focused on how to best promote economic development in Latin America, African nations largely adopted this approach as they gained their independence.

The import substitution approach built on the "infant industry" theory developed by Friedrich List, a nineteenth-century German. This theory held that industries must be protected in their early years when they are weak and unformed and would not be able to survive if exposed to strong international competition. (In fact, both the United States and Germany followed this model in protecting their infant industries against British competition in the nineteenth century, and Japan followed it in the postwar years.)

This approach, of course, is fundamentally different from the policies that are implied by David Ricardo's theory of comparative advantage. Under Ricardo's approach, a country would produce those products where it had a comparative advantage, and for developing countries, by and large, this would be primary products for export to the developed countries. Under import substitution policies, however, countries would seek to move up the value chain by protecting targeted industries until they could compete in world markets.

Although this approach had worked for Germany and the United States and most recently for Japan, it did not work well for African and smaller Latin American nations in the 1970s and 1980s. To be successful, a country needs to be big enough to generate the economies of scale needed for many industries, such as steel or automobiles, to become globally competitive. Second, it requires a government that can identify industries that have the potential to become competitive and to ensure that industries do not come to rely on permanent protection.

All these problems plagued the newly independent African countries, which were generally small nations with corrupt governments. Prebisch himself came to the view that import substitution was the wrong approach; when he was appointed to head the United Nations Conference on Trade and Development in the 1960s, he advocated that small countries seek to expand their market size through regional integration. He also pushed for special trade preferences by the developed countries that could help developing nations gain market opportunities to allow for economies of scale, and in 1971 the GATT did authorize these special preference schemes for developing countries.

By 1980, it was becoming increasingly clear that import substitution was not working for Latin America. Nancy Birdsall, Augusto de la Torre, and Felipe Valencia Caicedo characterized this period as "the dark side of inward-looking industrialization, . . . [which] was manifested in a well-known catalog of maladies. These included internationally uncompetitive industries; severely distorted relative prices leading to inefficient allocation of resources; rent-seeking and corruption in the administered allocation or rationing of credit, fiscal, and foreign exchange resources; bottlenecks and economic overheating; large public deficits; excessive foreign borrowing by Latin sovereigns; rising and unstable inflation (and actual hyperinflation in several countries)."[2]

During this same period, South Korea, Taiwan, Hong Kong, and Singapore—the so-called Asian Tigers—were growing rapidly by focusing on global markets. These economies all concentrated on export markets and became export powerhouses. However, their import policies were radically different. South Korea and Taiwan pursued protectionist import policies, following the path set out by Japan several decades earlier. However, Hong Kong and Singapore pursued the opposite strategy and reduced their barriers to imports, and they became two of the most open markets in the world.

In the 1980s and 1990s, India and China both shifted to a more outward-looking development strategy. However, both continued to have high import barriers and only began to reduce import barriers after

---

2. Nancy Birdsall, Augusto de la Torre, and Felipe Valencia Caicedo, *The Washington Consensus: Assessing a Damaged Brand*, Working Paper 213 (Washington, D.C.: Center for Global Development, 2010), 4.

high growth rates had been achieved. In addition to a high level of import barriers, China maintained—and still maintains—a sharply undervalued currency (an undervalued currency acts as both an import barrier and an export subsidy). This was the same model Japan followed until the mid-1980s and, like Japan before it, China accumulated a massive trade surplus.

The Washington Consensus

As a result of the success of the Asian Tigers in focusing on global markets and the relatively sluggish Latin America performance, economic thinking more and more turned to reliance on market forces to promote economic development and away from state control. The 1989 fall of the Iron Curtain seemed to symbolize the weaknesses of state planning and the strength of market-driven systems.

In 1989, John Williamson, an economist at the Institute for International Economics, outlined a "Decalogue" of policy principles that emphasized reliance on markets, such as privatizing state enterprises, abolishing regulations that restrict competition, establishing property rights, removing barriers to foreign direct investment, and reforming tax systems to broaden the tax base along with moderate marginal tax rates. With regard to trade policy, Williamson advocated replacing quantitative restrictions with tariffs, and then progressively reducing these to a uniform range of around 10 percent. He posed an exception to this in noting that it may be good policy to provide substantial but temporary import protection to infant industries to allow them to develop economies of scale. He dubbed these ten policy measures the "Washington Consensus."

In the 1990s, many Latin American countries implemented these recommendations, removing import quotas and reducing tariffs from nearly 50 percent in the early 1980s to around 10 percent by 1999. A group of African countries have also been pursuing a strategy along the lines suggested by Williamson. Steven Radelet of the U.S. Agency for International Development has identified seventeen African countries that have adopted this strategy to varying degrees and have been experiencing solid annual growth of more than 3.2 percent since 1996; Radelet dubbed these countries the African "Cheetahs."[3] The Cheetahs have

3. The seventeen Cheetahs are Botswana, Burkina Faso, Cape Verde, Ethiopia, Ghana, Lesotho, Mali, Mauritius, Mozambique, Namibia, Rwanda, São Tomé and

seen their trade double, while education, health, and the distribution of income have all improved. Seven of these countries apply an average tariff on manufactured goods of 10 percent or less, and the rest have average tariffs of 10 to 20 percent (data are not available for São Tomé).[4]

Over the fifteen years after Williamson articulated the Washington Consensus, however, the International Monetary Fund and a number of economists took these ideas to the extreme. The IMF required developing countries to sharply reduce tariffs in a very short time period as a condition for receiving an IMF loan. This produced a sharp backlash, as these countries were generally dependent on customs revenues for financing the government, and as their weak domestic industries faltered under sudden international competition.[5] Additionally, given the experience of some countries in achieving rapid growth through aggressive export promotion coupled with import protection, questions began to be raised about the Washington Consensus.

Today, almost all economists agree that policies to promote exports are important to economic development. Exporters need to compete with the best foreign firms, and this forces them to be efficient, and export earnings pay for financing the importing of needed raw materials and intermediate goods. Additionally, exporting can help firms in small countries gain economies of scale.

As noted in chapter 3, however, import policies are more controversial. Advocates of the desirability of reducing import barriers make a number of points. First, tariffs on raw materials and intermediate inputs can raise the costs of manufacturing and can make exporters uncompetitive in world markets. Additionally, tariffs on products not produced in the country raise the costs to consumers, thereby reducing aggregate demand for other products. Advocates of import liberalization point to economies such as Botswana, Hong Kong, Singapore, and Chile that have achieved high growth while sharply reducing import barriers.

Príncipe, the Seychelles, South Africa, Tanzania, Uganda, and Zambia. See Steven Radelet, *Emerging Africa: How 17 Countries Are Leading the Way*, Center for Global Development Report (Washington, D.C.: Brookings Institution Press, 2010).

4. See http://stat.wto.org/TariffProfile/WSDBTariffPFView.aspx?Language=E&Country=BW.

5. Because customs duties are easier to collect than taxes, particularly in countries with a high level of corruption, many developing countries today rely on customs duties for more than one-quarter of their tax revenues. Even the United States relied on tariffs for about half of total government revenue until 1910.

A number of economists, however, argue that reducing barriers to imports is not important for promoting economic growth. For example, Joseph Stiglitz argues that "it is exports—not the removal of trade barriers—that is the driving force of growth. Studies that focus directly on the removal of trade barriers show little relationship between liberalization and growth."[6] Dani Rodrik adds that "the available studies reveal no systematic relationship between a country's average level of tariff and nontariff restrictions and its subsequent economic growth rate. . . . The only systematic relationship is that countries dismantle trade restrictions as they get richer."[7]

Most of the criticisms of the Washington Consensus as it applies to trade policy, however, are not really relevant to Williamson's original formulation. As Rodrik summarizes the view, "Most well-trained economists would agree that the standard policy reforms included in the Washington Consensus have the potential to promote growth. What the experience of the last few decades has shown, however, is that the impact of these reforms is heavily dependent on circumstances."[8]

The U.S. Responsibility in Trade Negotiations

Wealthy nations such as the United States generally have large teams of negotiators who are able to actively participate in all the many issues that are covered in a trade negotiation, and they have staff members back in the capital who can research the implications of all the various proposals. In negotiations with other developed countries, U.S. negotiators can operate on the assumption that their counterparts will work with them to develop agreements that are win-win, where on balance all parties come out with an agreement that they consider to be in their national interest. They can assume that their counterparts understand the issues and how their country will be affected by the different proposals on the table.

Many developing countries, however, have very small negotiating teams and are not able to follow all issues; in fact, sixteen developing

6. Joseph E. Stiglitz, *Making Globalization Work* (New York: W. W. Norton, 2006), 72.

7. Dani Rodrik, *One Economics—Many Recipes: Globalization, Institutions, and Economic Growth* (Princeton, N.J.: Princeton University Press, 2007), 217.

8. Ibid., 56.

countries do not even have a permanent mission at WTO headquarters in Geneva.[9] Additionally, if a developing country does not pay its WTO dues, it is designated "inactive," which means that it does not receive a number of benefits, such as the distribution of documents. In 1997, twenty-three developing countries were so designated; and in 2011, there were still nine such countries.[10]

The reality is that many developing countries are not able to effectively promote their national interests in trade negotiations. More advanced developing countries—such as China, India, and Brazil—of course are totally capable of defending their own interests, and in fact they do so very effectively. However, many developing countries, particularly some of the smaller and poorer African and Latin American countries, cannot adequately advance their own interests in trade negotiations.

As noted, it is generally considered to be in the U.S. national interest that these countries grow and develop economically. In fact, in many cases, the United States explicitly negotiated the agreement to promote its foreign policy interests by promoting economic development. And the Doha Development Round was launched in the belief that over the long run, the developed countries would benefit from helping the poor countries become an active part of global commerce.

So how should the United States approach negotiations with developing countries that do not have the capacity to fully advance their own interests? First, it should seek to ensure that it does them no harm. This requires U.S. negotiators to understand the impact of proposed provisions of trade agreements on poor countries, which are basically in very different circumstances than developed countries. And then it requires U.S. negotiators to recognize these effects in developing their positions, even in cases where it may cost some domestic political support. As we shall see, there are several provisions in the WTO and in U.S. bilateral FTAs that do in fact cause poor countries significant difficulty—or even injury.

Second, there are a number of areas where agreements could be reached that would benefit both U.S. developing-country partners and the country's own commercial interests. These need to be aggressively

9. World Trade Organization, "WTO Organizes 'Geneva Weeks' for Non-resident Delegations," http://www.wto.org/english/tratop_e/devel_e/genwk_e.htm.

10. World Trade Organization, "Minutes of General Council Meeting of February 22, 2011 (WT/GC/M/130)," April 5, 2011, 22.

pursued and brought to closure, and given a higher priority than might be the case if the United States were only focused on its own immediate commercial interests.

Which Are the Developing Countries?

The GATT and now the WTO have never defined what a "developing country" is. Instead, they leave it up to each member to self-designate itself as a developing country if it so chooses. However, a country's self-selection as a developing country is subject to challenge by other contracting parties, and other members may or may not accept that self-designation.

Although there is no WTO definition of "developing country," the WTO is clear as to what a "least-developed country" (LDC) is. The WTO uses the United Nations definition of "least-developed country," which is an annual per capita gross domestic product (GDP) of under $992 based on a three-year average, coupled with a human resource weakness and an economic vulnerability, for inclusion on the list. (If per capita GDP increases to more than $1,190, the country is considered to have "graduated" and is removed from the list of LDCs.) The United Nations lists forty-nine nations as LDCs, of which thirty-four are members of the WTO.[11] Of the forty-nine LDCs, thirty-four are in Africa, fourteen are in Asia, and one is in Latin America.

Although the WTO does not define "developing countries," the World Bank does classify countries based on per capita gross national income (GNI).[12] By the World Bank's definitions, a "low-income developing country" has a per capita GNI of less than $1,025. The World Bank defines a "lower-middle-income" country as one with a per capita GNI of $1,026 to $4,035 and an "upper-income" developing country as one in the range of $4,036 to $12,475. Both lower-middle-income and upper-income countries can be considered to be "developing" countries, along with low-income developing countries not classified as least developed.

11. The United Nations list of least-developed countries is available on the UN Web site at http://www.unohrlls.org/en/ldc/164.
12. The World Bank categorization of countries by development status is available at http://data.worldbank.org/about/country-classifications.

Countries classified as "high-income countries," which have per capita incomes of $12,476 or more annually, can be basically considered to be "developed countries." The 2011 per capita GNI for the United States was $48,620, more than four times as high as the poorest countries in the "high-income" category. The World Bank ranked the United States as the ninth-wealthiest country in 2011, although it was well behind Switzerland, at $76,400, and Norway, at $88,890.

It is important to emphasize, however, that developing countries and LDCs do not all have the same problems or objectives, and this is true for countries in each category of development. Some countries are food exporters, while others cannot produce enough food to satisfy their needs, and some are oil producers with all the advantages and disadvantages that brings. Twenty-five are nations with populations of less than 1 million, while India and China have populations greater than 1.1 billion each. Some are rapidly growing and have clearly embarked on self-sustaining growth, while others are stagnant or even going backward into deeper poverty.

Some of the developing countries—such as Brazil, Russia, India, and China (known as the BRICs)—are commercial powerhouses and have a major impact on world trade. Indeed China and India, both classified as lower-middle-income countries and home to more than half the world's population living on less than $2 a day, nonetheless have a significant impact on the economic situation in the United States. In fact, from an economic development and from a trade policy perspective, every country must be considered based on its own unique conditions.

The Evolution of the Trade System

From its early days, the GATT had been sensitive to the problems of developing countries. In 1954, the members of the GATT added a new article to the agreement that called for special treatment for developing countries.[13] Consistent with economic theory at that time, this article recognized that "countries in the early stages of development" may need to impose import restrictions to facilitate the establishment of an industry.

---

13. This new article, "Governmental Assistance to Economic Development," became Article XVIII of the General Agreement on Tariffs and Trade.

Additionally, it recognized that developing countries may need "to apply quantitative restrictions for balance of payments purposes."

In 1965, the GATT agreed to a new Part IV, titled "Trade and Development," which allowed for *special and differential treatment* of developing countries. One provision noted that the "developed contracting parties do not expect reciprocity for commitments made by them in trade negotiations to reduce or remove tariffs and other barriers to the trade of less-developed contracting parties."

Part IV also called on the developed countries to make positive efforts to remove or reduce barriers to trade in the primary products particularly produced by developing countries. However, the language of Part IV is basically more hortatory than binding. For example, it includes language such as "shall to the fullest extent possible." Nonetheless, it did set the stage for some concrete measures to provide special assistance to developing countries.

In the late 1960s and early 1970s, a number of developed countries implemented special preferences for developing countries in arrangements known as the Generalized System of Preferences. Under these arrangements, the developed countries would accord a reduced tariff or no tariff on the importing of specified products from the developing countries while applying the full most-favored-nation (MFN) tariff to imports of the same product from nonbeneficiary countries. Another measure stimulated by Part IV occurred in 1976 and 1977, when most developed countries eliminated or reduced import barriers on tropical products, such as mangoes and bananas.

In the Tokyo Round, these provisions were carried a step further with the 1979 "Decision on Differential and More Favourable Treatment, Reciprocity, and Fuller Participation of Developing Countries." This decision authorized groups of developing countries to enter into preferential trade arrangements among themselves, without the requirement imposed on free trade areas and customs unions that barriers be eliminated on substantially all items.

In each of the multilateral rounds of trade negotiations under the GATT, the developing countries were not asked to reduce tariffs to the same extent as the developed countries, and they were given longer transition periods to implement tariff reductions. The LDCs were not required to make any concessions. Additionally, only a few developing countries signed on to the codes of conduct on nontariff measures that were negotiated in the Tokyo Round. In addition to granting developing countries preferential access to developed-country markets and to allowing delayed implementation of the rules or tariff concessions, or even permanent exemption from the rules, "special and differential" treatment of the developing countries called for special efforts to assist these countries in implementing GATT commitments, although the amount of such assistance has been small.

The New World of the WTO

When the GATT became the WTO as a result of the Uruguay Round in 1995, however, things changed dramatically. Toward the end of the Uruguay Round, the developed countries pressed for a "single undertaking," which required all WTO members to adhere to all the agreements except government procurement. And under the new WTO binding dispute settlement mechanism, they could be subject to trade sanctions if they did not implement these agreements.

The existing developing-country members were allowed to continue to have significantly higher tariffs than the developed countries, but suddenly they were required to sign on to all the codes. In addition, they were required to sign on to the new agreements negotiated in the Uruguay Round on intellectual property protection, investment, and services. However, the developing countries were given more time to implement the WTO codes than were the developed countries, and the LDCs were given the longest transition periods.

The WTO agreements did have a number of important benefits for the developing countries. First, the developed countries reduced their tariffs by some 30 percent on average, and a number of developing countries have benefited from this, including China and India.

Second, though commitments in the services sector were limited, they still offer potential economic benefits for the developing countries. Many services are labor intensive, and many developing countries have a comparative advantage in low-cost labor and should also be able to benefit from greater access to the developed-country markets.

Opening their own markets in services can also benefit the developing countries. Efficient and productive service industries in such areas as communications, business services, and transportation can promote efficiency throughout the economy, and allowing service providers from other countries to compete in their market can promote efficiency.

However, countries need to consider the overall economic context when they liberalize services trade, including the effectiveness of their regulatory regimes such as their antitrust and tax policies. Some developing countries could easily have problems from an abrupt liberalization of service sectors such as finance and telecommunications without an appropriate regulatory regime in place.

The developing countries can also benefit from adopting many of the rules of the WTO, to which they had not had to adhere under the GATT. For example, one agreement that is in the long-run interest of developing countries is the customs valuation code; traders need to know how products will be valued in crossing borders, and this code provides greater certainty.

The new WTO dispute settlement mechanism can also help the developing countries on some occasions, because they can now pursue disputes in a more legalistic approach, whereas under the GATT system they had little real power to take on a major trade partner. In fact, under the new WTO system, a number of developing countries have won dispute settlement cases against the major developed-country WTO members. And as part of the agreement on dispute settlement, the developed countries, including the United States, agreed to forgo the use of unilateral measures such as "voluntary restraint agreements" to force action by a trade partner.

Unfortunately, however, there are several aspects of the new WTO that have not benefited many of the poorest countries. First, the developing countries believed that they would benefit from improved access to developed-country markets in the textile and apparel areas as a result of the Uruguay Round, which required the developed countries to give up import quotas maintained under the Multi-Fibre Arrangement. Second, they looked to future benefits from the commitment in the Uruguay Round to launch negotiations by 2000 to improve access to developed-country agricultural markets and to reduce developed-country trade-distorting agricultural subsidies.

However, these expected benefits have not materialized. China, which was not a member of the WTO in 1995, has gained the lion's share of the benefits of improved market access to developed-country textile and apparel markets, as well as other labor-intensive product areas. Additionally, expected improved access to developed-country agricultural markets has not occurred, and the developed countries have not made WTO commitments to reduce subsidies to their farmers.

Many of the developing countries had a poor understanding of the implications of the WTO codes for their economies. What they found out was that the implementation of the WTO codes can cost upward of $100 million per country. Although this expense might seem trivial to the developed world, it can represent a significant fraction of a poor country's budget.

TRIPS and Developing Countries

The most expensive of these codes to implement is the Agreement on Trade-Related Intellectual Property (TRIPS); in addition to its expense, the TRIPS agreement has a number of severe negatives from the developing-country perspective. The first major problem developing countries faced was that the new WTO rules made it more difficult to obtain affordable drugs to combat the AIDS epidemic. As described in chapter 2, developed-country negotiators had to agree to establish a procedure whereby small countries could import generics to deal with emergencies in order to gain a consensus to launch the Doha Round.

The developing countries had until 2005 to implement the TRIPS pharmaceutical provisions, and the LDCs have until 2016. This meant that developing countries such as India could produce generic, first-generation AIDS antiretroviral drugs up to 2005. At that time, they were required to have implemented their TRIPS commitments, which meant that they could not manufacture generics of any new antiretroviral drugs developed after that date. This is very significant because these drugs are being constantly improved and countries such as India could not make cheaper generics of these latest versions.

The second major problem for the developing countries caused by the TRIPS agreement is that many of these countries did not have a system for protecting intellectual property in place, and implementing such a system is very expensive. Michael Finger of the World Bank estimates that for some developing countries the costs of implementing a regime to protect intellectual property is greater than the foreign aid they receive annually. As a result, some developing countries have not yet implemented the agreement or have only partially done so. (The World Intellectual Property Organization has provided technical assistance to developing countries to implement the TRIPS agreement, and this can offset the costs to some extent.)

The third problem for the LDCs is that the TRIPS regime does not protect the type of intellectual property found in some developing countries, namely, traditional and indigenous knowledge, such as knowledge of specific plants that have medicinal properties. There have been instances where pharmaceutical companies have come in and taken this traditional knowledge and patented it, making it harder for the developing countries to even use their own knowledge, much less benefit from it.

The Doha Development Round

To help overcome the argument by the developing countries that the Uruguay Round was unbalanced in favor of the developed countries, the new trade round launched at Doha in 2001 was called the "Doha Development Agenda." However, from the beginning some old trade hands were skeptical of this approach of emphasizing economic development in the mandate of a trade round, arguing that the WTO is essentially a trade organization, not a development organization. For example, Jan Woznowski, the former director of the Rules Division in the WTO, says: "The term 'Doha Development Agenda' does not make much sense because it neither reflects all negotiators' real intentions and objectives for the negotiations nor the Doha Declarations' content, nor the negotiating process in the Round. The name DDA is a largely political creature and, in fact, is somewhat misleading."[14]

In fact, U.S. and other developed-country negotiators by and large approached the Doha Development Round as a standard trade round, and primarily sought to promote U.S. commercial interests. Given the need to gain congressional approval for any trade package, the negotiators know that they must have some powerful industries that benefit from any agreement and will be willing to lobby Congress for passage. They also need to minimize the number of industries that are hurt by trade liberalization and that would likely lobby against passage.

Over the twelve years since the Doha Round was launched, negotia-

14. Jan Woznowski, "Anti-Dumping Negotiations in the GATT and the WTO: Some Personal Reflections," in *Opportunities and Obligations: New Perspectives on Global and US Trade Policy*, edited by Terence P. Stewart (Amsterdam: Kluwer Law International, 2009), 94.

tors have produced vast reams of paper outlining various country positions, but unfortunately the gaps between key players seem to be too large to bridge. In particular, the gaps between the developed and developing countries in the critical areas of agriculture and nonagriculture market access have been major stumbling blocks.

The agricultural negotiations have stonewalled over the unwillingness of the United States, the EU, and Japan to substantially reduce their trade barriers and subsidies. Many in the U.S. agricultural community have decided that they like government subsidies, and since 2000 they have been lobbying for larger subsidies, not reduced subsidies, as U.S. trade partners were demanding. In 2002 they pushed a new farm bill through Congress that nearly doubled U.S. farm subsidies, and the 2008 Farm Bill increased these subsidies even further. So U.S. negotiators had limited flexibility and basically only proposed binding current subsidy levels in the Doha Round, and not reducing subsidies as expected following the Uruguay Round.

The developing countries themselves have different views with regard to the elimination of trade-distorting developed-country subsidies for agriculture. The developing countries and regions that export or have the potential to export agricultural products, such as Brazil and the cotton growers in West Africa, want significant reductions in developed-country agricultural subsidies. However, countries that are dependent on food imports because they are unable to produce enough for domestic consumption welcome these subsidies, because they result in lower prices. On balance, however, the developing countries would benefit from the elimination of trade-distorting agricultural subsidies.[15]

In the tariff negotiations on nonagricultural goods, the negotiators have generally agreed on a formula for reducing bound tariff rates. Under this formula, the developed countries would reduce the tariff rates they

15. E.g., William Cline, an economist at the Peterson Institute, says that "concerns about losses for food-importing developing countries have been exaggerated. Most of the world's poor live in countries that are net agricultural exporters. Even most of the least developed countries (with the notable exception of Bangladesh) have a comparative advantage in agricultural goods, and so should benefit rather than lose from a rise in world agricultural prices following industrial country liberalization." William R. Cline, *Trade Policy and Global Poverty* (Washington, D.C.: Peterson Institute for International Economics, 2004), 4.

actually apply, because their bound and applied rates are the same. The developing countries would also reduce their bound rates, but because most of them have applied rates that are much lower than their bound rates, their applied rates would be basically unchanged because the proposed formula does not cut deep enough to impact their applied rates.

U.S. industry views these proposed formula cuts as grossly unfair, because major exporters such as China, India, and Brazil, which already enjoy a trade surplus with the United States, would be gaining market access without any reciprocal benefits to U.S. exporters. To compensate for this problem with the tariff formula approach, U.S. industry has been pressing for duty-free trade in key sectors—including chemicals, paper and forest products, information technology, machinery, and health products—but the developing countries have refused to make deeper cuts in these sectors.

Reductions in developed-country tariffs on nonagricultural goods would benefit those developing countries that have globally competitive industries, such as China, India, and Brazil. However, some of the poorer countries in Africa and Latin America would lose by these tariff reductions, because they currently enjoy duty-free access to the developed-country markets in many products under their FTAs or from developed-country preference schemes such as the African Growth and Opportunity Act (AGOA) and the Generalized System of Preferences.

This means that if the developed countries reduce their MFN tariff rates, the margin of preference currently enjoyed by these countries would be less and their trade would suffer as the more competitive countries like China, India, and Brazil pick up market share. A number of developing countries, such as Mauritius, have been deeply concerned about this potential *erosion of preference margins*, and this has been another impediment to completing the tariff negotiations.

In both the nonagriculture market access and agricultural areas, the developing countries have argued that they need "policy space," that is, room to maneuver in the future if unexpected circumstances arise. The developed countries, conversely, have pressed for firm commitments so that their exporters could be assured that market access commitments would not be undermined in the future.

On July 28, 2008, the negotiations basically collapsed, as noted in chapter 2, although there have since been occasional efforts to craft a Doha deal, and the negotiations have not been officially pronounced as being over. Though the negotiations have not lived up to the name

"Doha *Development* Round," there are two elements that could benefit developing countries, and that might be salvaged in a "small package" at the December 2013 Ministerial Meeting.

The first is an issue called "trade facilitation." The trade facilitation negotiations seek to reduce barriers to trade in the areas of fees and documentation requirements for imports and exports, the publication and administration of trade regulations, and freedom of transit for landlocked countries. If successful, these negotiations could be of benefit to many developing countries, which often have very cumbersome procedures for trade, including requirements for excessive documentation and fees for imports and exports. Landlocked countries have a particular problem because they need trade corridors to ports through other countries that would enable them to efficiently import and export, and these corridors often do not exist.

Some developing countries, such as Mauritius, have made enormous progress in reducing their own barriers to imports and exports and are as efficient as most developed countries. However, most of the LDCs and middle-income developing countries still have a long way to go in improving trade facilitation.

The World Bank has compiled a number of indices to measure the efficiency of trade facilitation, one of which is the Logistics Performance Index.[16] Bernard Hoekman and Alessandro Nicita at the World Bank estimate that "if low-income countries were to converge to a set of policies that would generate the observed average levels of the various indicators in middle-income countries" their imports might increase by some 15.2 percent and their exports by 14.6 percent.[17]

Another area that could benefit the developing countries, called "aid for trade," is aimed at improving both the "hard" infrastructure for trade, such as roads, and the "soft" infrastructure, such as trade finance. To some extent, these negotiations have already resulted in greater funding to help the poorer countries expand trade. At the 2005 WTO Ministerial Meeting, "Japan announced development assistance spending on trade, production and distribution infrastructure of $10 billion over three years, the United States announced Aid-for-Trade grants of

16. This index is available on the World Bank Web site, http://www.worldbank .org/lpi.

17. Bernard Hoekman and Alessandro Nicita, *Trade Policy, Trade Costs, and Developing Country Trade*, Policy Research Working Paper 4797 (Washington, D.C.: World Bank, 2008), 18.

$2.7 billion a year by 2010, and the EU and its member States announced trade-related development assistance spending of €2 billion per year by 2010."[18] Additional aid for trade could become part of a December "small package."

The Shift to Bilateral Agreements

Of the twenty countries with which the United States has an FTA, seven are developed, seven are upper-level developing countries, six are mid-level developing countries, and none is an LDC.[19] These agreements all built on existing commercial arrangements that the United States already had in place with these countries. First, the United States only negotiates FTAs with countries that are members of the WTO, and the various chapters of the FTA build on the WTO obligations. Second, the United States often has trade and investment framework agreements with countries before negotiating an FTA with that nation; these framework agreements establish councils that generally meet at least annually to encourage the liberalization of trade and investment, but they do not have nearly the breadth and scope of U.S. FTA agreements.

Additionally, many U.S. FTAs are negotiated with countries with which the United States already has a bilateral investment treaty (BIT) in place, although this is not always the case (e.g., among the Central American Free Trade Agreement (CAFTA) countries, only Honduras had an existing BIT with the United States). For countries that did not have an existing BIT, the investment chapter imposes new requirements, and for those that did already have a BIT, the investment provisions are now subject to the dispute settlement mechanism of the FTA. By and large, these investment commitments increase the attractiveness of U.S. developing-country partners to U.S. investors, and this can have a positive impact on economic development. Foreign investors bring in capital, management skills, and new technology, which all tend to diffuse out to other sectors in the country. However, for foreign direct investment to

18. World Trade Organization, "Building Trade Capacity," http://www.wto.org/english/tratop_e/devel_e/build_tr_capa_e.htm.

19. Developed-country partners are Australia, Bahrain, Canada, Israel, South Korea, Oman, and Singapore. Upper-level developing countries are Chile, Colombia, Costa Rica, Dominican Republic, Mexico, Panama, and Peru. Mid-level developing countries are El Salvador, Guatemala, Honduras, Jordan, Morocco, and Nicaragua.

be beneficial, the right regulatory environment needs to be in place in U.S. developing-country partners to prevent monopoly practices or other unfavorable outcomes.

All thirteen U.S. developing-country FTA partners were also eligible for one or more of the special preference programs administered by the United States, such as the Generalized System of Preferences, which provide duty-free treatment on their imports into the United States for most products. However, under the FTA, U.S. developing-country partners gain almost complete duty-free access to the U.S. market, whereas only some 91 percent of products were duty free without the FTA (54 percent under the preference program, and 37 percent because of a zero U.S. MFN duty). Additionally, the FTA basically provides for permanent duty-free entry, whereas the preference programs have to be periodically renewed by Congress, and there have been a number of lapses in authorization, which creates considerable uncertainty.

In addition to expanded duty-free coverage and greater certainty, the United States has sometimes provided funding to its developing-country FTA partners for capacity-building efforts to better enable them to benefit from the agreement.

In view of the fact that they already enjoy preferential access to the U.S. market, the question might be asked why a developing country would want to negotiate an FTA with the United States. There are a number of reasons why some countries have chosen to move on to an FTA. First, because of the huge size of the U.S. market, some of its partners calculated that reciprocal duty-free access would be in their commercial interest. Second, some hoped that strengthening the rules for investment would encourage foreign direct investment. Third, some developing-country partners wanted an FTA in order to cement a close political relationship with the United States. Fourth, the CAFTA countries wanted an FTA to level the playing field with Mexico. And fifth, a number of U.S. developing-country partners wanted the FTA as a way to lock in their own trade liberalization for the future and thereby provide traders and investors with a more certain commercial environment.

U.S. agreements with developing countries either call for it and its partner to completely eliminate tariffs by the same year or allow its developing-country partner to have a longer implementation schedule. Additionally, the United States commits to immediately eliminating duties on a substantial portion of its imports from its partners; for example, 95 percent of Chile's exports to the United States have immediate duty-free access, and 99 percent of Peru's and Colombia's exports receive immediate duty-free access. U.S. trade partners also provide immediate duty-free access to many U.S. exports, although to a lesser degree than the United States gives its partner; for example, 85 percent of U.S. exports to Chile have immediate duty-free access, and 80 percent have immediate duty-free access to Peru.

In the services area, as noted in chapter 2, the North American Free Trade Agreement (NAFTA) followed the approach taken in the WTO's General Agreement on Trade in Services, whereby the partners notified only services commitments that they were willing to undertake (the positive list). In subsequent U.S. FTA agreements, however, the parties agreed to a negative list approach, whereby all trade barriers were removed except those that were notified as remaining in effect. In NAFTA and subsequent U.S. agreements, both the United States and its developing-country partners have made commitments that go beyond concessions made in the WTO, although most of these commitments are in the form of additional bindings.

The Dark Side of U.S. Bilateral Agreements

Whereas the FTA partners of the United States seem to have generally benefited from these agreements, three features are not in their interest and are in the FTAs largely because of pressure from special interests in the United States. The first is the agriculture sector—a sector where most developing countries are relatively competitive. Unfortunately, the United States has insisted on full access to its partners' markets while continuing to give its growers huge subsidies, putting its developing-country partners at a competitive disadvantage. And in CAFTA, with regard to sugar, the United States will maintain its tariffs and only liberalize its quota to a small extent for the CAFTA countries. (To get around the U.S. quota, El Salvador expanded its ethanol production, which is then given duty-free/quota-free entry to the United States.)

A second feature is the provision in most U.S. FTAs in the services chapter that appears to prohibit U.S. partners from imposing controls on the flow of speculative capital into and out of their country. Such speculative capital is very different from foreign direct investment in manufacturing plants or business enterprises, which has a long-term commitment to the country. Speculative capital can move across borders with the click of a computer's mouse, and often moves for reasons that have nothing to do with economic events within the country.

Speculative capital that flows into an economy can cause asset bubbles that distort the economy and can cause the currency to appreciate to levels where many sectors in the real economy that had been competitive can no longer compete. And when speculative capital suddenly decides to leave an economy, it can cause a sudden devaluation of the currency and economic collapse. This is what happened to Thailand, Indonesia, and South Korea, and to a lesser extent Hong Kong, Malaysia, Laos, and the Philippines, in 1997, when they were hit with a severe financial crisis, which many blamed on speculative capital flows and weak regulatory regimes.[20]

A third area where the United States has pressed for a provision that is not in the interests of its developing-country partners is the protection of pharmaceuticals in the intellectual property chapter that goes beyond the WTO's TRIPS agreement or what is in U.S. law. As noted above, there is an important balance that needs to be in place between the holders of intellectual property rights and consumers. Too much protection means that poor countries—and indeed consumers in the developed countries—do not have reasonable access to low-cost generics, yet insufficient protection will reduce the incentive for the pharmaceutical companies to develop new drugs. The TRIPS agreement came out of a negotiation between countries that have much intellectual property to protect, and countries that have very little and want access to intellectual property at a reasonable price. Accordingly, it represents somewhat of a balance between the need to promote innovation and the needs of consumers.

However, in many U.S. FTAs with developing countries, the United States has insisted on what is called TRIPS Plus. As noted in chapter 4 on U.S. commercial interests, the aspect of TRIPS Plus that pertains to strengthened enforcement is well justified. However, some provisions provide added protection for pharmaceutical patents over what is provided for in the WTO agreement, and these provisions can be damaging to developing-country interests.

The potential problems for U.S. developing-country partners are aptly summed up by Carsten Fink and Kimberly Elliott: "Most notably, U.S. negotiators generally seek to extend the length of the patent term to compensate for delays in regulatory approvals; to allow for patents for new uses of existing compounds; to limit the grounds for issuing compul-

---

20. Until recently, the IMF also pressed countries to allow the free flow of speculative capital. However, in February 2010, the IMF changed its position to recognize the potential danger of speculative capital to developing countries.

sory licenses; to force drug regulatory agencies to play a role in enforcing patent rights, even though they typically have no expertise in that area; and to create another layer of market exclusivity through rules for the protection of pharmaceutical test data, further complicating the use of compulsory licensing."[21]

Not surprisingly, some potential U.S. FTA partners refused to agree to these provisions, and U.S. insistence on TRIPS Plus reportedly was a factor in the hesitancy of the Southern African Customs Union and Thailand to conclude FTAs. It also appears to be a factor in the current negotiations for the Trans-Pacific Partnership.

These provisions also energized nongovernmental organizations in the United States concerned about global health and economic development, and these organizations lobbied Congress to force the George W. Bush administration to negotiate a May 10, 2007, deal to scale back the TRIPS Plus provisions as they apply to pharmaceutical products. Among other provisions, this deal allowed for a more flexible approach for U.S. developing-country partners on extending the length of patent terms to compensate for delays in regulatory approvals, and clarified that the period for protection of pharmaceutical test data will not be longer for the same product than it is in the United States. Though agreements negotiated after May 10, 2007, follow these guidelines, some nongovernmental organizations focused on health are concerned that the old provisions may reappear in the Trans-Pacific Partnership negotiations.

NAFTA's Impact on Mexico

The 1994 U.S. FTA with Mexico is the only FTA that has been in effect long enough for serious analysis as to its impact on one of the U.S. developing-country partners. This is also a good agreement to consider in more depth, because the economic impact of this agreement would be expected to be larger than the other U.S. agreements because of Mexico's proximity to the U.S. market.

---

21. Carsten Fink and Kimberly Elliott, "Tripping over Health: U.S. Policy on Patents and Drug Access in Developing Countries," in *The White House and the World: A Global Development Agenda for the Next U.S. President*, edited by Nancy Birdsall (Washington, D.C.: Center for Global Development, 2008), 222.

Mexico entered into NAFTA as part of a long-term strategy to become more market oriented, which included such measures as joining the GATT in 1985 and easing restrictions on foreign investment in 1989. As is always the case in real-world economics, there were a number of exogenous events that make analysis of NAFTA's impact difficult. One of the largest exogenous events was the Mexican peso crisis in 1995, which had an enormous economic impact, but other events include the U.S. dot-com bubble, which burst in 2000; the global world recession of 2008; a number of other Mexican FTAs; and China's joining the WTO and becoming a major player in world trade.

A number of economists believe that NAFTA did increase foreign direct investment in Mexico. For example, Gordon Hanson concludes that "NAFTA appears to have raised capital inflows in part by raising investor confidence in the country's commitment to free trade. From 1980 to 1994, foreign direct investment (FDI) averaged 1.3% of Mexico's GDP, while from 1995 to 2000, it averaged 2.8% of GDP."[22] And a 2004 Congressional Research Service report notes that from 1994 to 2002, U.S. foreign direct investment in Mexico rose from $16.1 billion to $58.1 billion.[23]

There also is a consensus that NAFTA has contributed to a significant increase in Mexico's trade. For example, Gordon Hanson notes that Mexico's policy of trade liberalization "helped increase the share of trade in Mexico's GDP from 11.2% in 1980 to 32.2% in 2000."[24]

One major problem of NAFTA, however, has been the agricultural sector. The agreement itself gave Mexico a long transition period to eliminate duties on grains, particularly corn, but Mexico decided to implement duty elimination on a much more rapid schedule. Joseph Stiglitz describes this situation as follows: "Poor Mexican corn farmers now have to compete in their own country with highly subsidized American corn. . . . A fairer trade agreement would have eliminated America's agricultural subsidies and its restrictions on imports of agricultural goods, like sugar, into the United States. Even if the United States did not eliminate all its subsidies, Mexico should have been given the right to

22. Gordon H. Hanson, *What Has Happened to Wages in Mexico since NAFTA? Implications for Hemispheric Free Trade*, NBER Working Paper 9563 (Cambridge, Mass.: National Bureau of Economic Research, 2003), 2.

23. J. F. Hornbeck, *NAFTA at Ten: Lessons from Recent Studies* (Washington, D.C.: Congressional Research Service, 2004), 3.

24. Hanson, *What Has Happened to Wages in Mexico*, 1.

countervail—that is to impose duties on U.S. imports to offset the subsidies. But NAFTA does not allow that."[25]

The result was that rural Mexican growers of corn could not compete with heavily subsidized corn from the United States. Agricultural employment in Mexico dropped from 8.1 million in the early 1990s to 5.8 million in 2008, to some extent because of increased imports, and many of the unemployed rural poor flooded into the country's metropolitan areas. Many of these may subsequently have become illegal immigrants into the United States.

Although NAFTA does seem to have contributed to an increase in investment and trade, there is no consensus as to whether the overall impact on Mexican growth has been positive or negative. Eduardo Zepeda, Timothy Wise, and Kevin Gallagher argue that "the evidence points overwhelmingly to the conclusion that Mexico's reforms, backed by NAFTA, have largely been a disappointment for the country. Despite dramatic increases in trade and foreign investment, economic growth has been slow and job creation has been weak."[26] However, J. F. Hornbeck quotes a World Bank study that argues without NAFTA, Mexico's GDP growth would have been 4 to 5 percent lower by 2002.[27]

Conclusion: Economic Development: Too Often Ignored

Economic theories of the role of trade in economic development have changed dramatically over the past sixty years. In the 1960s, most economists argued that poor countries should impose high import barriers to allow domestic industries to grow to a level where they could compete in world markets. By the late 1990s, the consensus view was radically different; the Washington Consensus held that developing countries should aggressively pursue export markets and should have relatively low and transparent barriers to imports to promote economic growth. Today, this model has been criticized for ignoring the experience of neomercantilist countries, such as China, which have achieved extremely rapid

---

25. Stiglitz, *Making Globalization Work*, 64.
26. Eduardo Zepeda, Timothy A. Wise, and Kevin P. Gallagher, *Rethinking Trade Policy for Development: Lessons From Mexico under NAFTA* (Washington, D.C.: Carnegie Endowment for International Peace, 2009), 1.
27. Hornbeck, *NAFTA at Ten*, 4.

growth while maintaining high import barriers, an undervalued currency, and low transparency.

The position taken here is that both the Washington Consensus and the neomercantilist approach can be effective in promoting economic development, provided other progrowth policies are pursued such as reducing corruption, promoting savings and education, and removing impediments to trade such as cumbersome customs procedures. However, it needs to be emphasized that the neomercantilist approach is essentially a beggar-thy-neighbor approach that does not comport with the theoretical benefit of international trade based on the law of comparative advantage.

The GATT did not require the LDCs to open their markets, and it gave middle-income countries a great deal of flexibility in trade liberalization and adherence to the various nontariff measure codes. However, the WTO radically changed the approach to the treatment of developing countries, requiring them to adhere to almost all the agreements, and subjecting their practices to the new robust dispute settlement mechanism. The WTO, however, did promise some benefits to developing countries, including tariff reductions by developed countries, a commitment to end the restrictive trade regime on textiles and apparel, and a promise to begin negotiations in 2000 to reduce agricultural subsidies.

By 2000, however, many developing countries came to believe that they had been sold a bill of goods. Some of the agreements, particularly the TRIPS agreement, were proving to be very expensive to implement and of negligible benefit to the LDCs. Furthermore, China was grabbing most of the benefits of trade liberalization in textiles, apparel, and other goods, and the agricultural negotiations were going nowhere as the farm lobby in the United States and other countries effectively blocked efforts to reduce agricultural subsidies and trade barriers.

Accordingly, to get agreement from the LDCs to launch a new trade round, the negotiators committed to make the Doha Round a "development round." However, this original objective has largely been lost sight of, as the United States, Europe, and others approached the negotiations as a standard trade negotiation, and the Doha negotiations have now apparently failed. But the negotiators did make progress on a "trade facilitation" agreement that would benefit both developing and developed countries, and this should be salvaged from the failed Doha Round.

U.S. bilateral and regional FTAs also have some features that can help U.S. developing-country partners economically, and some negative features. On the positive side, these agreements give U.S. partners nearly complete, assured access to the U.S. market, and the United States often provides capacity-building assistance. On the negative side, the United States demands free access for its agricultural exports that it heavily subsidizes, such as corn and cotton, which poses unfair competition to producers in its partner. Other negatives sometimes include provisions on pharmaceuticals that go beyond the WTO's TRIPS agreement, and limitations on the ability of the parties to the agreement to restrict speculative capital flows to protect the integrity of the capital markets in U.S. developing-country partners.

The United States often has important foreign policy objectives in negotiating its trade agreements, including both in the WTO and in its bilateral agreements with developing countries. However, all too often there seems to have been overreliance on the assumption that expanded trade will lead to economic growth, and too great a willingness to demand special interest provisions that may injure a U.S. trade partner in order to gain domestic U.S. support for the agreement.

One of the reasons that U.S. negotiators do not always take into account the developmental impact of U.S. proposals is that the interagency process that helps the president formulate the nation's approach is not designed to consider these issues. The U.S. Agency for International Development (USAID), which is the key federal agency designed to promote economic development, only participates in the staff-level Trade Policy Staff Committee, and not the sub-Cabinet Trade Policy Committee.

To remedy this, USAID should be added to the Trade Policy Committee, and USAID and the Department of State should be given a specific mandate to consider the impact of the U.S. proposals on its developing-country partners. Additionally, the U.S. International Trade Commission should be charged with conducting an analysis of the impact of U.S. proposals on developing countries as soon as possible in the negotiating process.

Trade policy can be an important tool to help promote economic development, but unfortunately it is a tool that is not being used to maximum effect at this time.

Chapter 7

Uneasy Neighbors:
Trade and the Environment

According to economic theory, trade liberalization can have both positive and negative effects on the environment, and environmental groups historically have had mixed views regarding the impact of trade liberalization on the environment. Environmentalists who believed economic growth per se was damaging to the environment opposed all trade agreements, while those who supported economic growth did not oppose trade agreements. However, developments in the mid-1990s united virtually all environmental organizations in opposition to trade agreements.

Since then, U.S. negotiators and the World Trade Organization (WTO) have made significant progress in better reconciling U.S. trade agreements with environmental stewardship, and as a result mainstream environmental groups are supportive of trade agreements that they believe have been crafted correctly. The trade community and the environmental community, which had a relationship somewhat akin to the Hatfields and McCoys, have reconciled to some extent and could now be called uneasy neighbors.

The environmental and health communities have long raised concerns regarding expanded trade. Although some environmentalists are intrinsically opposed to trade liberalization and its resulting growth, more moderate groups argue that trade liberalization can be positive if care is taken in trade agreements to protect—or even advance—environmental stewardship. These moderate groups supported trade liberalization up through the Uruguay Round and the negotiations for the North American Free Trade Agreement (NAFTA). However, by 1999 events in the

WTO and NAFTA had raised the concerns of almost all environmental groups. By the time of the WTO Seattle Ministerial Meeting in 1999, almost all environmental groups opposed further trade liberalization. Conversely, staunch free trade advocates, including most businessmen and many academics, historically argued that trade expansion promotes efficiency and creates economic growth. This new economic wealth, according to this argument, can be used to strengthen environmental stewardship and promote health and safety. Free traders argued that any environmental effects of trade agreements would be minor and, in any case, the best way to protect the environment was through separate agreements on environment and safety.

A third view was expressed by developing countries, which generally have been skeptical of including environmental provisions in regional trade agreements. The major concern of the developing world is that environmental provisions could be used as new trade barriers to restrict their access to developed-country markets. Accordingly, they tended to resist including environmental provisions in the WTO and bilateral agreements.[1]

However, the issue of how to reconcile trade and environmental protection has evolved enormously during the past two decades. Trade negotiators now are more sensitive to the concerns of the environmental community, and trade agreements better deal with environmental and health/safety concerns. Today there is much greater acceptance by the business community of the legitimacy of including environmental provisions in trade agreements. Parallel to this, a number of environmental groups have moved back to supporting trade agreements where they believe the provisions adequately address environmental concerns. And though developing countries as a whole continue to oppose including environmental provisions in the Doha Round negotiations,

---

1. A quotation from by A. V. Ganesan, a former commerce secretary of India and a nongovernmental delegate to the Seattle Ministerial Meeting, gives a flavor of developing-country objections to including environmental provisions in trade agreements: "Environmental degradation is being caused by two segments of people: the affluent and the poor, or the greedy and the needy. The former are polluting the environment by excessive levels of consumption and the latter are forced into unsustainable practices by poverty. The approach needed to tackle these two varieties is different, but trade rules applied in a simplistic manner can hardly solve the fundamental problems." Quoted in the *Washington Post*, December 5, 1999, and posted on the Indian Embassy's Web site, http://www.indianembassy.org/Policy/WTO/wto_india/battle_seattle_dec_05_99.htm.

many have accepted far-reaching environmental provisions in bilateral trade agreements.[2]

How We Got Here

The original General Agreement on Tariffs and Trade (GATT), negotiated in 1947, recognized the right of the parties to abrogate trade commitments as necessary to protect human, animal, or plant life or health, or for the conservation of exhaustible natural resources provided these derogations were not disguised protectionism (Article XX).[3] Other than this, however, the original GATT did not acknowledge environmental concerns.

The U.S. free trade agreement (FTA) with Israel—the first post–World War II U.S. agreement—went into force in 1985. This agreement included the GATT Article XX exception, but otherwise gave short shrift to environmental considerations, and in fact leaned the other way. One article of the Israel agreement specifies that "the Parties shall review their current and future rules on veterinary and plant health matters to insure that these rules are applied in a non-discriminatory manner, and that these rules do not have the effect of unduly obstructing trade."

2. Progress on integrating trade and environment so far in regional trade agreements (RTAs) has been substantial, while progress in the WTO has been far less. As the Organization for Economic Cooperation and Development put the matter: "While RTAs have contributed to better integration of trade and environment at bilateral and regional levels, this progress is not yet visible in the multilateral arena. Indeed, it is striking that a number of countries have been prepared to incorporate environmental provisions in RTAs, but are not prepared to countenance similar outcomes at the multilateral level." Organization for Economic Cooperation and Development, "Environment and Regional Trade Agreements, 2007," 17, http:// www.oecd.org/document/8/0,3746,en_2649_34287_38768584_1_1_1,00&&en-USS_ 01DBC.html.

3. The language of GATT Article XX relevant to the environment is the following: "Subject to the requirement that such measures are not applied in a manner which would constitute a means of arbitrary or unjustifiable discrimination between countries where the same conditions prevail, or a disguised restriction on international trade, nothing in this Agreement shall be construed to prevent the adoption or enforcement by any contracting party of measures:. . . (b) necessary to protect human, animal or plant life or health; . . . (g) relating to the conservation of exhaustible natural resources if such measures are made effective in conjunction with restrictions on domestic production or consumption. . . ."

The concerns of environmentalists with trade were fanned in 1991 when the GATT ruled that a U.S. law prohibiting imports of tuna caught by purse seine nets, which often killed dolphins, was a violation of U.S. trade commitments. Mexico brought this case to the GATT but decided not to pursue a resolution because of concerns that it would cost them a potential FTA with the United States.[4] Nonetheless, the case became a cause célèbre for the environmental community, which dubbed it GATTzilla versus Flipper. This tuna-dolphin dispute became a symbol for the environmentalists that the trade rules would be used to systematically undermine international and national environmental rules.

With the commencement of negotiations for NAFTA in June 1991, environmental considerations received greater emphasis. Environmentalists were extremely concerned about the negative environmental impact this agreement could have on the United States, because Mexican environmental protection lagged far behind that of the United States and because the United States and Mexico share a 2,000-mile border. Among other negative effects, environmentalists believed this trade agreement could lead to a reduction in U.S. standards in an effort to remain competitive with imports from Mexico and could worsen Mexico's already-threatened environment.

To address these concerns, negotiators conducted the first-ever U.S. environmental review of a trade agreement and incorporated far more provisions addressing environmental concerns than ever before. When the agreement was signed by President George H. W. Bush in December 1992, the agreement was the greenest in U.S. history. Its preamble specifically recognized the need for environmental protection and conservation and the promotion of sustainable development, and it called for strengthening development and enforcing environmental laws and regulations.

NAFTA also contains a chapter on sanitary and phytosanitary measures, which allows the parties to impose more stringent health and safety standards than those in international agreements. Its chapter on technical barriers to trade specifically allows the parties to choose "the levels of protection considered appropriate" for that country. And the agreement provides that certain specified multilateral environmental

---

4. When Mexico failed to push the GATT decision, the European Community filed its own case against the United States, and in May 1994 the GATT again ruled that the U.S. law violated U.S. trade commitments.

agreements (MEAs) take precedence over NAFTA's trade liberalizing rules.[5]

One element of NAFTA, however, raised particular concern among environmental groups, and this was the provision in the investment chapter that allows investors to initiate a claim against a government if they believe their rights have been infringed. Environmentalists argued that this provision could be used by companies to block important environmental and health/safety regulations.

Even though NAFTA negotiated by the Bush administration recognized environmental concerns to a great extent, U.S. politics had changed even more dramatically. While the NAFTA negotiations were proceeding, the U.S. presidential contest was under way. Labor and many environmental nongovernmental organizations (NGOs) opposed NAFTA, and on October 5, 1992, a month before the election, candidate Bill Clinton moved to accommodate NAFTA opponents by committing to renegotiate NAFTA to include labor and environmental side agreements.

As one of his first acts as president, Clinton launched discussions with Mexico and Canada to negotiate subsidiary agreements covering labor and the environment, which concluded in September 1993. The revised NAFTA went into effect January 1, 1994, with side agreements on labor and the environment.

The Clinton changes were enough to gain support for passage of NAFTA from mainstream environmental groups, such as the World Wildlife Fund and the Audubon Society. Other environmental groups, such as the Sierra Club and Public Citizen, however, opposed NAFTA, arguing that it would weaken laws and regulations to protect the environment and health and safety, and would lead to environmental degradation.

While the NAFTA negotiations were proceeding, 123 countries were negotiating multilaterally in the Uruguay Round. The resulting agreement went into effect on January 1, 1995, and established the WTO,

---

5. The agreements given precedence over the NAFTA rules were the Convention on International Trade in Endangered Species (known as CITES), the Montreal Protocol on Substances that Deplete the Ozone Layer, and the Basel Convention on the Control of Transboundary Movements of Hazardous Wastes and Their Disposal, and two bilateral agreements, one with Canada regarding transboundary movement of hazardous wastes, and one with Mexico on cooperation on protecting the environment in the border area.

which incorporated the original GATT along with the many new elements negotiated in the Uruguay Round.

The WTO expanded environmental considerations substantially over the GATT. Among other elements, the preamble recognizes the objective of sustainable development, a new committee on trade and environment was established with the charter to enhance positive interaction between trade and the environment, and a new agreement was reached which recognized that members have the right to take sanitary and phytosanitary measures necessary for the protection of human, animal, or plant life or health, provided that such measures are not disguised restrictions on trade and do not discriminate between members. Additionally, a new agreement on services, the General Agreement on Services, also explicitly recognized the right of members to maintain service provisions to protect their environment.

Following passage of the Uruguay Round agreements and NAFTA, however, it looked like the worst fears of the environmental community were coming true. In 1998 a WTO Appellate Body ruled against a U.S. law that placed an embargo on the importation of shrimp caught without turtle-excluder devices, which were designed to allow endangered sea turtles to escape from shrimp nets. The dispute was brought by four Southeast Asian countries, and the panel based its ruling on the fact that the United States had not taken into account unique conditions in those countries and had not attempted to negotiate a multilateral agreement with those countries.

The ruling, however, took an enormous step in recognizing the concerns of environmentalists by setting out the view that an international agreement could enable the U.S. law to fall under the WTO/GATT Article XX exemptions permitting derogation from most favored trade provisions.[6] Nonetheless, the initial reaction of the environmental community was that once again trade trumped reasonable measures to protect the environment.

And then in June 1999 a Canadian company, Methanex, filed a case under the NAFTA investor-state dispute settlement provisions against a

6. In October 2001, the Appellate Body ruled in favor of the United States in a complaint brought by Malaysia in what is known as Shrimp-Turtle II. Following the first ruling, the United States sought negotiations with the Southeast Asian nations and allowed sufficient flexibility in compliance by requiring other country programs simply to be comparable in effectiveness to the U.S. program, rather than essentially the same.

California law that banned MTBE, a gasoline blending additive. California's ban was based on studies that indicated MTBE was increasingly found in drinking water. (MTBE is an ether that otherwise has a number of favorable properties.) These developments enraged the environmental community, and the moderate groups that had previously supported free trade were forced to the sidelines.

President Clinton tried to move the debate forward by issuing an executive order on November 18, 1999, requiring that environmental impact studies be conducted of all future trade agreements. But it was too little, too late. Many from the environmental community descended on Seattle from November 30 to December 3, 1999, to protest the WTO Ministerial Meeting, which had hoped to launch a new trade round, with protesters dressed as turtles joining labor union activists in hard hats and a myriad of other protesters in the Seattle streets.

Then on September 11, 2001, al Qaeda terrorists hit the World Trade Center and the Pentagon. Policymakers recognized that failed states provided a breeding ground for potential terrorist activities, as noted above, and that the WTO could play a role in helping developing countries. In this context, on November 14, 2001, the WTO finally succeeded in launching a new round of multilateral trade negotiations. This new round, the Doha Development Round, was couched in terms of supporting national security by promoting economic development, a hoped-for antidote to failed states.

Additionally, however, the mandate for this new round had an environmental component. Specifically, the Ministerial Declaration directed that the negotiations should consider the relationship between WTO rules and trade obligations in MEAs, procedures for the WTO and MEAs to share information, and the reduction of trade barriers on environmental goods and services.[7] Additionally, ministers committed to improve WTO disciplines on fisheries subsidies. They also agreed that the WTO Committee on Trade and Environment should give attention to the effect of environmental measures on market access, the relevant provisions of the Agreement on Trade-Related Aspects of Intellectual Property Rights, and labeling requirements for environmental purposes.

One month later, the U.S. FTA with Jordan went into effect. This agreement included environmental provisions modeled after NAFTA,

---

7. The Ministerial Declaration is available on the WTO Web site, http://www .wto.org/english/thewto_e/minist_e/min01_e/mindecl_e.htm.

although not as extensive. Additionally, both the United States and Jordan had conducted environmental assessments of the likely impact of the trade agreement.

In August, President George W. Bush signed the 2002 Trade Act, legislation driven by the Republican chairman of the House Ways and Means Committee, Bill Thomas (R-Calif.). For the first time, legislation giving the president trade negotiating authority included significant provisions aimed at ensuring that trade and environmental policies were mutually supportive. For example, objectives for trade negotiations specified in the legislation included ensuring that parties to the agreement effectively enforce environmental laws in a manner affecting trade, strengthening the capacity of U.S. trade partners to protect the environment, and opening market access for environmental goods and services, as well as ensuring that environmental policies do not unjustifiably discriminate against U.S. exports.

The provisions of this legislation shaped subsequent U.S. FTAs with Chile, Singapore, Australia, Morocco, the members of the Central American Free Trade Agreement (CAFTA; later, including the Dominican Republic, known as CAFTA-DR), and Bahrain; in fact, language closely parallel to language in the 2002 trade bill was included in many of these agreements. Even though this legislation represented a major evolution in U.S. trade policy toward recognizing the environmental implications of expanded trade, still-suspicious environmental groups generally opposed the 2002 bill.

In 2006, the Democrats won control of Congress and immediately pressed for stronger environmental and labor provisions. Without such provisions, congressional leadership refused to consider pending agreements with Colombia, Panama, Peru, and South Korea. To meet congressional concerns, on May 10, 2007, the administration and congressional leaders announced an agreement under which environmental provisions would have the same enforcement rules as commercial disputes and that foreign investors would have no greater substantive rights than U.S. citizens in investor-state disputes.

Trade's Impact on the Environment

Expanded trade may have an impact on the environment in a number of different ways, and depending on the specific conditions may have either positive or negative effects. First, as trade barriers are eliminated, trade increases, and this spurs economic growth and increased consumption and production, producing what is called *scale effects*. All other things being equal, this greater economic activity raises demand for energy and raw materials, and increases emissions and waste generation.

The impact of expanded trade on specific sectors, such as would occur if subsidies for agriculture were reduced, are called *structural* or *composition effects*. Production and consumption of some products are more polluting than others. For example, increased coal mining has profound impacts on water and ground pollution, and increased coal consumption has major effects on air quality. By contrast, the production and consumption of software have only a minimal impact on the environment. If the sectors that expand are more polluting, the environmental impact will be negative for a country; and if the sectors that are less polluting expand, the environmental impact will be positive.

A third impact, often called the *technique effect*, refers to changes in production methods that follow from trade liberalization. For example, if trade barriers are eliminated, trade in goods and services that protect the environment would likely increase. Liberalizing investment rules along with trade barriers will significantly amplify technique effects; for example, firms with more efficient production technology may invest overseas. Their production techniques may then be emulated by local companies.

And finally, *regulatory effects* refer to the impact the agreement might have on the ability of the parties to the agreement to implement environmental regulations. This impact also might be either positive or negative. It would be negative, for example, if the agreement's trade rules could be used to block rules and regulations to protect the environment or health and safety. Alternatively, the impact would be positive if the parties to the agreement were required to implement stronger environmental and health/safety regulations.

A major concern of environmentalists has been with what has been dubbed a race to the bottom, whereby the parties to a trade agreement seek to gain a competitive advantage by lowering environmental and health standards, creating so-called pollution havens. Alternatively, a race to the bottom may occur as companies move to areas with lower standards (pollution havens) to cut production costs.

Initially, free trade advocates tended to dismiss the concern about a potential race to the bottom, arguing that the costs of complying with environmental regulations are only a small percentage of total production costs. Other factors such as wages and proximity to market or vital resources were deemed to be much more critical to decisions as to where to produce. And initial academic studies of the issue tended to support this view.

However, more recent studies have found "statistically significant pollution haven effects of reasonable magnitude," according to a thorough review of the literature by Smita Brunnermeier.[8] These studies indicate that some firms that face high costs of complying with environmental rules and intense price competition may be influenced by the costs of complying with environmental regulations. According to the Organization for Economic Cooperation and Development, "the sectors prone to relocation tend to face high environmental costs, are relatively 'footloose'—not tied to specific locations by the need for particular mineral resource inputs, for example—and are traded between industrialized and developing countries."[9]

The impact of a trade agreement on the environment depends on the interaction of the scale, composition, technique, and regulatory effects. For example, expanded trade will increase the risks of an invasive species entering a new market that may cause extensive environmental damage, and it will increase the risks of oil spills and pollution from increased transportation. However, these adverse effects can be offset by improved regulation and capacity building to prevent environmental or health problems.

Some analysts argue that as countries grow from an impoverished level, first there are negative environmental effects and then, after a certain level of growth is reached, there are positive effects. This theory, known as the Environmental Kuznets Curve, is that after reaching a certain level of income, a society has the means and the will to spend on reducing pollution, and at that time technique effects and a strengthened regulatory system will more than counterbalance the scale effects.

Overall, studies of a possible environmental Kuznets curve indicate that the relationship seems to hold for a number of pollutants—such as

8. Smita B. Brunnermeier and Arik Levinson, "Examining the Evidence on Environmental Regulations and Industry Location," *Journal of Environment Development* 13, no. 1 (March 2004): 6–41, at 38.

9. Organization for Economic Cooperation and Development, "Environment and Regional Trade Agreements, 2007," 27.

sulfur dioxide, lead, and sewage—but not for other environmental threats —such as carbon emissions and deforestation.

Developing-Country Views

Poverty is the major cause of environmental degradation in most developing countries. Poverty forces people on the verge of starving to over-fish and to chop down forests for fuel for heating and light. Because of poverty, farmers engage in nonsustainable agriculture. And because of poverty, governments do not have the resources to enforce environmental laws and regulations.

Developing countries often look to trade agreements as a way to develop economically, and thus it is no surprise that they view proposals to include environmental provisions in trade agreements with substantial skepticism. Many developing countries lack the capacity to negotiate on environmental issues in trade agreements, and they suspect that developed countries may use environmental provisions to block their access to markets. They are also concerned that the implementation of environmental provisions will constitute an excessive burden on their limited financial and human resources.

Finally, many developing countries tend not to see any benefits to themselves from environmental provisions. They generally do not have companies that make products or create services that promote environmental stewardship.

For many developing countries, of course, their environment—whether a rain forest, a pristine seacoast, or unique wildlife—is a treasure of inestimable value, but it is a treasure only in the long term, and in the short term poverty is the main focus. However, developing countries have been willing to accede to including environmental provisions in bilateral FTAs, particularly when capacity building is provided to help them comply with their commitments.

Environmental Reviews of FTAs

The United States first undertook an environmental review of a trade agreement in 1991, with an early review of the potential NAFTA, which identified issues of possible concern. Eight years later, President Clinton issued Executive Order 13141, which mandated that environmental reviews of trade agreements be "undertaken sufficiently early in the process to inform the development of negotiating positions."[10]

This order required that public comments be solicited, and that the draft review be made available for public comment and the final review made public. Although the executive order defined the focus of these reviews as the impact on the United States, it provided that such reviews could also consider global and transboundary effects.

A precedent for environmental reviews of U.S. trade agreements is the requirement for environmental impact statements under the 1969 National Environmental Policy Act. However, this act's statements are an analysis of a fixed project, such as a dam, which is known in advance. Environmental assessments of a possible trade negotiation's result, however, have to address a moving target, as the outcome of a trade negotiation is never known until its very end. A second critical difference is the enormous complexity in predicting the results of a trade agreement, which may cover many different issues and two or more countries. Third, data to analyze the potential environmental effects are often very sketchy, particularly when one of the parties to the trade agreement is a developing country with limited statistical information.

Guidelines for implementing the executive order identified a number of "reasonably foreseeable environmental impacts arising from a proposed trade agreement" that should be considered.[11] Possible effects included the potential positive and negative implications of the proposed trade agreement for U.S. environmental regulations, and potential economic and environmental effects.

Negotiations for an FTA with Jordan were launched in June 2000, and this became the first agreement subject to the requirement to conduct an environmental review under Executive Order 13141. Because of critical foreign policy interests to bolster the Middle East peace process, these negotiations were on a very fast track and concluded in October 2000. The final environmental review found that the agreement would have no measurable impact on total U.S. imports, exports, production,

---

10. Executive Order 13141 is available at http://www.ustr.gov/assets/Trade_Sectors/Environment/Guidelines_for_Environmental_Reviews/asset_upload_file 570_5735.pdf.

11. "Guidelines for Implementation of Executive Order 13141," http://www.ustr .gov/assets/Trade_Sectors/Environment/Guidelines_for_Environmental_Reviews/ asset_upload_file556_5734.pdf.

or employment, and accordingly the environmental effects on the United States were expected to be de minimis.[12]

The review went further and found two positive effects on the environment. Because the agreement included provisions that help to maintain current legal and regulatory discretion, the FTA would encourage the parties to improve their environmental protection regimes (regulatory effect). Additionally, by eliminating trade barriers on environmental goods and services, the agreement would have a positive impact on environmental technologies (technique effect).

All subsequent FTA negotiations followed the requirement of the executive order and the Jordanian precedent for ex ante environmental reviews. And like the Jordan review, the environmental reviews of all subsequent agreements found that environmental effects on the United States were expected to be de minimis, based on the analysis that the impact on U.S. production from each agreement was expected to be small. Other than NAFTA, U.S. imports from its partner countries in each of its FTAs accounted for no more than 2.5 percent of its total imports, and its exports to each of its partners accounted for no more than 3.4 percent of its total exports in 2006. (Data for 2006 are used here because that was roughly the year when the International Trade Commission conducted many of these studies.)

Furthermore, because of the provisions in each of the FTAs requiring each of the parties to enforce their environmental rules, each of the reviews has concluded that the relevant agreement would encourage the parties to improve environmental protection. Each of the reviews, however, did identify some unique environmental implications of the FTAs, such as the following:

- Chile's economy is heavily dependent on natural resource sectors, such as mining and metals, forestry, fisheries, and agriculture, and this helped identify priorities for the environmental cooperation provisions.
- Singapore is a major transit center for endangered species.
- An increased risk of invasive species was identified as a potential environmental concern in the Australian and South Korean FTAs.

12. The Final Environmental Review of the FTA with Jordan is available at http://www.ustr.gov/assets/Trade_Agreements/Bilateral/Jordan/asset_upload_file64 _5111.pdf.

- Provisions in the Australian FTA to allow trade in remanufactured goods would have positive environmental benefits, because remanufacturing reduces the volume of material entering the waste stream by redirecting waste products to remanufactured goods and reducing energy consumption.
- CAFTA-DR, through increased economic activity in its partner countries, could have indirect effects on the U.S. environment through the transboundary transmission of air and water pollutants and their impact on migratory species of wildlife.
- Oman's trade in the horn of the rhinoceros, a highly endangered species, was flagged as an area of concern that should be addressed through environmental cooperation.

In its review of the experiences with environmental reviews, the Organization for Economic Cooperation and Development notes that it does not seem as if there have been any changes to final texts of U.S. FTAs as a result of its environmental reviews: "However, there are typically changes in the form of mitigation or enhancement measures: proactive policies such as capacity building for environmental management or increased cooperation that try to address the concerns raised. Indeed, there have been numerous instances of assessments feeding into the work programs of any related environmental cooperation or capacity building efforts."[13]

Like the United States, several other developed countries undertake environmental reviews, including Canada and New Zealand.[14] The European Union conducts sustainability impact assessments, which are broader than U.S. environmental reviews, as these consider labor and social effects as well as environmental, and they consider effects both in the EU and in the partner country. Additionally, a very few developing countries, most notably Chile, also regularly conduct environmental reviews of their FTAs.

Some international governmental organizations—including the African Development Bank, the Economic Commission for Africa, the Food and Agriculture Organization, the Inter-American Development Bank,

13. Organization for Economic Cooperation and Development, "Environment and Regional Trade Agreements, 2007," 58.
14. For a comprehensive listing of environmental reviews, see WTO Committee on Trade and Environment, "List of Environmental Reviews," WT/CTE/W/245, June 4, 2007.

and the United Nations Environment Program—have conducted or been involved in reviews. Finally, some NGOs also conduct environmental assessments, including the University of Manchester's Impact Assessment Research Centre and the World Wildlife Fund.

However, there is no agreed-on international methodology for conducting environmental reviews, and different countries use differing methodologies. Most countries still do not undertake environmental reviews, either because they do not recognize their importance or more often because they lack the resources to undertake them.

Almost all environmental assessments to date have been ex ante; that is, they were conducted before the agreement was adopted. NAFTA is one of the few U.S. agreements for which an ex post assessment (i.e., one that assesses the actual consequences after the agreement is in effect) has been conducted. This was conducted by the North American Commission for Environmental Cooperation (CEC) in 2005, ten years after NAFTA had gone into effect.

In 1999 the CEC issued a public call for research papers, which were financially supported by the CEC and selected by a trinational multidisciplinary advisory group. Papers selected were presented in 2000, 2003, and 2005. Between 200 and 300 trade and environment stakeholders participated. Some of the findings of the researchers were that the agreement had positive effects on the environment, and some found negative effects. According to the CEC report, some of the findings include the following:

- Fredriksson and Millimet failed to find evidence supporting the hypothesis that there would be a race to the bottom in U.S. environmental policies following NAFTA. In fact, they found that their three measures of environmental quality improved during the 1990s and did not seem affected by NAFTA's ratification.
- Carpentier considered whether NAFTA had created any "pollution havens" and interestingly found only one case, and that concerned Canada (as opposed to Mexico as was originally feared). Canada experienced a nearly fivefold jump in hazardous waste imports from the United States in the few years after NAFTA came into effect, primarily in steel and chemicals. (The CEC found it reassuring that only one case of a pollution haven was documented.)
- Dyer-Leal and Yunez-Naude found that increased corn imports displaced domestic Mexican production and traditional technologies.

This led to the expansion of cultivated area into marginal and for-ested lands and increasing adult male migration to the big cities. Ackerman concluded that this result, and the higher pesticide and water intensity in the U.S. corn sector, led to negative environmental and social effects.

- Porter reported that adoption of drip-irrigated technologies in Mex-ico's tomato production doubled yields and decreased the total area under cultivation by 15 percent, and displaced 15 percent of tomato production from the environmentally stressed Florida region.
- Reinert and Roland-Holst found that NAFTA appears to have led to increases in particulate matter, carbon monoxide, sulfur dioxide, nitrous oxide, and volatile organic compound emissions in the petro-leum, base metals, and transportation equipment sectors.
- IFC Consulting reported that expanded road freight transportation has led to an absolute increase in air emission concentrations at the Mexico–United States and United States–Canada border-crossing points.

Perhaps a major shortcoming of the environmental review process is that—except for Canada, Jordan, Chile, Singapore, and Australia—the U.S. FTA partners have not conducted reviews of the environmental im-pact of the agreement on their countries. Although these agreements are likely to have only minimal effects on the United States, they may well have very significant effects on smaller U.S. trade partners. For example, Honduras's exports to the United States account for more than 40 per-cent of its gross domestic product, and Nicaragua's exports to the United States account for slightly more than 28 percent of its gross domestic product.

U.S. negotiators believe they cannot require other parties to FTAs with the United States to undertake environmental reviews, as these are sovereign nations. Additionally, they do not believe that the United States should undertake its own analysis of the potential environmental impact on U.S. trade partners, because such a study would lack credibil-ity in the other party and would be viewed as condescending.

Provisions of U.S. FTAs

The U.S. approach to the environment in negotiating FTAs has been to seek a balance between two somewhat conflicting objectives. The first is a recognition that, as a sovereign nation, each party to the agreement has the right to determine its own approach to environmental protection. This is appropriate, as each country faces different environmental problems and has a different level of capacity and political will to deal with these problems. The second basic objective has been to ensure that neither party to the agreement lowers its environmental standards or enforcement of standards already in place to gain a commercial advantage.

Accordingly, environmental chapters in U.S. FTAs have included language to accomplish both objectives. For example, the basic language, as set out in Article 5:3 of the Jordan agreement, is as follows: "(a) A Party shall not fail to effectively enforce its environmental laws, through a sustained or recurring course of action or inaction, in a manner affecting trade between the Parties. . . . (b) The Parties recognize that each Party retains the right to exercise discretion with respect to investigatory, prosecutorial, regulatory, and compliance matters and to make decisions regarding the allocation of resources to enforcement with respect to other environmental matters determined to have higher priorities."

Along with the commitment not to lower environmental standards or enforcement, recent U.S. agreements all contain hortatory language to the effect that the parties "shall ensure that [their] laws and regulations provide for the highest levels of environmental protection and shall strive to continue to improve those laws and regulations."

Starting with the United States–Chile agreement, agreements have also included hortatory language on voluntary instruments and mechanisms that can contribute to enhancing environmental stewardship. In the case of Chile and Singapore, the agreements simply stated that each party should encourage enterprises operating within its jurisdiction to voluntarily incorporate sound principles of corporate stewardship. The Australian agreement had a different emphasis on encouraging flexible, market-based mechanisms that encourage the protection of natural resources and the environment. The Moroccan agreement expanded this further to include a listing of complementary voluntary mechanisms, such as partnerships involving business, NGOs, government agencies, and so on, and market-based incentives to encourage conservation and the protection of natural resources. The Moroccan model was continued in CAFTA, and in the Bahrain, Colombia, South Korea, Oman, Panama, and Peru agreements.

The environmental side agreement to NAFTA has an elaborate institutional structure for administering the environmental provisions, including the CEC, a Secretariat, and a public advisory committee. The

CEC, which is the governing institution, is composed of the environment ministers from each country, and meets at least once a year.

The post-NAFTA agreements all have less elaborate institutions. For example, institutional arrangements in some other U.S. FTAs include the following:

- Chile: a Commission that meets at least once every two years;
- Morocco: a Working Group on Environmental Cooperation that meets at least once a year;
- Bahrain and Oman: a Joint Forum to meet regularly; and
- CAFTA-DR: an Environmental Affairs Council.

Initially, a number of environmental groups objected to institutional structures that are less elaborate than NAFTA's. However, it is unrealistic to expect Cabinet officials to attend annual meetings for all the FTAs. Additionally, because the amount of trade and potential environmental impact on the United States of these other agreements is considerably less than for NAFTA, the less elaborate structure is preferable.

A very important feature of U.S. FTAs with developing countries, where institutions and expertise for environmental protection may be lacking, has been the provisions for capacity building. Some examples of the capacity-building assistance that the United States has given its trade partners include the following:

- Mexico: Established a chemicals department in the environment agency; improved management of toxic chemicals (Mexico's successful approach at phasing out DDT is now being adopted in Central America); development of a mandatory pollutant release and transfer registry; and conservation of wildlife habitat;[15]
- Morocco: Capacity-building efforts have addressed areas such as pollution prevention, cleaner production, and the principles of environmental law and enforcement; and
- CAFTA-DR: Programs are designed "to strengthen environmental management systems, including reinforcing the institutional and legal frameworks and the capacity to develop, implement, administer, and enforce environmental laws, regulations, standards, and policies."[16]

15. Organization for Economic Cooperation and Development, "Environment and Regional Trade Agreements, 2007," 81–82.
16. Ibid., 80.

Adequate financing, of course, is crucial to good capacity building. However, an important question is whether the funding is new money that would not otherwise have been forthcoming or reprogrammed funding. If it is the latter, has the funding for trade-related capacity building been more or less effective than would have been the case if the money had been used for other projects to promote environmental protection? In the case of CAFTA-DR, funding for capacity building appears to be new money. However, for the other agreements, it generally appears to be reprogrammed funding. It must also be noted that "some developing countries have complained that once the momentum of the negotiation is gone, and commitments on environmental issues agreed, the necessary resources for the implementation of environmental co-operation provisions does not always follow, or the allocation of resources is not necessarily in line with recipients' priorities."[17]

All the U.S. FTAs also have dispute settlement provisions. Until the May 10, 2007, agreement between the administration and congressional leaders on treating the environment in trade agreements, the penalty for a violation of environmental laws was a fine (up to $15 million for most of the agreements, and $20 million for Australia and the first year of NAFTA, which then changed to a percentage of trade). The fines were to go to a fund that would be used to provide capacity building to the developing country to remedy the problem.

However, as a result of the May 10 agreement, the most recent agreements with Colombia, South Korea, Panama, and Peru subject violations of environmental provisions to the same dispute settlement process as commercial disputes, which could mean trade retaliation. These newest agreements also extend the scope of violations further to include a commitment to enforce environmental regulations and other measures, as well as laws.

The agreements with Peru, Colombia, Panama, and South Korea also have provisions to subject obligations under MEAs to dispute settlement. And the level of obligation in these agreements is also strengthened, from a soft obligation found in some of the agreements ("shall seek to") to a no-derogation provision ("shall not lower").

U.S. FTAs, from NAFTA on, have also included investor-state provisions, which allow foreign investors to initiate binding arbitration to determine if the company is due financial compensation because of a government action or regulation that results in a "taking" of the compa-

17. Ibid., 100.

ny's property. U.S. business organizations have argued these provisions are necessary because they do not trust foreign courts. In the view of many, however, these provisions give foreign investors greater rights than domestic companies, because this procedure is not open to a domestic firm, and it also gives foreign investors an additional avenue for redress because they can also seek redress through the domestic court system or through the agreement's dispute settlement mechanism. Additionally, environmental groups argue that investors might use this system to undermine those domestic regulations that are intended to protect the environment and human health.

However, three events have reduced concerns regarding this issue. First, the 2002 trade act requires U.S. negotiators to pursue investment agreements in a manner "consistent with U.S. legal principles and practice," to provide foreign investors with no "greater substantive rights with respect to investment protections" than those enjoyed by U.S. investors in U.S. courts, and to establish an appellate process in dispute resolution and ensure appropriate public involvement in dispute hearings.

Second, concern regarding investor-state provisions was reduced in August 2005, when a NAFTA tribunal dismissed the case filed by Methanex. (In 1999, as noted above, Methanex had challenged a California regulation banning the gasoline additive MTBE in a case that had seemed to confirm the concerns of many environmentalists.) Not only did the tribunal dismiss Methanex's case; it also awarded $4 million in damages to the U.S. government. The U.S. government views the decision as a "vindication of the prerogative of states to take action to protect public health and the environment without running afoul of the investment protection provisions of international trade agreements and investment treaties."[18] Finally, the May 10, 2007, agreement between the administration and congressional leaders specified that these provisions do not give investors the right to challenge legitimate environmental and safety measures.

One of the greatest benefits of including environmental provisions in U.S. FTAs has been that it has improved the way some of its developing-country partners treat environmental protection. For example, at the time of the NAFTA negotiations, Mexico was still developing its environmental legislation, and its trade and environmental ministries had

18. U.S. Department of State, press release, http://www.state.gov/r/pa/prs/ps/2005/50964.htm.

not worked together to any great extent. El Salvador had similar problems in the United States–CAFTA-DR negotiations. For Morocco,

the negotiation of the [trade agreement] with the United States accelerated the adoption of several environmental Acts that had been pending for years. For Chile, the negotiations with Canada and the United States provided momentum for a thorough overhaul and codification of its environmental legislation, which up to then was scattered in numerous Acts and regulations. Without the "external" impulse given by the negotiation of this kind of provision, these changes may not have occurred, or would have occurred at a later stage. Another positive outcome has been enhanced regional cohesion in environmental matters. For Central American countries involved in the negotiations of the U.S.-CAFTA-DR, the experience of working on common "regional" positions, in preparation of the negotiations with the United States, enhanced regional cohesion and facilitated (for the first time) discussions on environmental and trade issues among experts of these countries.[19]

Negotiations currently under way for a Trans-Pacific Partnership (TPP) trade agreement, if successful, appear likely to improve synergy between trade liberalization and environmental protection even farther than has been accomplished in U.S. free trade area agreements to date. The U.S. proposal would continue the provisions of its agreements that require members to enforce their environmental laws and avoid weakening them for competitive reasons. In addition, the U.S. proposal would require that TPP signatories uphold the provisions of seven MEAs, provided that they are a party to the agreement, including the Convention on International Trade in Endangered Species and the Montreal Protocol on Ozone Depleting Substances. (This provision would be similar to that in the United States–Peru agreement.)

In addition, the United States has tabled a proposal aimed at addressing illegal trade in forest products, endangered wildlife, and illegal fishing activities. This would include information sharing among the TPP parties, including for law enforcement purposes, and measures to sup-

---

19. Organization for Economic Cooperation and Development, "Environment and Regional Trade Agreements, 2007," 48.

plement the Convention on International Trade in Endangered Species agreement.

However, some environmental groups have raised concerns that U.S. proposals on investor/state dispute settlement in the TPP might be tilted in favor of multinational corporations at the potential cost of inhibiting regulators from developing regulations that would better protect the environment and health and safety.

WTO Dispute Settlement

As noted above, the WTO, which came into being on January 1, 1995, recognized the need for the trade rules to be compatible with the needs of sustainable development to a far greater extent than had its predecessor, the GATT. However, the environmental community had significant concerns with the WTO's new dispute settlement mechanism, which could result in real sanctions being imposed for violations and which had sharp timelines for resolving disputes. Many viewed this new mechanism, which is arguably significantly more far-reaching than any other international organization's dispute resolution procedure, as a threat to domestic environmental and safety regulations, and also to MEAs. Many were also concerned that the new WTO dispute settlement system lacked transparency, and there was no assurance that it would consider the views of outside experts.

The original GATT, which was now incorporated into the WTO, requires in Article III that imported products be treated no less favorably than "like" domestic products. Traditionally, the phrase "like" products was interpreted by the trade rules as two products that compete against each other in the market as substitutes without consideration of how the product was produced. However, many environmental rules and agreements specifically address the way in which the product is made, known as "production process method" (PPM) rules.

Under the GATT's perspective, tuna were tuna regardless of whether they were caught in a net that inadvertently killed dolphins or not; but to an environmentalist concerned about preserving endangered dolphins, this was the key distinction. Two GATT dispute settlement cases (one brought by Mexico and one by the EU)—which ruled that U.S. provisions requiring that tuna be caught in a way that avoided inadvertently killing dolphins, were GATT illegal—particularly upset environmentalists.

The trade rules traditionally took a very dim view of drawing trade distinctions based on the way a product is made, because it is extraordinarily easy to design a protectionist standard based on such a rule. (To the trade community, this is known as "green protectionism," i.e., the use of a trade measure under the guise of an environmental objective when the real intent is to protect a domestic industry.) Now, however, for environmentalists the new dispute settlement mechanism raised the specter of the WTO ruling against environmental and safety measures based on PPMs in domestic law and MEAs.

However, WTO dispute settlement cases have since gone a long way to allow environmental and safety rules that are based on the way the product is produced, provided it is not trade protectionist. A major case was the Appellate Body's second ruling in October 22, 2001, on the shrimp-turtle case. Although the initial ruling by a dispute settlement panel in 1998 alarmed environmentalists, the Appellate Body's second ruling went a long way to easing the environmental community's concerns. The initial ruling had found the United States in violation of its trade obligations in banning shrimp imported from four Southeast Asian nations because they did not harvest the shrimp in nets incorporating turtle excluder devices. This decision was based to a large extent on the fact that the United States had not sought an international agreement on protecting endangered sea turtles in harvesting shrimp. Following this ruling, the United States sought such an international agreement and allowed countries greater flexibility in how they protected turtles when harvesting shrimp, provided that the effectiveness of the protection was comparable to the U.S. level.

Malaysia launched a second complaint, and this time the Appellate Body ruled in favor of the United States. This new ruling specified that trade measures were acceptable provided that they met the test of one of Article XX's specific exceptions (necessary to protect human, animal, or plant life; or relating to the conservation of natural resources) and did not constitute a disguised restriction on trade. As a result of this decision and others, the WTO would seem to provide flexibility for countries to impose production process method standards for environmental protection.

Another major issue for the WTO in the trade-environment nexus is the treatment of the "precautionary principle," and progress here is not as great as for the PPM issue. The Rio Declaration on Environment and Development stated that where there are threats of serious or irreversible damage, the lack of full scientific certainty shall not be used as a reason for postponing cost-effective measures to prevent environmental degradation.[20] However, WTO members—particularly the United States and the EU—disagree sharply as to the test for what constitutes the threat of serious damage.

This issue of what is the legitimate use of the precautionary principle has come to a head several times in disputes between the EU and the United States. In 1996, the United States brought a dispute regarding EU restrictions on the importation of meat products with traces of meat hormones. In 1998, the WTO ruled that the EU restrictions were inconsistent with the sanitary and phytosanitary measures agreement. However, rather than remove the restrictions, the EU opted to allow the United States to impose sanctions on imports of other products (valued at $116.8 million) from the EU.

In 2003, the United States brought a dispute regarding national marketing and import bans on biotechnology products that a number of EU member states maintain, even though those products have already been approved by the EU for importing and marketing in the EU. This is also an issue with enormous implications for many developing countries, which hope to be able to use genetically modified organisms (GMOs) to raise more drought- and disease-resistant crops, and unfortunately the EU's restrictions have scared some African countries away from GMO crops, even though such crops have enormous potential for that continent. Accordingly, a number of developing countries have joined the dispute—including Chile, Colombia, India, Mexico, Peru, El Salvador, China, Honduras, Thailand, and Uruguay. In January 2008, the WTO sided with the United States and gave the EU a deadline to speed up the approval process of GMOs and lift member states' bans on GMOs that have been found safe by EU regulators.

It seems that from these cases, the WTO gives members substantial latitude in determining acceptable levels of risk in applying the precautionary principle, but that the procedural risk assessments of the sanitary and phytosanitary measures code must be followed.

The Unfulfilled Environmental Promise of the Doha Round

In launching a new multilateral trade round in November 2001, the WTO committed to become more environmentally friendly. In the words

20. Available at http://www.oardc.ohio-state.edu/plantranslab/HCS597/precprinc.htm.

of WTO director-general Pascal Lamy, these negotiations represent a "very modest start that the international community has agreed to make to address environmental challenges through the prism of trade."[21]

A small initial positive step was taken as the round was launched. As noted in chapter 2, to gain the developing countries' support for launching the Doha Round, the developed countries had to agree to a procedure under which waivers from the requirements of the Trade-Related Aspects of Intellectual Property Rights (TRIPS) agreement could be approved to allow small developing countries facing a national emergency, such as the AIDS crisis, to be able to import inexpensive generic drugs. Rwanda, which was facing a severe AIDS crisis and whose impoverished population could not afford patented retroviral drugs that cost several hundred thousand dollars a year, was the first to apply for a waiver.

Unfortunately, it took until July 2007 before Rwanda could use this provision so that they could import generics that only cost several hundred dollars a year—still a huge sum for a country with a per capita income of less than $200 annually, but it has brought the cost down to the realm where governmental programs and donors can make these drugs available to infected citizens.

Another positive step is that several countries have conducted environmental assessments of the potential impact of a successful round, including the European Union and Canada. The EU conducted an assessment of the overall impact—as well as specific ones on fisheries, forestry, environmental services, pharmaceuticals, and agriculture—and the EU studies do raise some specific problems that would need to be addressed as the negotiations progress. For example, the study on the forestry sector concludes that "trade liberalization could accentuate negative sustainability trends unless appropriate forest governance systems are in place and enforced. Cumulative impacts and the threshold effect mean small incremental changes could result in significant negative impacts in individual countries with sustainability and governance problems. In biodiversity hotspot countries such as Brazil, Indonesia, the Congo Basin countries and Papua New Guinea possible negative impacts could be irreversible."[22]

The Doha Round had also sought to make progress in better reconciling trade and the environment in two other areas, but unfortunately these are unlikely to be achieved given the apparent failure of the Doha

21. Available at http://www.wto.org/english/news_e/sppl_e/sppl54_e.htm.
22. European Commission, Directorate-General for Trade, "Trade SIA of the Forest Sector under DDA Negotiations: Position Paper," Brussels, June 26, 2006, 3.

Round. The first of these relates to the problem of overfishing. A number of countries that are major exporters of fish provide an estimated total $30 to $34 billion in subsidies to their fishing industries, according to a study by the University of British Columbia's Fisheries Center. Most of these subsidies have gone to expand fishing capacity, and this has contributed to far too much fishing capacity globally.

Although estimates of the seriousness of this problem vary, a study published in *Science* projected that 29 percent of the species that are fished commercially had collapsed by 2003. The environmental community describes the current situation as "too many boats chasing too few fish." In addition to its environmental impact, overfishing has serious repercussions for maintaining an acceptable diet in many developing countries, which often depend on fish as a major protein source. Overfishing off the coast of many of these developing countries is threatening the sustainability of this critical food source for these nations.

To help address this problem, the United States and others have been pressing for a code in the Doha Development Round that would prohibit fisheries subsidies that lead to overcapacity. Under the draft text published November 30, 2007, subsidies that support acquisition, construction, repair, renovation or modification of fishing vessels, or support operating costs such as fuel or bait, or price supports for products of wild capture fishing would all be prohibited.[23]

Subsidies that assisted sustainable fishing would be permitted—for example, retraining workers into occupations unrelated to fishing or decommissioning fishing vessels. The least-developed countries would be exempted from most of the disciplines of the draft code, and the developing countries would be permitted to subsidize inshore operations and subsidies for boats not greater than 10 meters in length for marine fishing.

Currently several MEAs would require parties to the agreement to curtail subsidies that contribute to overcapacity. The advantages of a WTO code, however, are that all WTO members would be obliged to curtail these subsidies, and a workable and effective dispute settlement procedure would be in place that could result in harsh sanctions for violations.

A number of countries—including South Korea, Taiwan, Japan, Portugal, France, and Italy—all subsidize their fishing fleets. Without an

23. A copy of the U.S. proposal is available at http://www.wto.org/english/news _e/news07_e/rules_draft_text_nov07_e.htm.

overall trade agreement whereby everyone agrees to forgo these subsidies simultaneously and in which they gain offsetting concessions, these countries will continue to subsidize overbuilding of capacity, and the survival of more and more species of fish will be in doubt.

The second area where trade negotiators had been hoping to reach an agreement that can both benefit trade interests and promote better environmental stewardship is by eliminating barriers to trade in environmental goods and services. The United States and EU tabled a proposal in 2007 to eliminate trade barriers on 43 products related to climate change and 153 goods associated with manufacturing or generating energy in an environmentally friendly way. (Developing countries would have "special and differential" treatment under the United States–EU proposal.) Brazil would add biofuels to the list of barrier-free products; however, the United States has a high duty on imported biofuels and opposes this.

Agreements to limit subsidies that promote overfishing and eliminate trade barriers on environmental goods and services should be high priorities in future negotiations.

Conclusion: Almost There

The environmental community strongly opposed trade agreements after some dispute settlement decisions in the GATT/WTO and NAFTA in the mid-1990s that seemed to show a disregard for measures taken to protect the environment. As a result, environmentalists marched with labor unions and other opponents of globalization in the Seattle streets in 1999 in an effort to block the launch of a new round of trade negotiations.

Shortly after the adverse dispute settlement panel decisions, however, the WTO Appellate Body reversed the panel decisions that were particularly egregious, and the United States and some other nations agreed to regularly undertake assessments of the potential environmental impact of proposed trade agreements. Additionally, the Doha Round promised to take additional steps to better reconcile trade liberalization with protection of health and the environment. To get developing countries to agree to a new trade round, negotiators had to agree to ease the TRIPS rules on compulsory licensing so that small poor nations could more easily import generic drugs in the event of a national emergency. They also committed to negotiations in two areas that could have positive effects for environmental stewardship: a possible agreement to end subsidies that contribute to overfishing, and a possible agreement to reduce trade barriers on environmental goods and services. Unfortunately, with the apparent failure of the Doha Round, agreements in these two areas are unlikely.

Meanwhile, U.S. FTAs have made significant progress in reconciling trade liberalization and environmental protection. Following the NAFTA precedent, all U.S. agreements require the parties to commit not to lower their environmental regulations to gain a commercial advantage. Many of these agreements include side provisions that the United States will provide funding for capacity building to alleviate environmental concerns identified in the assessment process. The more recent U.S. agreements require the parties to implement their obligations under some of the MEAs or be subject to dispute settlement. Another major step has been taken in the negotiations for the TPP agreement, where U.S. negotiators have submitted proposals to positively benefit both forest and fisheries resources.

However, one area where trade policy needs to better recognize the legitimate concerns of the environmental community is to conduct environmental assessments of the likely impact of the U.S. agreements on its developing-country partners. Although the United States must respect the sovereignty of these countries, it could offer to fund a study of the possible impact on the environment of its developing-country partners, and it could encourage an international organization, such as the United Nations Environment Program, to undertake such assessments.

Overall, however, in view of these developments since the mid-1990s, it can be said that trade and environmental protection are now *uneasy neighbors*. Some mainstream environmental groups have moved back to accepting further trade liberalization but continue to cast a wary eye on the negotiations to ensure that there is continued progress in making trade and environmental stewardship genuinely synergistic.

Chapter 8

The Labor Dilemma

According to the factor price equalization theorem, wages around the world would tend to equalize under conditions of free trade. This would mean that unskilled workers in the United States would be injured, either through increased unemployment or reduced wages or both, as we saw in chapter 3. Thus, it is not surprising that the major industrial trade unions in the United States have been the strongest and most consistent opponents of America's trade agreements for the past thirty years. To try to offset this injury and to minimize organized labor's opposition to trade agreements, Congress has included a Trade Adjustment Assistance (TAA) program in trade legislation since the 1962 Trade Expansion Act.

In addition to TAA, the AFL-CIO has successfully demanded that U.S. negotiators seek to include provisions in U.S. trade agreements that commit the parties to the agreement to respect the core standards of the International Labor Organization (ILO). These provisions are now a standard part of U.S. bilateral and regional free trade agreements (FTAs), but U.S. trade partners have refused to consider such provisions in the World Trade Organization (WTO) or the Doha Round.

From the end of World War II through the 1960s, the two major unions in the United States—the American Federation of Labor (AFL) and the Congress of Industrial Organizations (CIO) supported America's trade agreements program. The AFL and the CIO, which merged in 1955 to become the AFL-CIO, were concerned that communism could spread from the Soviet Union to Western Europe and Japan, and they agreed that trade agreements could help those countries regain their economic footing and strengthen democracy. For example, in 1962 the AFL-CIO supported the Trade Expansion Act, which President John F. Kennedy touted as a "jobs bill"; in his remarks signing this legislation, Kennedy said, "Increased economic activity resulting from increased trade will provide more job opportunities for our workers."[1]

By the early 1970s, however, U.S. industry was losing competitiveness as Europe and Japan recovered from the wartime devastation, and U.S. industries, such as consumer electronics and machine tools, were being wiped out by foreign competition. The AFL-CIO switched from supporting trade liberalization to seeking protection from foreign competition. (However, the United Auto Workers continued to support open trade in automobiles until the early 1980s, when small, fuel-efficient cars from Japan and Europe began to grab a significant share of the U.S. market.)

In 1971, the AFL-CIO worked with Congress to push the Burke-Hartke Bill, and this "marked the formal conversion of the politically powerful AFL-CIO . . . to a protectionist stance. . . . [This legislation] called for across-the-board import quotas and changes to U.S. international tax laws so sweeping that most foreign direct investment would have become immediately unprofitable for U.S. companies."[2]

In the face of strong opposition from the White House and industry and threats of retaliation from U.S. trade partners, the Burke-Hartke Bill failed to pass Congress. Nonetheless, since that time the AFL-CIO has generally continued to oppose new agreements; although it has not been successful in blocking new negotiations, labor's opposition has slowed down the passage of several trade agreements—most recently, and most notably, the U.S. agreement with Colombia—and has had a significant effect in shaping legislation that authorizes new trade negotiations.

In the most recently enacted legislative authority for negotiating trade agreements—the 2002 Trade Act—U.S. labor unions did play a significant role in shaping the objectives of the nation's trade agreements. One objective stated in this legislation is "to promote respect for worker rights and the rights of children consistent with core labor standards of

---

1. President John F. Kennedy, October 11, 1962, "Remarks upon Signing the Trade Expansion Act."
2. Stephen D. Cohen, Robert A. Blecker, and Peter D. Whitney, *Fundamentals of U.S. Foreign Trade Policy: Economics, Politics, Laws, and Issues* (Boulder, Colo.: Westview Press, 2003), 39.

the ILO."[3] Another is to specifically promote universal ratification of ILO Convention 182 for the prohibition of the worst forms of child labor. And a third is a requirement to ensure that the parties to U.S. trade agreements do not weaken the protections of their labor laws as an inducement to trade and investment.

The Economic Theory of Trade and Labor

On the basis of standard economic theory, it is easy to understand why the labor movement opposes new trade agreements that would lead to expanded international trade. As discussed in chapter 3, under free trade countries export products where they have a comparative advantage and import products where they have a disadvantage, and their comparative advantage is in products that are produced with the factor of production (e.g., labor or capital) that is in relative abundance for that country.

The United States has a relative abundance of capital and a relative scarcity of unskilled labor. The factor price equalization theorem predicts that under free trade, the price of factors of production would tend to equalize between nations. Joseph Stiglitz describes the situation as follows:

> Standard economic theory, which underlies the call for trade liberalization, has a scenario for what should happen with full liberalization—a scenario that its advocates seldom mention. . . . With full global economic integration, the world will become like a single country, and the wages of unskilled workers will be the same everywhere in the world, no matter where they live. Whether in America or in India or in China, unskilled workers of comparable skills performing comparable work will be paid the same. . . . In practice, given the relative size of the populations, the likelihood is that the single wage to which they will converge will be closer to that of China and India than to that of the United States or Europe.[4]

Totally eliminating trade barriers, of course, would not remove all the obstacles to trade. There would still be transportation costs (which, as

3. The 2002 Trade Act is available at http://heinonline.org.
4. Joseph E. Stiglitz, *Making Globalization Work* (New York: W. W. Norton, 2006), 271.

we have seen, are higher today on average than developed-country tariffs on nonagricultural goods). Additionally, the costs of converting currencies and the general uncertainty and complexity of trade would prevent the full equalization of factor costs.

More important, under conditions of decreasing costs of production, the prices of the factors of production do not equalize. And many products are produced in industries that experience decreasing costs of production as the volume of production increases; these tend to be high-value-added products like automobiles, steel, semiconductors, and aircraft.

However, for industries that experience constant or increasing costs of production, such as textiles and wine, there would be some equalization of the prices of factors of production, which for the United States would mean that the wages of unskilled labor would fall closer to world levels. Economists tend to assume this problem away. As Dominick Salvatore puts it in his economics textbook: "Since . . . international trade causes real wages and the real income of labor to fall in a capital abundant and labor-scarce nation such as the United States, shouldn't the U.S. government restrict trade? The answer is almost invariably no. The reason is that the loss that trade causes to labor . . . is less than the gain received by owners of capital. With an appropriate redistribution policy of taxes on owners of capital and subsidies to labor, both broad classes of factors of production can benefit from international trade."[5]

In theory, as jobs and capital are displaced from industries that have a comparative disadvantage, these factors of production will move to new areas where the United States has a comparative advantage. However, there are several problems with this theory. First, there are adjustment costs as labor and capital shift to more efficient uses; for example, workers may have to move to a new state or undergo expensive retraining. More fundamentally, not all workers are the same; some simply do not have the education or ability to move to industries that are hiring, and they join the ranks of the permanently unemployed or take jobs that pay very low wages.

Workers who lose their jobs because of import competition can drive down the wages of unskilled workers throughout the economy. As Daniel Drezner says: "Reduced demand for low-skilled labor in the import-competing sectors decreases overall domestic demand for unskilled la-

---

5. Dominick Salvatore, *International Economics*, 8th ed. (Hoboken, N.J.: John Wiley & Sons, 2004), 134.

bor. When demand declines, so do wages. This phenomenon affects low-skilled workers in both tradable and non-tradable sectors. This negative effect has the widest range, in that unskilled workers working in a purely domestic sector still experience a small negative shock from trade expansion."[6] Josh Bivens at the Economic Policy Institute adds that "waitresses, for example, do not generally lose their jobs due to trade, but their pay suffers as workers displaced from tradable goods industries crowd into their labor market and bid down wages."[7] To a small extent, workers hurt by trade will at least benefit by cheaper prices; however, this is small consolation to someone out of work and running out of money.

Economic theory also holds that increased international competition can undermine the bargaining power of labor unions. Companies facing increased competition often cannot afford wage increases because they have to cut costs to remain competitive, and they will consequently be more resistant to labor's demands. Additionally, the company can threaten to move overseas, or the foreign competition may invest in a U.S. state where it can resist unionization.

In a 1996 study of the effects of a threat of closing the plant on the right of workers to organize, Kate Bronfenbrenner, director of labor education research at Cornell University, reported that where "employers can credibly threaten to shut down and/or move their operations in response to union activity, they do so in large numbers; . . . 62 percent in mobile industries such as manufacturing, transportation, and warehouse/distribution . . . In more than 10 percent of the campaigns with threats, the employer directly threatened to move to Mexico if the workers were to organize."[8]

Trade Adjustment Assistance

In response to pressure from labor unions (particularly David McDonald, the former president of the United Steelworkers Union) and bol-

---

6. Daniel W. Drezner, *U.S. Trade Strategy: Free Versus Fair.* Critical Policy Choices Series (New York: Council on Foreign Relations, 2006), 76.

7. Josh Bivens, "Marketing the Gains from Trade," Economic Policy Institute, June 2007, http://www.epi.ort/publications/entry/ib233.

8. Kate Bronfenbrenner, "Final Report: The Effects of Plant Closing or Threat of Plant Closing on the Right of Workers to Organize," Digital Commons@ILR: Cornell University ILR School, 1966, 2, http://digitalcommons.ilr.cornell.edu/intl/1/.

stered by economic theory, Congress established the TAA in the 1962 Trade Expansion Act. Under TAA, workers who have lost their jobs due to import competition can receive retraining, financial support for moving to a new job, and extended unemployment insurance; and firms affected by import competition could originally receive loans and loan guarantees, tax relief, and technical assistance.

TAA was little used until its benefits were expanded in the Trade Act of 1974, and since then the program has been modified several times. In 1986, the program to provide loans and loan guarantees for firms was eliminated due to limited effectiveness. In 2002, new benefits were added; and in 2009, the program was expanded so that service firms and workers would be eligible for adjustment assistance, and a new community support program was added. Most recently, the TAA program was extended in the trade bill passed in November 2011, which also ratified the FTAs with South Korea, Panama, and Colombia.

However, benefits are somewhat limited. Assistance for firms is aimed at small and mid-size firms, with average support being roughly $60,000, and the company must pay half the costs of adjustment for projects greater than $30,000. Agricultural producers are limited to benefits of $10,000. Workers can receive 130 weeks of income support (156 if they are older), up to 65 percent of the premium for health insurance, and reimbursement of up to $1,250 for relocation expenses.

In 2008, a fairly typical year, 2,146 petitions for adjustment assistance were filed, of which 1,368 were certified, covering an estimated 126,529 workers.[9] A total of 38,000 workers entered training, 405 were assisted in their job search, and 757 benefited from relocation assistance. The year's total outlays for the TAA program were $259 million.

One of the main criticisms of the TAA program is that it assists firms and workers adversely affected by trade, but not those affected by technology, changes in consumer tastes, or other events. Another major criticism is that the benefits of the program do not appear to justify the costs. Supporters, conversely, argue that TAA reduces opposition to trade liberalization and that it eases the adjustment of resources to industries where the United States has a comparative advantage or where trade does not have a significant impact. In any case, supporters argue that TAA helps companies and workers adversely affected by a government

---

9. In 1980, when TAA was at its peak, some half a million workers received assistance.

policy (i.e., trade liberalization), while other changes are often the result of natural economic forces.

Evaluations of the TAA program are not definitive. In his review of TAA for firms, J. F. Hornbeck of the U.S. International Trade Commission says: "Anecdotal evidence points to numerous 'success' stories, but more sophisticated analysis is needed to estimate the effectiveness of this program approach. It is difficult to isolate the effects of the firm TAA program in determining why a particular firm might succeed in its turnaround effort. Previous studies . . . have suggested that many firms might have been able to do so on their own."[10]

The WTO and the International Labor Organization

The original General Agreement on Tariffs and Trade (GATT) 1947 did not address labor issues, other than through a brief nod in the preamble to the importance of promoting full employment, and a very brief note in Article XX that countries may take action to block the import of goods produced by prison labor.[11] The founders of the post–World War II policy architecture probably assumed that labor issues would be addressed in the ILO, which was established in 1919, and accordingly would have seen no need for the GATT to get into the labor arena.

The ILO, which today has 183 member countries, is a tripartite organization consisting of representatives of the member governments, employers, and workers. Its objective is to promote and improve working conditions by adopting various "conventions," each of which addresses different specific labor issues. Today there are 189 such conventions, many of which overlap. The ILO has no enforcement mechanism to ensure compliance, but it does have the power to publicize violations of labor rights.[12]

Eight of the ILO conventions are considered "core," and these address four key areas:

10. J. F. Hornbeck, *Trade Adjustment Assistance for Firms: Economic, Program, and Policy Issues* (Washington, D.C.: Congressional Research Service, 2011), 6–7.

11. The Preamble of the 1947 GATT states: "Recognizing that their relations in the field of trade and economic endeavor should be conducted with a view to raising standards of living, ensuring full employment . . ."

12. For a listing of the ILO conventions and other information on the ILO, see http://www.ilo.org/global/lang--en/index.htm.

- freedom of association and the right to collective bargaining (conventions 87 and 98);
- elimination of forced labor (conventions 29 and 105);
- abolition of child labor (conventions 138 and 182); and
- nondiscrimination with respect to employment and occupation (conventions 100 and 111).

The United States joined the ILO in 1934, but has only ratified some of the conventions. As a member, the United States is obligated to respect the principles of the core conventions, but of the eight core conventions, the United States has only ratified two, specifically the ones pertaining to the abolition of forced labor (convention 105) and child labor (convention 182). The United States has not ratified the other conventions because some of their provisions conflict with U.S. laws, such as the National Labor Relations Act and the Landrum-Griffin Act. Even though the United States has not ratified these conventions, its actual practices need to respect their principles.

In 1977, the United States dropped out of the ILO because of concerns that the organization had become too politicized and was "appallingly selective" in condemning countries for human rights violations. (For example, the ILO was highly critical of Israel, largely for political reasons, while refusing to condemn some nations that did not respect human rights.) The United States rejoined in 1980 under assurances that the ILO would be less political in the future.

The GATT largely stayed away from labor issues throughout its almost fifty years. However, at the WTO Ministerial Meeting in Seattle in 1999, which was supposed to launch a new round of multilateral trade negotiations, President Clinton called for the formation of a working group to consider the issue of establishing labor standards for international trade, and he said he ultimately would support sanctions against countries that violate labor standards. This came as a surprise to all the negotiators and enormously upset many developing countries.[13]

The secretary of commerce for India at the time, A. V. Ganesan, put the issue this way: "Those who want to link labor standards to the trade

---

13. I was at the Seattle Ministerial Meeting and vividly remember a businessman from India who was so upset he was visibly shaking; he said something to the effect that "our children work not because we want them to; they work because they have to survive."

rules of the WTO have an ulterior motive. . . . The labor organizations of the United States and Europe have complained that the liberalization of trade and investment regimes will lure investment away from wealthy nations to countries where wages are low. But low wages, the result of lower levels of national income, are the primary comparative advantage developing countries have to attract investment and create jobs. This advantage will be destroyed if labor standards are linked to WTO's rules."[14] When the Doha Development Round was finally launched in November 2001, the U.S. proposal to include labor standards was dropped from the negotiating mandate in the face of this strong opposition from developing countries.

U.S. Free Trade Agreements

Promoting labor rights was not an element in the first U.S. FTA, the one with Israel, and was only addressed in a very minimal way in the early negotiations for the North America Free Trade Agreement (NAFTA). However, as noted in chapter 7, NAFTA became embroiled in the 1992 presidential race when Bill Clinton pledged to strengthen the protections for workers' rights. Shortly after he became president, Clinton ordered the negotiations for side agreements on both labor and environment, which then became part of the final NAFTA package.

Under pressure from trade unions, all U.S. bilateral trade agreements since NAFTA have addressed workers' rights. The basic approach taken has been to encourage the advancement of workers' rights within the context of respecting each partner country's national sovereignty, and to require each partner to enforce its own labor laws. Labor's basic concern is that U.S. trade partners might suppress independent unions or allow low-paid child labor in order to gain an unfair advantage in competing with U.S. firms—the so-called race to the bottom.

However, concern with promoting workers' rights had been an element of U.S. trade policy even before these trade agreements were in force. Under the U.S. Generalized System of Preferences (GSP), one of

14. A. V. Ganesan, a former commerce secretary of India and a nongovernmental delegate to the Seattle Ministerial Meeting, as quoted on the Indian Embassy's Web site, http://www.indianembassy.org/Policy/WTO/wto_india/battle_seattle_dec_05_99.htm.

the considerations made by the U.S. government in granting eligibility to developing countries is whether the country respects internationally recognized worker rights, "including (1) the right of association, (2) the right to organize and bargain collectively, (3) freedom from compulsory labor, (4) a minimum age for the employment of children, and (5) acceptable conditions of work with respect to minimum wages, hours of work and occupational safety and health."[15] These GSP provisions have produced some results; for example, in 1987 and 1988 the United States successfully pressed Indonesia to introduce a higher minimum wage and to allow some scope for independent labor unions to operate.

The basic approach taken by the United States in negotiating its FTAs built on the GSP and NAFTA provisions, although specific elements have changed in response to domestic political pressures and the demands of U.S. negotiating partners. For example, the provisions in the U.S. FTAs do not include any reference to minimum wage. Additionally, the dispute settlement provisions have changed from the NAFTA side agreement, which allowed for the imposition of fines only in the event of violations, rather than the trade sanctions that could follow from a commercial dispute. Organized labor objected to the lack of trade sanctions and to the cumbersome nature of the labor dispute settlement mechanism, and it successfully demanded that sanctions be applicable for labor disputes as well as commercial disputes under the FTA dispute settlement mechanism. (It is noteworthy, however, that a number of complaints have been considered under the NAFTA mechanism. By March 2004, fourteen cases had been accepted for review against Mexico, eight against the United States, and one against Canada.)

The next U.S. agreement after NAFTA—that with Jordan—consequently included labor provisions in the main body of the agreement, subject to the same dispute settlement mechanism as commercial disputes, and accordingly the AFL-CIO supported congressional approval of this agreement.

The agreements with Chile and Singapore, two countries that had adequate labor laws before the negotiations, required the parties to the agreement to enforce their labor laws; with regard to ILO workers' rights

15. Office of the U.S. Trade Representative, fact sheet, http://www.ustr.gov/trade-topics/trade-development/preference-programs/generalized-system-preference-gsp/gsp-program-inf.

provisions, the parties only committed to "strive" to honor the core rights. These agreements both reverted to a system of possible fines in the event of a violation, rather than trade sanctions, with any revenue from fines to be used to address the underlying labor problem. Only if the party in violation refused to pay the fine could trade sanctions be imposed.

In contrast to Chile and Singapore, Morocco's labor laws were considered inadequate. Accordingly, before concluding a trade agreement, Morocco agreed to a number of improvements in its labor practices, such as raising the minimum employment age from twelve to fifteen years, reducing the work week from 48 to 44 hours, and guaranteeing the right of association and collective bargaining. Subsequently, Oman, where workers' rights were also considered inadequate, followed a similar path of improving its labor practices; in 2006, the government issued a decree that allowed for collective bargaining, prohibited the dismissal of workers for union activity, guaranteed the right to strike, and raised the penalties for child labor violations.

The six U.S. partners in the Central American Free Trade Agreement–Dominican Republic (CAFTA-DR) were also considered to have weak protection of worker rights. Accordingly, it was agreed to set up a body to help the CAFTA countries improve their labor practices, particularly with regard to honoring ILO standards. Additionally, the United States committed $60 million to capacity building in the areas of environment and labor. (The Chile and Singapore agreements had also included some technical cooperation projects.)

However, organized labor considered CAFTA-DR to be a step back from the Jordan agreement, because violations are only subject to fines, which are capped at $15 million. Additionally, organized labor believed that the CAFTA-DR rules on workers' rights are weaker than they are under GSP. Nonetheless, this agreement has so far been the only one except for NAFTA where a labor complaint has been pursued under the dispute settlement mechanism, and that has been a complaint against Guatemala. In 2008 the AFL-CIO and six Guatemala labor unions filed a complaint alleging that Guatemala had failed to allow freedom of association and other violations. The Labor Department conducted an examination of the issue and concluded that Guatemala in fact was not meeting its obligations. The United States requested consultations in July 2010, but consultations did not resolve the issue, and in August 2011 the United States requested the establishment of an arbitral panel, as provided for in the agreement.

Organized labor has been most strongly opposed to the agreements with Colombia and South Korea—Colombia because of its human rights record, and South Korea because of concerns regarding potential job losses. With regard to the Colombia agreement, the AFL-CIO was particularly concerned with what it perceived as a systematic effort to murder union organizers. For example, John Sweeney, then president of the AFL-CIO, wrote in an April 14, 2008, op-ed article in the *Washington Post* that "it's of little use to include a paper commitment to respect 'freedom of association' when workers who organize and speak out for economic freedom—and their families—face an implicit death sentence."[16]

Proponents of the agreement disagreed and argued that Colombia was just a violent country and that unionists were not targeted. For example, an April 19, 2008, *Washington Post* editorial stated: "Colombia is, indeed, violent—though homicide has dramatically declined. . . . There were 17,198 murders in 2007. Of the dead, only 39—or 0.226 percent—were even members of trade unions, let alone leaders or activists." In any case, Colombia took a series of measures to reduce violence, particularly against labor leaders, and in November 2011 Congress finally approved the agreement.

With regard to current negotiations, the AFL-CIO has been skeptical of the Trans-Pacific Partnership (TPP) negotiations but generally supportive of the Trans-Atlantic Trade and Investment Partnership (TTIP) negotiations. The AFL-CIO considers it critical that the TPP agreement include enforceable commitments to the ILO's core labor standards, and it opposes inclusion of the Investor State Dispute Mechanism. Additionally, the AFL-CIO has expressed concern that other countries might be able to join the TPP after the agreement is reached, regardless of the country's commitment to democracy and labor rights.[17]

The AFL-CIO has been more supportive of negotiating a free trade agreement with the European Union because EU members are all developed countries with generally high labor standards. However, with regard to the portion of the TTIP that will address regulatory barriers, the AFL-CIO emphasizes that, "instead of harmonizing regulations down to the

16. Available at www.washingtonpost.com/up-dyn/content/article/2008/04/18/AR2008041802900.html.
17. This is from AFL-CIO, "Trans-Pacific Free Trade Agreement," http://www.aflcio.org/Issues/Trade/Trans-Pacific-Free-Trade-Agreement.

lowest level, the U.S. and EU should work together to raise occupational safety and health standards and labor rights guarantees for *all* workers."[18]

Should Labor Standards Be Included in U.S. FTAs?

The issue of whether or not labor standards should be included in the U.S. FTAs is controversial. For example, the Princeton economist Jagdish Bhagwati argues that "simply proscribing the use of child labor is unlikely to eliminate it; it will only drive poor parents to send their children to work by stealth and often into even worse 'occupations' such as prostitution."[19] Additionally, Bhagwati argues that trade sanctions are the wrong remedy since "trade often accounts for a tiny fraction of the sales of products made with offending processes such as child labor. Only 5 percent of the output of child labor is estimated to enter trade, so trade sanctions are not even an appropriately targeted policy."[20]

Many in business argue that the best approach is to promote economic growth through expanded trade, because expanded economic activity and employment tend to lead to improved labor standards. Furthermore, business and some other opponents are concerned that the United States itself has some practices that could be found in violation of the core ILO provisions.

On the other side, U.S. labor believes that without commitments to respect workers' rights and end child labor, and requirements that countries will not weaken their labor laws for reasons of competitive advantage, there could be a race to the bottom whereby nations weaken their labor rights to increase their exports and attract foreign investment. The Harvard economist Dani Rodrik adds that "nondiscrimination, freedom of association, collective bargaining, prohibition of forced labor do not 'cost' anything; compliance with these 'core labor rights' does not harm, and indeed possibly benefits, economic development."[21]

18. This is from AFL-CIO, "What Would a Free Trade Agreement with the EU Look Like?" http://www.aflcio.org/Blog/Global-Action/What-Would-a-Free-Trade-Agreement-with-the-EU-Look-Like.

19. Jagdish Bhagwati, *In Defense of Globalization*, Council on Foreign Relations Report (New York: Oxford University Press, 2004), 71.

20. Ibid., 249.

21. Dani Rodrik, *One Economics—Many Recipes: Globalization, Institutions, and Economic Growth* (Princeton, N.J.: Princeton University Press, 2007), 229.

Provided U.S. negotiators show flexibility with and understanding of the realities that many of our developing-country partners face, including labor standards will lessen labor's opposition to trade agreements and provide some benefit to the workers in U.S. trade partners.

The Impact of the GATT/WTO on U.S. Labor

As a result of the widespread trade liberalization since World War II, world trade has expanded enormously. What has been the impact of this huge increase in trade on workers in America? To what extent has the increase in trade caused the substantial increase in income inequality that the United States has experienced during the past thirty years? And to what extent has it contributed to unemployment in the United States, which reached more than 9 percent in 2009, 2010, and 2011?

With regard to income inequality, incomes in the United States have grown substantially more unequal over the past forty years, in contrast to the 1947–68 period, during which incomes in the United States had become more equal. Although statisticians have many ways of measuring income inequality, all show a similar pattern of rising inequality in the United States. For example, in 1969 the average income of households in the top 10 percent was 8.93 times that of those in the bottom 10 percent; but by 2009, it was 11.36 times as high, an increase of 27 percent.[22] Another common way to measure income inequality is the Gini Coefficient, which ranks inequality on a scale from 0 to 1, with zero indicating complete equality and one indicating complete inequality (i.e., where one person has all the wealth). In 1969, the Gini Coefficient for the United States was 0.391, but by 2009 it had risen to 0.468, an increase of some 18 percent.

Although income inequality has been increasing in a number of countries, it has increased to a greater extent in the United States than almost all other developed countries. For example, measured by the Gini Coefficient, income inequality rose in Japan from 0.24 in the early 1990s to

22. Census Bureau data on income inequality in the United States are available at www.census.gov/hhes/www/income/data/historical/inequality. In addition, see the excellent paper from the World Bank, "Measuring Inequality," http://web.worldbank .org/WBSITE/EXTERNAL/TOPICS/EXTPOVERTY/EXTPA/0,,contentMDK: 20238991~menuPK:492138~pagePK:148956~piPK:216618~theSitePK:430367,00 .html.

about 0.39 in 2007. According to Elhanan Helpman, the income gap in the United States "increased by 29 percent, more than in any other country. But it also increased by 27 percent in the U.K., 15 percent in New Zealand, 14 percent in Italy, and 9 percent in Canada."[23] In fact, income inequality in the United States is even greater than for some developing countries; for example, the Gini Coefficient for Indonesia is just 0.37, while Russia's is 0.42, according to the World Bank.

Economists are not sure of the exact causes of this increase in inequality among American households, but, as we have seen, economic theory would indicate that increased world trade could be a partial explanation. According to the law of comparative advantage, the United States would tend to export those products that are produced with the factors that it has in relative abundance, which are capital and technology, and import products made by the factors of relative scarcity, such as unskilled labor, which would mean that U.S. wages for unskilled labor would fall. And that is exactly what has happened since 1970.

There are many other factors that may be causing the increase in income inequality, and it is impossible to identify the exact role of expanded trade. Some of the factors commonly mentioned by economists include increasing automation, particularly of low-skilled jobs; the declining clout of labor unions; the shift from manufacturing to services since the 1980s; changes in business practices, such as the increased use of temporary workers; and sociological changes such as higher divorce rates.

Estimates of the impact of expanded trade on income inequality vary widely, with some analysts arguing that it has been a major factor. At the other extreme, Bhagwati argues that "trade has actually helped the workers, not just harmed them insignificantly, by moderating the decline that was instead caused by technical change that economized on the use of unskilled labor."[24]

However, the consensus among economists seems to be that expanded trade accounts for some of the rising income inequality in the United States, although it is not the major cause. As J. F. Hornbeck notes, "The USITC [U.S. International Trade Commission], in summarizing the vast literature on the observed rising U.S. income gap between more-skilled

23. Elhanan Helpman, *The Mystery of Economic Growth* (Cambridge, Mass.: Belknap Press of Harvard University Press, 2004), 95–96.
24. Bhagwati, *In Defense*, 122–23.

and less-skilled workers, suggests that while estimates varied, trade in general has contributed to no more than 10–20% of the wage gap."[25]

With regard to the static impact of trade on employment in the United States, exports create both production and jobs, while imports tend to displace production and employment, as noted in chapter 3. The U.S. trade deficit as a percentage of its gross domestic product has increased enormously over the past three decades, rising to more than 5 percent between 2004 and 2007, before declining due to the U.S. recession, which curbed import demand even more than recession in other countries reduced demand for our exports. Logically, this trade imbalance would seem to be a cause of our high unemployment.

However, unemployment has many causes. Increases in productivity have played a major role, as companies today can produce more with fewer workers. Additionally, the business cycle is a major determinant of the employment level, and unemployment today is high to a large extent because of the deep recession that started in 2008. In fact, changes in the business cycle have a far more significant impact on unemployment year to year than does the impact of the U.S. trade balance.

America's economy naturally has a great deal of "churn"; as some companies and industries grow and others decline, employees may find themselves unemployed or may decide to switch into another company or even a different career. International trade, of course, can accelerate the level of churn through the creative destruction it causes. This churn can cause substantial pain, because many employees in industries that suddenly cannot compete because of foreign competition do not have skills that are readily usable in other industries, and thus they may face permanent unemployment or need to accept a job with lower pay. Till von Wachter, an economist at Columbia University, estimates that workers who lose a stable job often suffer a 20 percent earnings loss for fifteen years or more.[26]

Not surprisingly, estimates of the impact of trade on unemployment in the United States vary substantially, although most would agree that

25. J. F. Hornbeck, *NAFTA at Ten: Lessons from Recent Studies* (Washington, D.C.: Congressional Research Service, 2004), 5.
26. Till von Wachter, "Challenges for the U.S. Economic Recovery," Testimony before the Senate Budget Committee, February 3, 2011, http://www.columbia .edu/~vw2112/Von_Wachter_Testimony_Before_Senate_Budget_Committee_2011 .pdf.

there is some impact. For example, the protrade economist Robert Lawrence estimates for the 2000 to 2005 period, when the U.S. trade deficit rose from 3.8 percent of gross domestic product to 5.7 percent, "that 1.3 million jobs in manufacturing were lost due to trade. So, about 1 million workers were displaced in a labor force of over 140 million."[27]

However, the actual impact of the U.S. structural trade deficit may be greater than this. First off, as we saw in chapter 6, developing countries that have grown the fastest have all pursued the objective of achieving a large structural trade surplus; there is no reason to believe that the large U.S. structural trade deficit would not have the opposite impact of depressing U.S. economic growth and employment. Second, as we saw in chapter 3, a structural deficit in goods and services trade would mean that the country is importing some products where it would actually have a comparative advantage, given more balanced trade. For industries that benefit from economies of scale, this may mean that the industry never gets back to producing those goods and services. The United States, of course, has a structural deficit in goods and services trade.

The Impact of U.S. FTAs on U.S. Labor

Organized labor strongly opposed NAFTA, even with the labor side agreement, fearing that many U.S. firms would move their production to Mexico to take advantage of cheap labor (Ross Perot's "giant sucking sound"). Even today, there is no solid consensus on the impact of NAFTA on U.S. labor, although Ross Perot's fears of a massive job loss clearly did not occur.

Other than NAFTA, most U.S. FTAs are with countries that are too small to have a significant impact on the U.S. economy or on U.S. labor. In addition, the United States already granted most of the imports from its developing-country partners—such as from the CAFTA countries Peru, Colombia, and Panama—duty-free access under the U.S. preference programs before the FTA, and accordingly U.S. imports are not expected to increase to a significant extent. On the contrary, these agree-

27. Robert Z. Lawrence, *Blue Collar Blues: Is Trade to Blame for Rising US Income Inequality?* (Washington, D.C.: Peterson Institute for International Economics, 2008), 42.

ments may have a slightly positive impact on U.S. labor; many of these countries have fairly high most-favored-nation tariffs, and U.S. exporters will now gain duty-free access to these markets as a result of the FTA, which will expand the demand for labor in U.S. exporting industries.

However, both Australia and South Korea are large enough economically to potentially have an impact on the U.S. economy and workers, although both countries are on the other side of the world and the impact of these agreements will be far less than would be the case for Mexico, which is about the same size economically but right next door. The Australian agreement is unlikely to have an impact on U.S. labor because Australia's comparative advantage is in agriculture and the United States will retain important trade barriers to potential Australian agricultural exports. However, the South Korean agreement is a different story.

South Korea has a globally competitive auto industry and currently exports 470,000 vehicles to the United States, compared with the less than 6,000 that the U.S. exports to South Korea. This imbalance is due to the relative openness of the U.S. market, which has minimal tariff and nontariff barriers (except for a 25 percent tariff on light trucks[28]), compared with the South Korean market, which is largely closed due to an array of nontariff barriers, including arbitrary standards, special taxes, ever-changing and nontransparent regulations, and a system of large business conglomerates (the *chaebol*) that have an anticompetitive effect.

Under the FTA, South Korea would immediately eliminate its 8 percent tariff on cars and a 10 percent tariff on pickup trucks. The United States would immediately eliminate its 2.5 percent tariff on most autos and auto parts and phase out its 25 percent tariff on light trucks over a ten-year period. In the short run, this would give Korean car makers an immediate savings from the tariff reductions, which would be about forty times larger than the savings for U.S. car makers due to the huge volume of South Korean exports to the United States compared with the small volume of U.S. exports to South Korea.

The AFL-CIO, the United Auto Workers, and Ford Motor Company strongly opposed the original agreement negotiated in June 2007. They

---

28. The United States imposed a 25 percent tariff on light truck imports in 1963 in retaliation for a tariff increase by the European Community on U.S. chicken exports, in a trade dispute dubbed "the chicken war." This 25 percent tariff still stands.

argued that the agreement did not contain sufficiently strong mechanisms to prevent South Korea from simply adopting new nontariff barriers to continue to block imports of autos from the United States. This opposition forced the administration to negotiate some additional changes in 2010 that make it more likely the U.S. auto industry and workers will not be put at a competitive disadvantage. As a result of these changes, Ford dropped its opposition to the agreement, although both the AFL-CIO and the United Auto Workers continued to oppose approval. Nonetheless, in October 2011 Congress approved the agreement.

In the long run, the impact of the South Korean FTA will depend on whether South Korea really opens its auto market to U.S. competition, and if not, whether the administration takes strong counteractions.

Conclusion: The Double Whammy

Economic theory predicts that unskilled workers in the United States will be worse from trade liberalization under conditions of balanced trade between the United States and its trade partners,. As a partial offset to these expected losses to labor, Congress has included TAA provisions in trade legislation; these provisions expand unemployment benefits, and they provide some funding for retraining and community assistance. However, these programs are only partially successful and do not fully offset the losses to labor.

Additionally, economic theory holds that a structural trade deficit means that a country is importing some products and not exporting other products where it otherwise would have a comparative advantage. This loss of production, of course, also represents a real loss to workers. The U.S. trade deficit equaled some $560 billion in 2012; if the United States closed this gap through expanded exports, some 2.8 million jobs would have been created, as described in chapter 4.

Thus labor faces a double whammy—first, from the losses from liberalized trade that would be expected under economic theory; and second, from the U.S. structural trade deficit, which was not anticipated under standard trade theory. Accordingly, it is no surprise that labor in the United States is a vocal and strong opponent of many of the nation's trade agreements.

The dilemma for policymakers is that trade liberalization done correctly benefits the economy broadly, although it hurts unskilled workers to some extent. To ensure that U.S. trade agreements better address labors' concerns, several steps should be taken. First, when negotiating trade agreements, the United States needs to do all it can to ensure that the agreement does not unduly affect American workers. For example, the agreement with South Korea as initially negotiated did not adequately ensure that the U.S. auto industry would not be injured by increased imports without offsetting export sales to South Korea.

Second, the United States needs better policies to help unemployed workers find new jobs. To some extent, this can be accomplished by strengthening TAA. However, it is probably preferable to adopt policies and programs that would help all unemployed workers gain new employment. And third and finally, the United States needs to deal with its structural trade deficit and the neomercantilist policies of some of its trade partners. These issues are addressed in the next chapter.

Chapter 9

The Way Forward

Since the end of World War II, the goal of the U.S. trade agreements has been to eliminate barriers to international trade to the greatest extent possible in order to promote economic efficiency and consumer benefit, as called for by Western economic theory. As a result of these U.S. trade agreements, there have been enormous reductions of trade barriers and steady expansions of the trade rules to cover a wide range of nontariff barriers, services, and even the protection of intellectual property. The United States and other countries have benefited greatly from the resultant expansion of world trade.

However, today there are two major problems with U.S. trade agreements program. First, the international trade rules developed in previous rounds of negotiations have significant gaps, and some neomercantilist countries have taken advantage of these loopholes to pursue commercial policies that injure the U.S. economy. Second, after a dozen years multilateral negotiations under the World Trade Organization (WTO)—the so-called Doha Development Round—have apparently failed. The United States has free trade agreements (FTAs) with twenty other countries, but seventeen of these are with small economies, and these agreements have only very minimal commercial benefit for the United States. The United States needs a strategy that will promote its commercial and foreign policy interests and strengthen the global trade system.

The law of comparative advantage—one of the fundamental pillars of modern economic theory—holds that total global welfare will increase under conditions of free trade, and that even if one nation maintains trade barriers, other nations may still benefit from reducing their own

231

trade barriers. Consumers will benefit from lower prices as tariffs are re-duced, and producers will be forced to become more efficient to meet international competition. However, economists note some very important caveats to the basic theory of comparative advantage, and these caveats are too often ignored by policymakers.

One caveat is that the law of comparative advantage assumes that trade is basically balanced and that any deficit or surplus is temporary or at least cyclical. If a country has a long-term structural deficit, as is the case for the United States, it means that the country is importing some products and not exporting other products where it actually has a comparative advantage.[1] The result is reduced economic output and a loss of employment opportunities.

A second important caveat is that countries can create comparative advantage in some products. The original theory expounded by David Ricardo assumes constant or increasing costs as production expands. However, in today's complex economy, the costs of production for many products, such as automobiles and semiconductors, decline as production increases. This means that for these products, countries can play an important role in creating comparative advantage. For example, a neo-mercantilist country might impose trade barriers to allow domestic producers to take advantage of the home market until sufficient market size can be obtained to be cost competitive, or it might provide subsidies to enable domestic producers to expand production and move down the cost curve. Or the country might maintain an undervalued currency that acts as both an import barrier and a subsidy and is perhaps the most egregious form of protectionism.

And a third important caveat is that the multilateral reduction of trade barriers under the WTO is generally preferable to trade liberalization as a result of a bilateral or regional FTA. Reducing or eliminating trade barriers between just a few countries may actually be a move away from trade based on global comparative advantage if the agreement leads to more trade diversion than trade creation. (A bilateral or regional FTA leads to trade diversion if members of the FTA expand their sales to a partner because of the tariff preference, thereby displacing a more efficient nonmember that has to pay the duty.)

---

1. The United States also had a trade deficit in the nineteenth century, but that financed investment and could be repaid at a later date. Its current deficit finances consumption of imported television sets, cars, etc.

Bilateral and regional FTAs also have cumbersome rules of origin, which are generally different in each agreement and which are often explicitly designed to increase trade diversion to benefit the parties to the agreement at the expense of nonmembers. Rules of origin that differ from one agreement to another mean that a country's products may qualify for duty-free treatment when exported to a partner in one of its bilateral agreements but not qualify for duty-free treatment under other agreements. In addition to this loss of efficiency, it is expensive for firms to track compliance with these rules of origin, and this also reduces global efficiency.

With these three caveats in mind, we look first at the huge U.S. structural trade deficit, which is caused partly by defective U.S. domestic policies and partly by the neomercantilist practices of some U.S. trade partners, such as maintaining an undervalued exchange rate and taking advantage of other loopholes in the world trade rules.

Then we consider what should be the U.S. strategy toward trade agreements in the current context of a failed round of multilateral negotiations—the Doha Development Round—under the WTO. How can the negotiations for a Trans-Pacific Partnership (TPP) trade agreement and for a Trans-Atlantic Trade and Investment Partnership (TTIP) further U.S. commercial and foreign policy interests? And how can America help revive the multilateral trade system and move back toward trade based on the most-favored-nation (MFN) principle?

The U.S. Trade Deficit

As described in chapter 4, the U.S. deficit in goods and services trade has increased enormously over the past thirty years, from $13.0 billion in 1980 to $560 billion in 2012. In 1980, the U.S. deficit in goods and services trade equaled about 0.5 percent of its gross domestic product, rising to just under 6 percent in 2005 and 2006 before falling during the global financial and economic crisis of 2008–9 to just under 3 percent in 2009. More recently, as the U.S. economy has been slowly recovering and demand for imports has been increasing, the U.S. deficit has been rising again and in 2012 equaled 3.6 percent of the nation's gross domestic product.

Economists, of course, generally focus on the current account, rather than the more narrow trade balance, when analyzing a country's international balance. However, the other items combined that make up the U.S. current account except for goods and services, such as earnings on investments or foreign aid, have a slight positive balance. Because the U.S. deficit in goods and services trade is far larger than its surplus on the other items, it has a large deficit in its current account, which equaled $475 billion in 2012, more than three-fourths the size of the deficit in goods and services trade by itself.

There are several major problems with the large U.S. structural current account deficit. The most immediate, as described in chapters 4 and 8, is that it represents a loss in U.S. economic output and reduced employment. Additionally, most economists believe that at some point in the future, America's continued trade deficits will become unsustainable. Much of U.S. debt to finance its current account deficit is held by just a few countries, primarily China and Japan. At some point these countries may decide to no longer accumulate dollars, or they may be unable to continue purchasing U.S. debt.

The risk that this would pose to the U.S. economy is vividly described by Daniel Drezner:

> Any decision by the major central banks to sell off dollars would make it impossible to finance the current account deficit at current price levels and interest rates. Under this worst-case scenario, a run on the dollar could commence. A drastic fall in the dollar's value would fuel inflation at home as the prices of imports shot up. The Federal Reserve Board would in all likelihood ratchet up the short-term federal funds rate in order to stanch outward capital flows. The result would be severe stagflation—higher prices combined with decreased output. At a minimum, such a move would trigger a severe economic slowdown.[2]

As described in chapter 4, the large U.S. current account deficit is partly caused by the neomercantilist trade practices of some other countries, which take advantage of loopholes in the trade rules, and partly by its own policies. U.S. policies that contribute to the nation's trade deficit include a low national savings rate exacerbated by consistent federal budget deficits, fiscal and monetary policies that do not encourage

2. Daniel W. Drezner, *U.S. Trade Strategy: Free Versus Fair.* Critical Policy Choices Series (New York: Council on Foreign Relations, 2006), 47.

household savings, and a corporate tax structure that discourages companies from repatriating profits earned overseas.

Because of the U.S. corporate tax code, many multinational companies choose to keep their profits overseas, rather than bring them back to the United States to give to shareholders or invest in United States–based production. U.S. companies such as Cisco, Microsoft, Bristol-Myers Squibb, and GE have more cash overseas than they have had for decades—an estimated $213 billion in 2012 for all U.S. companies.

This element of U.S. tax policy is in direct opposition to some elements of its policy regarding trade agreements. In particular, trade negotiators have pushed for access for direct investment by U.S. companies in both the WTO services agreement and the investment provisions of U.S. bilateral agreements. However, significant benefit for the U.S. economy from these provisions occurs only if the companies repatriate their profits. Fixing U.S. budget and tax problems will put the country on a much stronger footing as it seeks to close the loopholes in the trade rules that permit the beggar-thy-neighbor trade practices that damage its economy.

Mind the Gap: The Exchange Rate Loophole

Manipulation of foreign exchange rates is the most egregious tool used by neomercantilist countries. The founders of the General Agreement on Tariffs and Trade (GATT) recognized the potential for currency manipulation to undermine the trade system, but to date negotiators have not successfully addressed this gap in the rules.

In an outstanding analysis by C. Fred Bergsten and Joseph E. Gagnon of the Peterson Institute, eight economies are listed as the most significant currency manipulators: China, Denmark, Hong Kong, South Korea, Malaysia, Singapore, Switzerland, and Taiwan. The report also notes that Japan "has been an occasional manipulator in the past but has not intervened recently."[3]

Because of its size and history of manipulating its exchange rate, China is the focus of concern by most analysts today. In its semiannual

---

3. C. Fred Bergsten and Joseph E. Gagnon, *Currency Manipulation, the U.S. Economy, and the Global Economic Order* (Washington, D.C.: Peterson Institute for International Economics, 2012), 2.

report on exchange rates released on November 27, 2012, the U.S. Treasury noted that China's currency is "undervalued by between 5 and 10 percent on a real effective basis, as of July 2012."[4] Though a considerable improvement from the extent of Chinese undervaluation of the past decade, this still represents a significant trade distortion. The report also notes that "China's official foreign exchange reserves remain exceptionally high compared to those of other economies," and it says that it is important that the Chinese government move toward greater disclosure of its activities in the currency market.[5]

The Chinese government pegs the renminbi to the dollar and maintains an undervalued rate by purchasing an average of $1 billion to $2 billion in the foreign exchange markets every day. As a result, China has accumulated foreign exchange reserves of some $3.3 trillion, of which about $1 trillion is in U.S. Treasury bills. China, of course, is home to half of all the people in the world living on less than $2 per day, and its leaders deliberately undervalue the exchange rate to boost exports in order to promote China's economic development and alleviate poverty.

Although the main focus today is on China, currency manipulation is not a new problem. In 1971, the United States believed that some other nations were pegging their currencies below the market value of the dollar to gain a trade advantage. President Richard Nixon imposed a 15 percent import surcharge, which was only removed after Germany, Japan, and other countries revalued their currencies. And then the problem resurfaced again in the mid-1980s, particularly with regard to Japan and some European currencies. At that time, the U.S. Congress threatened to impose an across-the-board import surcharge, which led Japan to agree to revalue the yen by some 80 percent and the Europeans to allow their currencies to appreciate by some 50 percent in the so-called Plaza Accord of 1985.

As noted in chapter 2, Article XV of the GATT specifies that members should not take exchange rate actions that "frustrate the intent of the provisions of this Agreement," and the International Monetary Fund's Article IV states that members should "avoid manipulating exchange rates . . . in order . . . to gain an unfair competitive advantage

---

4. U.S. Department of the Treasury, Office of International Affairs, "Report to Congress on International Economic and Exchange Rate Policies," November 27, 2012, 13.
5. Ibid.

over other members." However, the WTO/GATT is to accept all findings of statistical fact presented by the IMF, and the IMF for its part has never taken action on exchange rate issues. The result is a huge gap in the international rules.

Ironically, the immediate problem with China's currency regime could have been resolved when China joined the WTO; as noted in chapter 2, at the insistence of the United States, the draft protocol on China's accession to the WTO would have required that China bring its foreign exchange regime into conformity with the obligations of the IMF. Unfortunately, the IMF staff forced the deletion of this provision on the grounds that such a provision was the IMF's jurisdiction, not the WTO's.[6]

So today the United States has two problems: the immediate one regarding currency manipulation by a number of countries, and the more fundamental problem that there are no effective rules on exchange rates. With regard to China, some progress has been made. In 2005, China pledged to allow the renminbi to appreciate about 5 percent a year, and today it is about 25 percent higher than it was then. Most economists would argue that it is in China's own interest to allow the renminbi to continue to appreciate. First, China is facing a problem of inflation; wages are rising about 10 to 15 percent a year, and there has been a precipitous rise in housing prices. Former premier Wen Jiabao said that "the biggest problem with China's economy is that the growth is unstable, unbalanced, uncoordinated, and unsustainable."[7]

A stronger renminbi would help curb Chinese inflation, and it would raise living standards in China. Additionally, the dollar will likely depreciate over time, given the huge U.S. current account deficits, and this means that by buying dollars to maintain its undervalued currency, China is basically investing in a declining asset. Thus it is not surprising that China has recently been trying to diversify its exchange holdings to include other currencies and gold. A reason that China has not moved faster is that Chinese leaders are concerned that too rapid appreciation of the renminbi would sharply curb exports and result in political instability.

6. This incident is reported by the International Monetary Fund, *IMF Involvement in International Trade Policy Issues* (Washington, D.C.: Independent Evaluation Office of the International Monetary Fund, 2009), 59.

7. Quoted from a report of a March 2007 news conference during the National People's Congress, according in an article by David Ignatius in the *Washington Post*, March 11, 2010.

Nonetheless, the fact is that the process is too uncertain and is moving too slowly. So how should the United States proceed in order to protect its own vital interests?

The United States actually has significant leverage in pressing for a solution with China. First, of course, it could follow the same approach of 1971 and 1985 and threaten or impose an across-the-board import surcharge on countries that consistently maintain an undervalued currency. Another approach to increasing its negotiating leverage would be to unilaterally intervene in global currency futures markets to bid up the renminbi—in essence, the mirror image of the way that China maintains an undervalued renminbi.[8]

So why has the United States not adopted either of these measures to press China to revalue its currency? There are two answers to this question: The first is the lack of a consensus among economists as to whether China's undervalued renminbi—and the overvalued dollar—is in the U.S. interest; and the second is that the United States has important foreign policy interests in resolving this issue in a less confrontational manner.

Some economists argue that because the renminbi and other currencies are undervalued in relation to the dollar, the United States is able to purchase more foreign goods for every dollar than it would be able to do if the dollar were valued at a competitive rate. This benefits importers and consumers. However, as we have seen, it hurts U.S. producers and workers, and this injury is significantly greater than the benefit to consumers. Furthermore, the undervalued renminbi reduces overall global welfare, because it represents a movement away from trade based on comparative advantage.

There is a critical distinction between a strong dollar that has a favorable exchange rate with other currencies because the U.S. economy is strong compared with an overvalued dollar that is artificially high because of U.S. fiscal and monetary policies, or because other countries buy U.S. Treasury notes as protection from global insecurity, or because other countries deliberately undervalue their currencies to gain a competitive advantage. An overvalued dollar in these conditions artificially

---

8. The recent "quantitative easing" by the U.S. Federal Reserve in effect accomplishes this same thing, i.e., a devaluation of the dollar. Brazil has strongly protested against U.S. quantitative easing precisely on these grounds, namely, that it puts Brazil's exporters at an unfair trade disadvantage.

expands U.S. imports beyond the level that would exist under comparative advantage, and similarly it reduces U.S. exports.

The second reason why the United States has not been more forceful on this issue is that it has important foreign policy interests in ensuring that a commercial dispute with China does not create significant enmity that could damage long-term relations between the two nations. Very aggressive unilateral action by the United States would be viewed as extremely antagonistic by its trade partners.

An Approach to Developing Rules on Exchange Rates

Although this is not the time to designate China or another country as a "currency manipulator," the United States cannot allow this issue to continue to fester because it is critical to its long-run economic health and indeed the health of the international trade system. Therefore, the United States should take a two-track approach to developing effective rules on exchange rates. Under the first track, the United States should take the issue of ineffective rules on currency manipulation to both the WTO and the IMF. In fact, Brazil has already proposed that the WTO undertake a work program to consider the relationship of exchange rates and international trade. In Brazil's view, the "WTO could and should . . . deal with the effects of [currency] fluctuations and misalignments." Among other things, this work program should "define methodologies to assess currency misalignments."[9] The United States should vigorously support this Brazilian proposal.

However, agreeing on general principles to identify unfair currency manipulation will be difficult. In the analysis by Bergsten and Gagnon noted above, four criteria are listed that may identify a country that is unfairly manipulating its currency: (1) The country's foreign exchange reserves must exceed six months' worth of its goods and services imports, (2) its foreign exchange reserves must have grown more rapidly than its GDP, (3) its current account must have been in surplus on average since 2001, and (4) its per capita gross national income must be at least $3,000.[10] Though these criteria are a good starting point for consid-

---

9. World Trade Organization, "The Relationship between Exchange Rates and International Trade," WT/WGTDF/W/68, November 5, 2012, 2.

10. Bergsten and Gagnon, *Currency Manipulation*, 5.

eration, it will take some time to gain an international consensus as to what constitutes unfair currency manipulation.

While this work is under way in the WTO and hopefully the IMF, the United States should press to have rules in both the TPP and the TTIP that address currency manipulation. Two countries that have been identified by Bergsten and Gagnon as currency manipulators, Malaysia and Singapore, and also Japan, which has a history of manipulating its currency, are in the TPP negotiations. Because of this, and because this is a complex issue that will take some time to address, it is likely that only limited progress can be made in the TPP. However, it should be possible to agree that (1) members will not seek to gain a commercial advantage by manipulating their currency; (2) members will ensure transparency with regard to their interventions in the foreign exchange market; and (3) members will commit to immediate consultations in the event that a member country has concerns with a TPP partner's actions with regard to the exchange rate.

In the TTIP, it should be possible to make greater progress on this issue. The European Union has also been injured by exchange rate distortions and will likely be more open to developing effective rules on currency manipulation. In addition to what might be agreed on in the TPP, in the TTIP it might be possible to define unfair currency manipulation and make it subject to the dispute settlement mechanism.

Responding to Trade Distortions and Barriers

In addition to currency manipulation, countries can take a number of other trade actions to tip the trade field in their own favor at the expense of their trade partners. Sometimes these policies are in violation of WTO rules, and sometimes they take advantage of loopholes in existing rules and are not technically in violation, although the policies may contradict the spirit of the trade rules, which are intended to promote competition based on comparative advantage.

The piracy of intellectual property is a particular area where a number of countries tolerate practices that disadvantage U.S. commercial interests. For example, a study by the U.S. International Trade Commission estimated that the piracy of other company trademarks, copyrights, and patents by Chinese companies resulted in losses of approximately $48.2 billion in 2009 to U.S. firms.[11] Some of China's and other countries' practices would likely be found to be in violation of WTO commitments in the event of a dispute settlement case, and the United States should continue to aggressively pursue these cases. However, many of these practices involve inadequate enforcement of the country's own existing laws; unfortunately the requirements of the Trade-Related Aspects of Intellectual Property Rights agreement for enforcement are vague, and pursuing dispute settlement cases would be difficult. Here, the United States needs to negotiate tighter rules regarding enforcement.

Some examples of other loopholes in the international trade rules:

- The services code (the General Agreement on Trade in Services, GATS) only covers specific commitments to which countries have agreed and have notified to the WTO, and countries are free to implement whatever policies they choose to in areas that have not been notified. China, for example, allows only twenty foreign films a year to be shown, and this is not in violation of China's GATS commitments; similarly, foreign financial services and insurance firms are largely blocked from the Chinese market.
- The WTO rules on investment allow for a range of domestic subsidies and practices, and a number of countries have given large subsidies to attract foreign investors. Singapore gave Intel $10 billion in tax subsidies, free land, and so on to establish a plant there, and a number of U.S. states give tax incentives to new investors (although the states have funding problems and cannot provide large subsidies). China requires foreign car companies to form a partnership with a Chinese automaker if they want to do business in China.
- Competition policy is not addressed at all by international trade rules. Some countries have business structures that can have the impact of excluding foreign competition; Korea's *chaebol* system and Japan's *keiretsu* system consist of families of companies in different business segments that give preferential purchasing to other family members and sharply limit the ability of nonnational firms to compete.

11. U.S. International Trade Commission, *China: Effects of Intellectual Property Infringement and Indigenous Innovation Policies on the U.S. Economy* (Washington, D.C.: U.S. Government Printing Office, 2011), xiv.

If there are domestic U.S. producers that are seriously injured by these or other practices, there will be an adverse impact on U.S. employment and production. Some models that some economists use to predict trade effects assume that any capital idled by this lost production or workers who have lost their jobs are instantly reemployed. However, this is usually not the case. Capital and labor often are not fungible. Workers who have lost their jobs in one industry due to imports often do not have skills that are readily transferable to other industries, and equipment that has been idled often cannot be readily redeployed to make other products. Further, if injury occurs in an industry with decreasing costs of production, the firm or industry can suffer permanent long-term damage as the foreign competitor gains global market share, thereby reducing its costs for later penetration of the global market.

So how should the United States respond to the practices of its trade partners that injure an industry? First, if the practice appears to violate an existing rule, of course, the response should be to bring a dispute settlement case. Although a number of companies and congressmen argue that the United States should be more aggressive in using the WTO dispute settlement mechanism (DSM), the United States has actually been one of the more aggressive countries in bringing disputes to the WTO. For example, the United States has brought eleven cases against China and won eight of these (four were settled before a WTO decision), with the other three pending. However, the DSM is somewhat time-consuming because the industry first must persuade the administration to file the case and then it has to wait a year or year and a half for the WTO to render a decision. And even once a decision has been rendered, it may be some time before the offending country changes its practices, and occasionally the country will decide to maintain the practice and provide other compensation that benefits another industry.

Second, as an alternative to a dispute settlement case or in parallel with one, it often is possible to offset the injury to the U.S. domestic economy from the trade practices of other countries by taking domestic policy actions. For example, China imposed restrictions on the exportation of rare earths, which are critical to the production of many high-technology products such as cell phones, ostensibly on the grounds that this was necessary to protect the environment. However, because China produces 97 percent of the world's supplies of rare earths and because China did not impose any restrictions on domestic producers, many saw this action as a blatant attempt to gain a commercial advantage by disadvantaging foreign competitors to Chinese industry. Accordingly, the United States, the EU, and Japan filed a dispute settlement case in the WTO against China's export restraints.

In parallel to this dispute settlement case, the United States could take domestic policy actions to offset the Chinese restrictions. As a case in point, a U.S. mine, the Mountain Pass Mine in California, ceased mining rare earths in 2002 because of weak demand and delays in environmental reviews. The United States could speed up the environmental review process of such a mine without weakening its protection of the environment, and it could even provide subsidies to reopen the mine. Other possible U.S. actions could include providing greater incentives for research into substitute materials for rare earths, promoting the recycling of products such as cell phones that use many of these minerals, and stockpiling vital minerals.

Third, the United States could seek to enter into negotiations with the country imposing the barrier or distortion. As a spur for such bilateral negotiations, the United States could take a unilateral action of its own that limits the other country's access to the U.S. market to be used as leverage to launch bilateral negotiations. For example, in the rare earths case, America could refuse to license the export of liquefied natural gas to China until China removes its export barriers on rare earths.

Needed: A New Negotiating Strategy

The WTO Doha Development Round of multilateral trade negotiations has essentially failed, although it may be possible to reach agreement on a few elements, particularly trade facilitation, at the December 2013 Ministerial Meeting. There are a number of reasons for failure, including the sheer complexity of trying to reach an agreement among more than 150 countries and the WTO's governance structure, which gives each member veto power over an agreement.

A major cause is the fundamental disagreement between the developed countries and the advanced developing countries—particularly China, India, and Brazil—over the level of obligations to be assumed by these emerging economic powerhouses. Although they are home to extensive poverty, these advanced developing countries have an enormous impact on the trade system and their trade partners. The major test for the trade system in the coming decade will be how to integrate these nations into a trade system that enjoys support in the developed countries and that still respects the legitimate needs of these nations to continue economic development.

The fundamental concept of a world trade system based on MFN rules is still valid. The founders of the trade rules after World War II believed that trade blocs had contributed to the political frictions that led to the war. Additionally, economists believe that bilateral and regional agreements often cause trade diversion away from trade based on comparative advantage, whereas multilateral agreements allow all WTO members to compete within the same rules-based system. Accordingly, MFN is one of the fundamental principles of the trade rules. However, bilateral and regional trade arrangements have proliferated, and today the MFN system is almost the exception rather than the rule.

The Organization for Economic Cooperation and Development sums up the pros and cons of multilateral versus bilateral trade agreements well:

Multilateral trade rules provide the best guarantee for securing substantive gains from trade liberalization for all WTO members. Nevertheless, . . . [regional trade agreements] have allowed groups of countries to negotiate rules and commitments that go beyond what was possible at the time multilaterally. In turn, some of these rules have paved the way for agreement in the WTO. . . . [However], there are concerns that the proliferation of RTAs could create problems of coherence and consistency in trade relations, put developing countries at a disadvantage when negotiating RTAs, and generally divert negotiating resources and energy from multilateral negotiations.[12]

Although multilateral negotiations are preferable to bilateral negotiations, the fact is that this genie is out of the bottle, given that 354 bilateral and regional trade agreements were in force as of January 2013, according to the WTO, and U.S. trade competitors are eagerly pursuing additional agreements. A strategy that can eventually put the FTA genie back in the MFN bottle is badly needed.

In the early 1980s, when faced with the reluctance of the developing countries in the GATT to launch a new multilateral round of trade ne-

12. Organization for Economic Cooperation and Development, "Environment and Regional Trade Agreements, 2007," 13, http://www.oecd.org/document/8/0,3746, en_2649_34287_38768584_1_1_1_1,00&&en-USS_01DBC.html.

gotiations, the then–U.S. trade representative, William Brock, considered a concept he called "GATT Plus." This would have been an arrangement between countries that were willing to undertake additional liberalization and expanded obligations beyond GATT provisions in exchange for greater market access to their GATT Plus partners. In essence, this would have been a two-tier system in which all GATT members would honor GATT liberalization and trade rules, and then a subset of GATT member countries would have additional rules and freer trade among themselves.

The intent was twofold. First, it was to promote the economic benefits of trade liberalization to the greatest extent possible, given international political realities at the time; and second, it was to put pressure on the recalcitrant countries to adhere to the new GATT Plus system at a later date. When the Uruguay Round negotiations were finally launched in 1986, this idea was dropped.

However, perhaps it is now time to consider the concept of a "WTO Plus" system. Under this approach, countries willing to strengthen the trade rules regarding currency manipulation, state-owned enterprises, and other loopholes in the current rules, and to develop rules for the new issues such as digital commerce and regulatory coherence would negotiate an FTA among themselves that would supplement the current WTO system. The negotiations for the TPP agreement and the TTIP could provide the basis for developing such a WTO Plus system.

This approach, which may well be the current U.S. strategy, would represent a temporary further movement away from MFN; however, the intent would be to create a system that other countries would join in the future or that could form a basis for a future multilateral WTO trade round. Because of the huge size economically of the TPP and the TTIP, trade diversion that might be caused by either agreement would be minimal.

Current U.S. bilateral and regional FTAs have several provisions that many other countries strongly oppose. If the TPP and TTIP are to become templates for future multilateral negotiations, these provisions must be handled in a way that meets the legitimate concerns of current and prospective U.S. trade partners. If the prospect of joining these agreements is to be attractive to other trade partners in the future, U.S. negotiators must avoid the temptation to muscle through provisions not in its partners' interest in order to gain support from U.S. special interests. As noted above, the particular provisions that many U.S. trade partners have found objectionable are those on intellectual property protection for pharmaceuticals that go beyond the WTO provisions; the investor-to-state dispute resolution mechanism; the maintenance of trade-distorting agricultural subsidies; and the restrictions on the use of capital controls by developing countries, which limit their ability to deal with currency speculation. These provisions have to be dealt with in a way that will not discourage other countries from joining these agreements at some point in the future.

The major problem confronting the world economy today is the enormous imbalance in trade between the United States, and to a lesser extent Europe, with the major Asian nations, particularly China and Japan. The United States and the EU basically have minimal barriers to imports, whereas Japan and China have greater barriers that limit imports and foreign investment. Additionally, the United States and the EU have very low levels of savings compared with China and several other Asian countries. These enormous imbalances undermine support for liberal trade policies in the West and threaten the stability of the international system.

If done correctly, the TPP and TTIP can be important mechanisms for addressing these imbalances. If Japan uses the TPP to actually eliminate its trade barriers and open its market, over the long term that would put its economy on a more solid footing. The same would be true for China if it should decide to adhere to the TPP sometime in the future.

However, many are skeptical that Japan, or at a later date China, will actually open its market. Japanese policymakers will face enormous opposition from its agricultural sector to eliminate trade barriers, and its barriers in the industrial side are deeply entrenched in domestic policies, including its business structure.

If the TPP and TTIP are not constructed correctly, they will exacerbate the already precarious world trade system. These agreements need to address the potential for currency manipulation, and they need to close many of the loopholes in the current system. Even more important, adherents to these agreements need to open their markets and remove barriers to imports.

A Return to a Multilateral System

Even if successful, the TPP and the TTIP cannot address three major trade problems. First, these agreements would not include most of the

WTO members, and particularly all the world's poorest countries, which now will be at an even greater disadvantage in exporting to the TPP and TTIP nations. Second, these agreements will not include effective rules that limit the enormous subsidies that the United States, the EU, and others give to their agricultural sector; these subsidies distort world trade and are not in the U.S. national economic interest. And third, the mishmash of differing rules of origin between these agreements and all the FTAs that have been negotiated will still be in place, and these will add to inefficiencies in the trade system.

However, the TPP and TTIP can be a mechanism to return the trade system to one based on MFN trade in either of two ways. First, other WTO countries can join these agreements, provided they commit to the additional disciplines, thereby expanding the number of countries participating in the WTO Plus agreements. Second, and more important, would be to launch a new round of multilateral trade negotiations at a future date. Many trade experts question whether a future WTO multilateral round is feasible, and certainly it will be difficult to launch a future round. But given the importance of multilateral negotiations, the effort should be made, using the TPP and TTIP agreements as a template.

Reducing the developed countries' tariffs on nonagricultural goods has been the centerpiece of multilateral trade negotiations since the Kennedy Round, including the recent Doha Development Round. However, U.S. and other developed-country tariffs on nonagricultural goods are now so low—with a few but significant exceptions—that further reductions would only have minimal consumer and economic benefits. Today, the tariffs that generally have the greatest commercial effects are developed-country agricultural tariffs and the tariffs of the advanced developing countries on all products.

If the advanced developing countries—particularly China, Brazil, and India—continue to refuse to make significant cuts in their tariffs on products of interest to U.S. exporters, the traditional formula approach to reducing tariffs would again be doomed to failure. U.S. industrial firms would oppose reducing U.S. tariffs, even though they are relatively low, without gaining real access to the large markets of the advanced developing countries.

Although a formula reduction of *tariffs* should not be the centerpiece of a future trade round, tariffs should be on the table. Though the average U.S. tariff rate is low, it does have some high tariffs that could be reduced significantly, and these concessions could be in its broader economic interest and would be important negotiating chips to gain access to other important markets. For example, the United States has a tariff equivalent to about 800 percent on ethanol, which adds to domestic transportation costs and hurts the consumer. The U.S. International Trade Commission estimates that eliminating this duty would increase U.S. welfare by $1.5 billion.[13] This concession would be important to Brazil and would be a very important bargaining chip. Similarly, reducing U.S. barriers on sugar would benefit downstream industries; the International Trade Commission estimates that this would increase welfare by $49 million.

Other areas where the United States has high import barriers that could be used as bargaining chips flagged by the International Trade Commission include dairy products, sugar, canned tuna, tobacco, textiles and apparel, footwear, costume jewelry, writing instruments, ball and roller bearings, tires, handmade tools, and ceramic tile.

The United States also has some important objectives for gaining tariff reductions from its trade partners. For example, one area is technology. The Information Technology Agreement, as noted above, now has seventy-four signatories, but some important countries, such as Brazil, are not signatories. Eliminating tariffs on information technology products worldwide would benefit U.S. exports, and also be in the interests of all importing countries, because information technology has become an integral building block for many other industries. Another example is environmental goods and services; eliminating trade barriers on these products would benefit both the environment and U.S. exporters.

Instead of the approach of reducing tariffs through formula cuts, negotiators might consider a request-offer approach, as was used before the Kennedy Round. For example, the United States could ask Brazil to eliminate its duties on information technology products in exchange for the United States' eliminating its tariffs on sugar. Or a sector approach might be possible in which the participating countries all agreed to eliminate trade barriers in the sector.

Agricultural subsidies should definitely be on the table. As we saw in chapters 2 and 4, the United States gives substantial subsidies to domes-

---

13. U.S. International Trade Commission, "The Economic Effects of Significant U.S. Import Restraints," August 2011, http://www.usitc.gov/publications/332/pub 4253.pdf.

tic farmers, and reining these in would be in the broader U.S. national interest. Many of these subsidies go to farmers with annual incomes greater than $250,000—something that is hard to justify at a time when the United States is experiencing the largest income inequality since 1928. Some aspects of these subsidies have been found to be in violation of America's WTO commitments; for example, the United States is paying Brazil $148 million annually as compensation for continued U.S. subsidies on cotton.

Some elements of the U.S. agricultural subsidy program, of course, are important. The agricultural sector is critical to the nation, and farming is an inherently risky business. In negotiations, the United States would have to retain the right to provide subsidies that serve its national interest, such as countercyclical payments in bad years.

Strengthening and reform of the trade rules could be on the table. From the U.S. perspective, rules on exchange rates must be developed and enforced, and the loopholes that allow countries to pursue beggar-thy-neighbor policies need to be fixed.

Conversely, several U.S. trade partners object to some of its practices, such as the way it administers antidumping actions. Provided that the antidumping or countervailing duty offsets only the original distortion, then from an economic theory perspective these duties basically restore trade based on comparative advantage and should not be viewed as "protectionist."

However, several countries believe the U.S. administration of dumping and subsidies agreements goes beyond offsetting the distortion and is protectionist. In fact, the United States has lost a number of WTO dispute settlement cases regarding U.S. administration of the antidumping statute.[14]

---

14. Jan Woznowski, the former director of the WTO Rules Division, notes that one of the reasons the United States has lost WTO disputes is that the WTO Appellate Body has ignored a provision in the Uruguay Round Anti-Dumping Agreement, which specified that panels must accept "the investigating authorities' evaluation of the facts if proper and unbiased, even though the panel might have reached a different conclusion. Furthermore, if a panel finds that a relevant provision of the agreement is subject to more than one permissible interpretation, the panel should find the measure to be in conformity with the agreement if it rests upon one of those permissible interpretations." Jan Woznowski, "Anti-Dumping Negotiations in the GATT and the WTO: Some Personal Reflections," in *Opportunities and Obligations: New Perspectives on Global and US Trade Policy*, edited by Terence P. Stewart (Amsterdam: Kluwer Law International, 2009), 106–7.

The United States has resisted proposals for negotiations on these rules because a number of politically powerful industries depend on the antidumping and countervailing duties provisions for protection against import surges. However, it might be politically possible to make some changes to U.S. antidumping practices if rules regarding currency manipulation and competition policy were developed, and safeguard actions were once again made a viable policy option. Certainly this is an area that could be explored to see if negotiations on rules might be possible.

Services is another area that needs to be effectively addressed in a future multilateral round. In the Doha Round, services were approached on a request-offer basis, similar to the way negotiators approached tariff negotiations in the first five rounds of GATT negotiations, and the results were similar—very minimal. In the next round, instead of a request-offer approach, services might be negotiated using a sector approach. In each sector under negotiation, the negotiators might have additional objectives in addition to seeking to gain access for exporters. The following two examples indicate the possibilities for negotiation in the medical and transportation sectors.

Costs are a major concern in the medical sector in the United States, and a properly structured negotiation might help reduce costs in a way that did not lessen the quality of care or create unemployment in the United States. A number of operations can be performed more cheaply in some other countries, but few Americans can take advantage of this because health insurance programs, including Medicare, are limited to a certified practitioner in the United States, and most other countries have similar restrictions. Mattoo and Rathindran of the World Bank estimate that extending health insurance coverage to overseas care for just fifteen types of tradable treatments could produce savings for the United States of more than $1 billion a year even if only one in ten American patients travels abroad.[15] The United States might only make this concession of allowing Medicare to cover treatment in designated hospitals in specified countries that had facilities comparable to its own and only in exchange for concessions of interest to the United States.

Costs are also a major concern in the transportation sector. As noted in chapter 4, transportation costs now are a larger factor in international

---

15. As cited by Joseph François and Bernard Hoekman, *Services Trade and Policy*, Working Paper 903 (Linz: Department of Economics, Johannes Kepler University of Linz, 2009), 24.

trade than are developed-country tariffs on nonagricultural goods, and these costs are particularly onerous for developing countries. The transportation sector is highly protected in most countries, but some liberalization could reduce these high costs. The major reason progress has not been made in this sector is that the United States has been unwilling to put on the table its major barrier, which is the Jones Act. This legislation limits shipping in American waters to United States–owned and –crewed vessels, and it was designed to protect the American shipping industry. However, today there are only about 3,000 or 4,000 workers affected by the Jones Act, which now applies principally to the shipment of Alaskan oil to the mainland, and eliminating this law could reduce the costs of shipping Alaskan oil to U.S. consumers.

Conclusion

The U.S. trade agreements policy is only part of its total trade policy, and its trade policy is only one of many critical national policies for ensuring its prosperity and more harmonious world relations. At this point, however, U.S. policy on trade agreements is stuck, unable to contribute to either its domestic economic needs or its foreign policy objectives.

Following are some key steps that the United States should take to reenergize its trade agreements policy:

- The lack of rules on exchange rates is a cancer eating away at the global trade system. Policymakers have long recognized that currency manipulation can be the most unfair trade practice of all, yet this issue has only been addressed sporadically and ineffectively. The United States needs to launch negotiations to fix this problem as its top priority.
- The United States needs to recognize that the neomercantilist practices of other countries can cause unacceptable damage to the U.S. economy. It thus needs to develop a mechanism to identify when its important interests are at stake, and then to develop a strategy to protect these interests, either through domestic actions or bilateral or multilateral negotiations.
- The U.S. trade agreements program has both contributed to the speed of globalization and been driven by globalization. However, its domestic policies have not kept up with today's globalized world.

Among other steps, it needs to recognize that its huge federal budget deficit has contributed to its trade problems, and it needs a tax system that promotes its global competitiveness.

- There is a fundamental disagreement between the developed countries and the advanced developing countries—such as China, India, and Brazil—over the appropriate trade obligations for these countries. Though these countries have enormous domestic poverty, the trade system needs to recognize that some of their practices can cause unacceptable injury to their trade partners.

- Negotiations for the TPP and the TTIP could be vehicles for establishing a WTO Plus system, provided that the United States negotiates a template for these agreements that establishes effective rules regarding neomercantilist practices and eschews special interest provisions that are not in the interests of our trade partners. Such a WTO Plus system would both open markets for countries willing to accept strengthened trade rules and put pressure on nonparticipating countries to further open their markets and adopt similar rules in a future multilateral trade round.

- Over time, the United States needs to move back to a trade system based on MFN trade rules rather than bilateral and regional trade agreements that provide favored access for members at the expense of nonmembers. As the United States negotiates the TPP and TTIP, it needs to lay the groundwork for a new multilateral trade round under the WTO's auspices.

U.S. trade agreements have an important role to play today in promoting both its commercial and foreign policy interests, just as they have since the 1930s. It is time for America to make some modifications in its approach to negotiating its trade agreements to meet the current and likely future realities of globalization.

Appendix:
Backgrounds of U.S. Trade
Representatives

Name	Years Served	Principal Career	Education
Christian Herter	1962–66	Politician	B.A. in architecture
William M. Roth	1967–69	Businessman/government	B.A.
Carl Gilbert	1969–71	Business executive	Law
William Eberle	1971–75	Businessman/politician	Law
Frederick Dent	1975–77	Business executive	B.A.
Robert Strauss	1977–79	Lawyer/politician	Law
Reubin Askew	1979–81	Politician: governor	Law
William Brock	1981–85	Politician: senator	B.S. in commerce
Clayton Yeutter	1985–89	Government	Ph.D. in agricultural economics
Carla Hills	1989–93	Lawyer/government	Law
Mickey Kantor	1993–97	Politician/lawyer	Law
Charlene Barshefsky	1997–2001	Lawyer	Law
Robert Zoellick	2001–5	Business/academia	Law/M.A. in public policy
Rob Portman	2005–6	Politician/lawyer	Law
Susan Schwab	2006–9	Government/academia	Ph.D. in international business
Ronald Kirk	2009–13	Politician/lawyer	Law

Bibliography

Altman, Roger C. "Globalization in Retreat: Further Geopolitical Consequences of the Financial Crisis." *Foreign Affairs*, July–August 2009, 2–7.

American Center for International Labor Solidarity/AFL-CIO. *Justice for All: A Guide to Worker Rights in the Global Economy*. Washington, D.C.: USAID, 2008. http://www.solidaritycenter.org/content.asp?contentid=481.

Anand, Sudhir, and Paul Segal. "What Do We Know about Global Income Inequality?" *Journal of Economic Literature* 46 (2008): 57–94.

Antweiler, Werner, Brian R. Copeland, and M. Scott Taylor. "Is Free Trade Good for the Environment?" *American Economic Review* 91, no. 4 (September 2001): 877–908.

Audet, Denis. "Government Procurement: A Synthesis Report." *OECD Journal on Budgeting* 2, no. 3 (2002): 149–94.

Audley, John. "Lemons into Lemonade? Environment's New Role in U.S. Trade Policy: The Trade Act of 2002." *Environment*, March 2003.

Behar, Alberto, and Lawrence Edward. *How Integrated Is SADC? Trends in Intra-Regional and Extra-Regional Trade Flows and Policy*. Policy Research Working Paper 5625. Washington, D.C.: World Bank, 2011.

Bellin, Eva. "Democratization and Its Discontents: Should America Push Political Reform in the Middle East?" *Foreign Affairs*, July–August 2008, 112–19.

Bergsten, C. Fred, ed. *The Long-Term International Economic Position of the United States*. Washington, D.C.: Peterson Institute for International Economics, 2009.

Bergsten, C. Fred, and Joseph E. Gagnon. *Currency Manipulation, the U.S. Economy, and the Global Economic Order*. Washington, D.C.: Peterson Institute for International Economics, 2012.

Bernanke, Ben S. "Lessons from Emerging Market Economies on the Sources of Sustained Growth." Speech at Cleveland Clinic "Ideas for Tomorrow" Series, September 28, 2011.

Bernstein, William J. *A Splendid Exchange: How Trade Shaped the World*. New York: Grove Press, 2008.

Bessma, Momani. "A Middle East Free Trade Area: Economic Interdependence and Peace Considered." University of Waterloo, November 2007. http://papers.ssrn.com/sol3/papers.cfm?abstract_id=1026742.

Bhagwati, Jagdish. *In Defense of Globalization*. Council on Foreign Relations Report. New York: Oxford University Press, 2004.

Birdsall, Nancy, Augusto de la Torre, and Felipe Valencia Caicedo. *The Washington Consensus: Assessing a Damaged Brand*. Working Paper 213. Washington, D.C.: Center for Global Development, 2010.

Bivens, Josh. "Marketing the Gains from Trade." Economic Policy Institute, June 2007. http://www.epi.ort/publications/entry/ib233.

Borchert, Ingo, and Aaditya Mattoo. *The Crisis-Resilience of Services Trade*. Policy Research Working Paper 4917. Washington, D.C.: World Bank, 2009.

Brack, Duncan, and Kevin Gray. *Multilateral Environmental Agreements and the WTO*. London: Royal Institute of International Affairs and International Institute for Sustainable Development, 2003.

Brewer, Thomas L. "U.S. Climate Change Policies and International Trade Policies: Intersections and Implications for International Negotiations." February 12, 2008. http://www.usclimatechange.com.

Bronfenbrenner, Kate. "Final Report: The Effects of Plant Closing or Threat of Plant Closing on the Right of Workers to Organize." September 30, 1996. Digital Commons@ILR, Cornell University ILR School. http://digitalcommons.ilr .cornell.edu/intl/1/.

Brunnermeier, Smita B., and Arik Levinson. "Examining the Evidence on Environmental Regulations and Industry Location." *Journal of Environment Development* 13, no. 1 (March 2004): 6–41.

Bush, George W. "Statement of the President," Executive Office of the President, February 26, 2003. http://www.whitehouse.gov/news/releases/2003/02/20030226-11.html.

Carpentier, Chantal Line. "NAFTA Commission for Environmental Cooperation: Ongoing Assessment of Trade Liberalization in North America." *Impact Assessment and Project Appraisal* 24, no. 4 (December 2006): 259–72.

Clarida, Richard H., Manuela Goretti, and Mark P. Taylor. "Are There Thresholds of Current Account Adjustment in the G7?" In *G7 Current Account Imbalances: Sustainability and Adjustment*, edited by Richard H. Clarida. Cambridge, Mass.: National Bureau of Economic Research, 2007. http://www.nber.org/chapters/c0120.

Cline, William R. *Trade Policy and Global Poverty*. Washington, D.C.: Peterson Institute for International Economics, 2004.

Cline, William R., and John Williamson. "Updated Estimates of Fundamental Equilibrium Exchange Rates." Peterson Institute for International Economics, November 2012. http://www.piie.com/publications/pb/pb12-23.pdf.

Clinton, William. "Message to the Congress Transmitting Proposed Legislation to Implement the North American Free Trade Agreement." Executive Office of the President, November 3, 1993. http://www.gpo.gov/fdsys/browse/collection.action? collectionCode=PPP&browsePath=president-58%2F1993%2F02%3BA%3B August+1+to+December+31%2C+1993&isCollapsed=false&leafLevelBrowse= false&isDocumentResults=true&ycord=61.

Co, Catherine Y., John A. List, and Larry D. Qui. "Intellectual Property Rights, Environmental Regulations, and Foreign Direct Investment." *Land Economics* 80, no. 2 (May 2004): 153–73.

Cohen, Stephen D., Robert A. Blecker, and Peter D. Whitney. *Fundamentals of U.S.*

Foreign Trade Policy: Economics, Politics, Laws, and Issues. Boulder, Colo.: Westview Press, 2003.

Cooper, Richard N. "Trade Policy Is Foreign Policy." *Foreign Policy*, Winter 1972–73, 18–36.

Cooper, William H. *Free Trade Agreements: Impact on U.S. Trade and Implications for U.S. Trade Policy.* Washington, D.C.: Congressional Research Service, 2005.

Cosbey, Aaron. *Mining, Minerals and Sustainable Development: The Links to Trade and Investment Rules.* MMSD Working Paper 40. London: International Institute for Environment and Development and World Business Council for Sustainable Development, 2001.

Deardorff, Alan V., and Robert M. Stern. *Empirical Analysis of Barriers to International Services Transactions and the Consequences of Liberalization.* Discussion Paper 505. Ann Arbor: Research Seminar in International Economics, University of Michigan, 2004.

Dong, Yan, and John Whalley. *Model Structure and the Combined Welfare and Trade Effects of China's Trade Related Policies.* NBER Working Paper 15363. Cambridge, Mass.: National Bureau of Economic Research, 2009.

Drezner, Daniel W. *U.S. Trade Strategy: Free Versus Fair.* Critical Policy Choices. New York: Council on Foreign Relations, 2006.

Dryden, Steve. *Trade Warriors: USTR and the American Crusade for Free Trade.* New York: Oxford University Press, 1995.

Eckersley, Robyn. "The Big Chill: The WTO and Multilateral Environmental Agreements." *Global Environmental Politics* 4, no. 2 (May 2004): 24–50.

Eicher, Theo S., and Christian Henn. *In Search of WTO Trade Effects: Preferential Trade Agreements Promote Trade Strongly, But Unevenly.* Working Paper 09/31. Washington, D.C.: International Monetary Fund, 2009.

Eisenhower, Dwight D. *Mandate for Change, The White House Years, 1953–1956.* New York: Doubleday, 1963.

Esty, Daniel C. "Bridging the Trade-Environment Divide." *Journal of Economic Perspectives* 15, no. 3 (Summer 2001): 113–30.

———. *Greening the GATT: Trade, Environment, and the Future.* Washington, D.C.: Institute for International Economics, 1994.

European Commission, Directorate-General for Trade. *Trade SIA of the Forest Sector under DDA Negotiations: Position Paper.* Brussels, June 26, 2006.

Feketekuty, Geza. *International Trade in Services: An Overview and Blueprint for Negotiations.* Cambridge, Mass.: American Enterprise Institute/Ballinger, 1988.

Feenstra, Robert C. *Advanced International Trade: Theory and Evidence.* Princeton, N.J.: Princeton University Press, 2004.

Fink, Carsten, and Kimberly Elliott. "Tripping over Health: U.S. Policy on Patents and Drug Access in Developing Countries." In *The White House and the World: A Global Development Agenda for the Next U.S. President,* edited by Nancy Birdsall. Washington, D.C.: Center for Global Development, 2008.

Fink, Carsten, and Keith Maskus. *Intellectual Property and Development: Lessons from Recent Economic Research.* Washington, D.C.: World Bank, 2004.

François, Joseph, and Bernard Hoekman. *Services Trade and Policy.* Working Paper 903. Linz: Department of Economics, Johannes Kepler University of Linz, 2009.

Fredriksson, Per G., ed. *Trade, Global Policy, and the Environment*. Discussion Paper 402. Washington, D.C.: World Bank, 1999.

Ginsberg, Julie. *Reassessing the Jackson-Vanik Amendment*. Council on Foreign Relations, July 2, 2009. http://www.cfr.org/publicaton/19734.

Gomory, Ralph E., and William J. Baumol. *Global Trade and Conflicting National Interests*. Cambridge, Mass.: MIT Press, 2000.

Goncalves, Marilyne Pereira, and Constantinos Stephanou. *Financial Services and Trade Agreements in Latin America and the Caribbean: An Overview*. Policy Research Working Paper 4181. Washington, D.C.: World Bank, 2007.

Goncharuk, Andrii. "The Path of Ukraine into the WTO." In *Opportunities and Obligations: New Perspectives on Global and US Trade Policy,* edited by Terence P. Stewart. Amsterdam: Kluwer Law International, 2009.

Griswold, Daniel T. "Trading Tyranny for Freedom: How Open Markets Till the Soil for Democracy." January 6, 2004. Cato Institute. http://cato.org/pubs/tpa/tpa-026.pdf.

———. "Unions, Protectionism, and U.S. Competitiveness." *Cato Journal* 30, no. 1 (Winter 2010): 181–96.

Hanson, Gordon H. *What Has Happened to Wages in Mexico since NAFTA? Implications for Hemispheric Free Trade*. NBER Working Paper 9563. Cambridge, Mass.: National Bureau of Economic Research, 2003.

Harrison Institute for Public Law, Georgetown University Law Center. "International Trade and Investment Rules and State Regulation of Desalination Facilities." March 2004.

Hayek, Friedrich von. "The Pretence of Knowledge." Lecture, Nobel Prize in Economics, December 11, 1974. http://nobelprize.org/nobel_prizes/economics/laureates/1974/hayek-lecture.html.

Helpman, Elhanan. *The Mystery of Economic Growth*. Cambridge, Mass.: Belknap Press of Harvard University Press, 2004.

Hills, Carla A. "The Stakes of Doha." *Foreign Affairs*, December 2005. http://www.foreignaffairs.org/20051201faessay84703/carla-a-hills/the-stakes-of-doha.html.

Hoekman, Bernard, and Alessandro Nicita. *Trade Adjustment Assistance for Firms: Economic, Program, and Policy Issues*. Washington, D.C.: Congressional Research Service, 2011.

———. *Trade Policy, Trade Costs, and Developing Country Trade*. Policy Research Working Paper 4797. Washington, D.C.: World Bank, 2008.

Hornbeck, J. F. *NAFTA at Ten: Lessons from Recent Studies*. Washington, D.C.: Congressional Research Service, 2004.

———. *Trade Adjustment Assistance for Firms: Economic Program and Policy Issues*. Washington, D.C.: Congressional Research Service, 2011.

Howse, Robert. "The Appellate Body Rulings in the Shrimp/Turtle Case: A New Legal Baseline for the Trade and Environment Debate." *Columbia Journal of Environmental Law* 491 (2002). http://worldtradelaw.net/articles/howseshrimp.pdf.

Hudgins, Edward. "Executive Memorandum 53: The Case for a U.S.-Israel Free Trade Area." Heritage Foundation, May 22, 1984. http://www.heritage.org/Research/TradeandForeignAid/EM53.cfm.

Hufbauer, Gary C., Daniel C. Esty, Diana Orejas, Luis Rubio, and Jeffrey J. Schott. *NAFTA and the Environment: Seven Years Later*. Washington, D.C.: Peterson Institute for International Economics, 2000.

Hughes, Kent H. *Building the Next American Century: The Past and Future of American Economic Competitiveness.* Washington, D.C.: Woodrow Wilson Center Press, 2005.

Hull, Cordell. *The Memoirs of Cordell Hull, Volume 1,* edited by Andrew Henry Thomas Berding. New York: Macmillan, 1948.

Hummels, David. "Transportation Costs and International Trade in the Second Era of Globalization." *Journal of Economic Perspectives* 21, no. 3 (Summer 2007): 131–54.

Ikenson, Daniel. *Protection Made to Order: Domestic Industry's Capture and Reconfiguration of U.S. Antidumping Policy.* Washington, D.C.: Cato Institute, 2010.

Imbs, Jean, and Romain Wacziarg. "Stages of Diversification." *American Economic Review* 93, no. 1 (2003): 63–86.

International Monetary Fund. *IMF Involvement in International Trade Policy Issues.* Washington, D.C.: Independent Evaluation Office of the International Monetary Fund, 2009.

Irwin, Douglas A. *From Smoot-Hawley to Reciprocal Trade Agreements: Changing the Course of U.S. Trade Policy in the 1930s.* NBER Working Paper 5895. Cambridge, Mass.: National Bureau of Economic Research, 1997.

———. *The Rise of U.S. Antidumping Activity in Historical Perspective.* Working Paper 31. Washington, D.C.: International Monetary Fund, 2005.

Jackson, James K. *Trade Agreements: Impact on the U.S. Economy.* Washington, D.C.: Congressional Research Service, 2006.

Jara, Alejandro. "DDG Jara Urges Another Way of Looking at Trade Statistics." World Trade Organization, May 26, 2010. www.wto.org/english/news_e/news10 _e/devel_26may10_e.htm.

Johnson, Martin, and Chris Rasmussen. *Jobs Supported by Exports 2012: An Update.* Washington, D.C.: International Trade Administration, U.S. Department of Commerce, 2013.

Kennedy, John F. "Remarks upon Signing the Trade Expansion Act." Executive Office of the President, October 11, 1962. http://www.jfklink.com/speeches/jfk/ publicpapers/1962/jfk449_62.html.

Konan, Denise Eby, and Keith E. Maskus. "Quantifying the Impact of Services Liberalization in a Developing Country." *Journal of Development Economics* 81, no. 1 (October 2006): 146–62.

Koncz, Jennifer, and Anne Flatness. "U.S. International Services: Cross-Border Trade in 2007 and Services Supplied through Affiliates in 2006." U.S. Bureau of Economic Analysis, October 2008. http://www.bea.gov/scb/pdf/2008/10%20 October/services_text.pdf.

Krist, William. "Making Doha a Development Round." Woodrow Wilson International Center for Scholars. http://www.wilsoncenter.org/publication/making-doha-developmental-round-what-do-the-developing-countries-want.

———. *Trade Policy and the Farm Bill.* Washington, D.C.: Woodrow Wilson International Center for Scholars, 2007.

Langenfeld, James, and James Nieberding. "The Benefits of Free Trade to U.S. Consumers." *Business Economics* 40, no. 3 (July 2005): 41–51.

Lawrence, Robert Z. *Blue Collar Blues: Is Trade to Blame for Rising US Income Inequality?* Washington, D.C.: Peterson Institute for International Economics, 2008.

Lee, Thea Mei. "The U.S.-Korea Free Trade Agreement." Testimony before the Senate Finance Committee, May 26, 2011.

Levitt, Theodore. "The Globalization of Markets." *Harvard Business Review*, May–June 1983, 92–102.

Li, Quan, and Rafael Reuveny. "Economic Globalization and Democracy: An Empirical Analysis." *British Journal of Political Science* 33 (2003): 29–54.

Li, Guan, and Drew Schaub. "Economic Globalization and Transnational Terrorism: A Pooled Time-Series Analysis." *Journal of Conflict Resolution* 48, no. 2 (April 2004): 230–58. http://www.jstor.org/stable/3176252.

Lopez-Cordova, Ernesto, and Christopher Meissner. *The Globalization of Trade and Democracy, 1870–2000*. NBER Working Paper 11117. Cambridge, Mass.: National Bureau of Economic Research, 2012. http://www.nber.org/papers/w11117.

Lynch, David A. *Trade and Globalization: An Introduction to Regional Trade Agreements*. Lanham, Md.: Rowman & Littlefield, 2010.

Mattoo, Aaditya, and Arvind Subramanian. *A China Round of Multilateral Trade Negotiations*. Washington, D.C.: Peterson Institute for International Economics, 2011.

———. *Currency Undervaluation and Sovereign Wealth Funds: A New Role for the World Trade Organization*. Washington, D.C.: World Bank, 2008.

McCormick, Rachel. "A Qualitative Analysis of the WTO's Role on Trade and Environment Issues." *Global Environmental Politics* 6, no. 1 (February 2006): 102–24.

McDaniel, Christine, Ken Reinert, and Kent Hughes. "Tools of the Trade: Models for Trade Policy Analysis." Woodrow Wilson International Center for Scholars, January 2008.

Michalopoulos, Constantine. *The Participation of the Developing Countries in the WTO*. Policy Research Working Paper 1906. Washington, D.C.: World Bank, 1998.

Momani, Bessma. "A Middle East Free Trade Area: Economic Interdependence and Peace Considered." *World Economy* 30, no. 11 (November 2007): 1682–1700.

Morici, Peter. *Reconciling Trade and the Environment in the World Trade Organization*. Washington, D.C.: Economic Strategy Institute, 2002. http://www.econstrat.org/images/ESI_Research_Reports_PDF/reconciling%20trade%20and%20the%20environment%20in%20the%20world%20trade%20organization%20(peter%20morici).pdf.

Mun, Thomas. Letter written to his son in the 1630s. http://socserv.mcmaster.ca/econ/ugcm/3ll3/mun/treasure.txt.

Organization for Economic Cooperation and Development. "Environment and Regional Trade Agreements, 2007." http://www.oecd.org/document/8/0,3746,en_2649_34287_38768584_1_1_1_1,00&&en-USS_01DBC.html.

———. "OECD in Figures 2008." Paris: Organization for Economic Development and Cooperation, 2008. http://www.oecd-ilibrary.org/economics/oecd-in-figures-2008_oif-2008-en.

Pahre, Robert. *Politics and Trade Cooperation in the Nineteenth Century*. Cambridge: Cambridge University Press, 2008.

Palley, Thomas I. *Explaining Global Financial Imbalances: A Critique of the Sav-*

ing Glut and Reserve Currency Hypotheses. Report 13/2011. Washington, D.C.: Macroeconomic Policy Institute, 2011.

Pastor, Robert A. "The Future of North America." *Foreign Affairs*, July–August 2008, 84-98.

Pollard, Robert A., and Samuel F. Wells Jr. "1945–1960: The Era of American Economic Hegemony." In *Economics and World Power*, edited by William Becker and Samuel F. Wells Jr. New York: Columbia University Press, 1984.

Portugal-Perez, Alberto, and John S. Wilson. *Why Trade Facilitation Matters to Africa*. Policy Research Working Paper 4710. Washington, D.C.: World Bank, 2008.

Posen, Adam, and Daniel K. Tarullo. *Report of the Working Group on Economics and National Security*. Princeton, N.J.: Princeton Project on National Security, 2005.

Prestowitz, Clyde. *The Betrayal of American Prosperity. Free Market Delusions, America's Decline, and How We Must Compete in the Post-Dollar Era*. New York: Simon & Schuster, 2010.

Radelet, Steven. *Emerging Africa: How 17 Countries Are Leading the Way*. Center for Global Development Report. Washington, D.C.: Brookings Institution Press, 2010.

Ramos, Laura Marquez, Inmaculada Martinez-Zarzoso, and Celestino Suarez-Burguet. *Trade Policy versus Trade Facilitation: An Application Using "Good Old" OLS*. Discussion Paper 2011-38. Economics: The Open-Access, Open-Assessment E-Journal, September 14, 2011. http://www.economics-ejournal.org/economics/discussionpapers/2011-38.

Ricardo, David. *On the Principles of Political Economy and Taxation*. London: John Murray, 1821. Available at http://www.econlib.org/library/Ricardo/ricP.html.

Rice, Condoleezza. "Rethinking the National Interest." *Foreign Affairs*, July–August 2008, 2–26.

Rodriguez, Francisco, and Dani Rodrik. *Trade Policy and Economic Growth: A Skeptic's Guide to Cross-National Evidence*. NBER Working Paper W7081. Cambridge, Mass.: National Bureau of Economic Research, 1999.

Rodrik, Dani. *One Economics—Many Recipes: Globalization, Institutions, and Economic Growth*. Princeton, N.J.: Princeton University Press, 2007.

Salvatore, Dominick. *International Economics*. 8th ed. Hoboken, N.J.: John Wiley & Sons, 2004.

Salzman, James. "Executive Order 13,141 and the Environmental Review of Trade Agreements." *American Journal of International Law* 95, no. 2 (April 2001): 366–80.

Samuelson, Robert J. "It's Not Easy Being Rich." *Washington Post*, October 10, 2011.

Schott, Jeffrey J., ed. *Free Trade Agreements: U.S. Strategies and Priorities*. Washington, D.C.: Peterson Institute for International Economics, 2004.

Seker, Murat. *Trade Policies, Investment Climate, and Exports*. Washington, D.C.: World Bank, 2011.

Sewell, John. "The New Realism: Globalization, Development and American National Interests." Unpublished paper, August 21, 2004.

Sha, Lynn, and Kent H. Hughes, eds. *New Thinking in International Trade: Global Competition and Comparative Advantage*. Washington, D.C.: Woodrow Wilson International Center for Scholars, 2009.

————. *New Thinking in International Trade: National Strategies to Build Comparative Advantage*. Washington, D.C.: Woodrow Wilson International Center for Scholars, 2009.

Smith, Adam. *An Inquiry into the Nature and Causes of the Wealth of Nations*, edited by Edwin Cannan. London: Methuen, 1904. Library of Economics and Liberty. http://www.econlib.org/library/Smith/smWN.html.

Stephanou, Constantinos. *Including Financial Services in Preferential Trade Agreements: Lessons of International Experience for China*. Policy Research Working Paper 4898. Washington, D.C.: World Bank, 2009.

Stiglitz, Joseph E. *Making Globalization Work*. New York: W. W. Norton, 2006.

————. "Progress, What Progress?" *OECD Observer*, no. 272. April 2009.

Stokes, Bruce. "Chinese Checkers." *National Journal*, February 20, 2010, 18–26.

Subramanian, Arvind, and Shang-Jin Wei. "The WTO Promotes Trade, Strongly but Unevenly." *Journal of International Economics* 72, no. 1 (May 2007): 51–175.

Tarasofsky, Richard, and Alice Palmer. "The WTO in Crisis: Lessons Learned from the Doha Negotiations on the Environment." *International Affairs* 82, no. 5 (2006): 899–915.

Tomz, Michael, Judith L. Goldstein, and Douglas Rivers. "Do We Really Know That the WTO Increases Trade? Comment." *American Economic Review* 97, no. 5 (2007): 2005–18.

Topoleski, John J. *Trade Adjustment Assistance for Workers (TAA) and Alternative Trade Adjustment Assistance (ATAA)*. Washington, D.C.: Congressional Research Service, 2011.

Truman, Harry S. "Address Before a Joint Session of Congress." Avalon Project, Yale University Law School: March 12, 1947. http://avalon.law.yale.edu/20th_centure/trudoc.asp.

Udall, Morris K. "The Trade Expansion Act of 1962: A Bold New Instrument of American Policy." University of Arizona. May 17, 1962. http://www.library.arizona.edu/exhibits/udall/congrept/87th/620517.html.

United Nations Industrial Development Organization. *Trade Capacity-Building Background Paper: Supply Side Constraints on the Trade Performance of African Countries*. Background Paper 1. Vienna: United Nations Industrial Development Organization, 2006.

United States Council for International Business. *U.S. Ratification of ILO Core Labor Standards*. New York: United States Council for International Business, 2007.

U.S. Department of Commerce, Economics and Statistics Administration, U.S. Census Bureau. *The Changing Shape of the Nation's Income Distribution*. Washington, D.C.: U.S. Government Printing Office, 2000.

U.S. Department of the Treasury, Office of International Affairs. "Report to Congress on International Economic and Exchange Rate Policies." November 27, 2012.

U.S. Government Accountability Office. *An Analysis of Free Trade Agreements and Congressional and Private Sector Consultations under Trade Promotion Authority*. Washington, D.C.: U.S. Government Printing Office, 2007.

————. *International Trade: Four Free Trade Agreements GAO Reviewed Have Resulted in Commercial Benefits, but Challenges on Labor and Environment Remain*. Report GAO-09-439. Washington, D.C.: U.S. Government Printing Office, 2009.

U.S. International Trade Commission. *China: Effects of Intellectual Property Infringement and Indigenous Innovation Policies on the U.S. Economy.* Investigation 332-519, Publication 4226. Washington, D.C.: U.S. Government Printing Office, 2011. http://www.usitc.gov/publications/332/pub4226.pdf.

————. *U.S.-Chile Free Trade Agreement: Potential Economywide and Selected Sectoral Effects.* Investigation TA-2104-5, Publication 3605. Washington, D.C.: U.S. Government Printing Office, 2003.

VanGrasstek, Craig. *U.S. Trade Promotion Authority and the Doha Round.* Geneva: International Centre for Trade and Sustainable Development, 2008.

Vaughan, Scott, and Greg Block. *Free Trade and the Environment: The Picture Becomes Clearer.* Montreal: Commission for Environmental Cooperation of North America, 2002.

Viner, Jacob. *The Customs Union Issue.* New York: Carnegie Endowment for International Peace, 1950.

Von Wachter, Till. "Challenges for the U.S. Economic Recovery." Testimony before the Senate Budget Committee, February 3, 2011. http://www.columbia.edu/~vw2112/Von_Wachter_Testimony_Before_Senate_Budget_Committee_2011.pdf.

Wanniski, Jude. "Why Wall Street Crashed." January 8, 2005. http://www.polyconomics.com/ssu/ssu-050108.htm.

Whalley, John. *Assessing the Benefits to Developing Countries of Liberalization in Services Trade.* NBER Working Paper 10181. Cambridge, Mass.: National Bureau of Economic Research, 2003.

Williamson, John. "What Washington Means by Policy Reform." In *Latin American Adjustment: How Much Has Happened?* Washington, D.C.: Peterson Institute for International Economics, 2002.

Woodrow Wilson International Center for Scholars and Heinrich Boll Foundation. *Trade and Environment, the WTO, and MEAs: Facets of a Complex Relationship.* Washington, D.C.: Heinrich Boll Foundation, 2001.

World Bank. Measuring Inequality (database). http://web.worldbank.org/WBSITE/EXTERNAL/TOPICS/EXTPOVERTY/EXTPA/0,,contentMDK:20238991~menuPK:492138~pagePK:148956~piPK:216618~theSitePK:430367,00.html.

World Trade Organization. "International Trade Statistics, 2009." http://www.wto.org/english/res_e/statis_e/its2009_e/its09_toc_e.htm.

————. "Minutes of General Council Meeting of February 22, 2011 (WT/GC/M/130)." April 5, 2011.

————. "The Relationship between Exchange Rates and International Trade" (WT/WGTDF/W/68). November 5, 2012.

————. "World Trade Report, 2007: Six Decades of Multilateral Trade Cooperation—What Have We Learnt?" http://www.wto.org/english/res_e/publications_e/wtr07_e.htm.

————. "World Trade Report, 2010: Trade in Natural Resources." http://www.wto.org/english/res_e/booksp_e/anrep_e/world_trade_report10_e.pdf.

Woznowski, Jan. "Anti-Dumping Negotiations in the GATT and the WTO: Some Personal Reflections." In *Opportunities and Obligations: New Perspectives on Global and U.S. Trade Policy,* edited by Terence P. Stewart. Amsterdam: Kluwer Law International, 2009.

Yang, Yongzheng, and Sanjeev Gupta. *Regional Trade Arrangements in Africa: Past Performance and the Way Forward.* IMF Working Paper WP/05/36. Washington, D.C.: International Monetary Fund, 2005.

Yi, Kei-Mu. *Can Vertical Specialization Explain the Growth of World Trade?* New York: Federal Reserve Bank of New York, 1999.

Zepeda, Eduardo, Timothy A. Wise, and Kevin P. Gallagher. *Rethinking Trade Policy for Development: Lessons From Mexico under NAFTA.* Washington, D.C.: Carnegie Endowment for International Peace, 2009.

Zoellick, Robert B. "Statement of the U.S. Trade Representative before the Committee on Finance, U.S. Senate." March 5, 2003, 19.

Index

Notes and tables are indicated by "n" and "t" following page numbers.